SWIMMING POOLS

SWIMMING POOLS

Projects For Hot Tubs, Spas, Lanais, Cabanas, Gazebos, Fountains, Ornamental Pools, Fences

Kent and Pamela Jacobs Keegan

CREATIVE HOMEOWNER PRESS®

A DIVISION OF FEDERAL MARKETING CORPORATION,
24 PARK WAY, UPPER SADDLE RIVER, NEW JERSEY 07458

Manufactured in United States of America

Current Printing (last digit)
10 9 8 7 6 5 4

Editor: Shirley M. Horowitz
Associate Editor: Gail N. Kummings
Art Director: Léone Lewensohn
Designers: Léone Lewensohn, Paul Sochacki
Additional Illustrations: Norman Nuding

Cover photograph courtesy of:
  Berkus Group Architects
  Santa Barbara, Calif.
Designed by: Barry Berkus
Photographer: Robert Kohn

We wish to extend our thanks to the many designers, companies, and other contributors who
allowed us to use their materials and gave us
advice. Their names, addresses, and individual
identifications of their contributions can be
found on *page 156*.

ISBN: 0-932944-50-7 (paperback)
ISBN: 0-932944-49-3 (hardcover)
LC: 81-69642

CREATIVE HOMEOWNER PRESS®
BOOK SERIES
A DIVISION OF FEDERAL
MARKETING CORPORATION
24 PARK WAY,
UPPER SADDLE RIVER, NJ 07458

PROJECTS AND TECHNIQUES

A properly installed and maintained pool will add enormously to the value of your house and its resale value. When you measure the pleasure that can be derived from the pool, consider also the probable investment return due to installation of the pool.

There are other forms of water recreation that do not take the form of a swimming pool, but which constitute a very important part of water recreation. Additional forms of water recreation covered in this book include: entry pools, ornamental pools and fountains, ponds, waterfalls for visual pleasure, spas and hot tubs incorporated into a deck or patio. Detailed instructions and art are offered for planning purposes, as well as to aid those who wish to handle the construction work.

SWIMMING POOL PROJECTS
Outdoor In-ground Concrete Swimming Pool, 17
Enclosed In-ground Concrete Swimming Pool, 57
Outdoor Above-ground Swimming Pool, 120
Vinyl-liner System Swimming Pool, 45

GARDEN POOLS, HOT TUBS, SPAS, PONDS
Eight-sided Tiled Ornamental Pool, 113
Square Timber-edged Concrete Garden Pool, 109
Shallow Saucer Ornamental Pool, 106
Vinyl-liner Ornamental Pool, 105
Home Spa Alternatives and Systems, 98
Redwood Hot Tub Installation, 99
Manmade Natural Pond, 125

GARDEN STRUCTURES
Basic Concrete Slab for Following Jobs, 136
Attached Lanai with a Fence Extension, 149
Four-sided and Eight-sided Lattice-finished Gazebos, 139
Cabanas Used as Pool Changing Rooms, 147
Fencing for Privacy or Windbreak, 152

CONTENTS

1
BACKYARD
WATER RECREATION

Landscaping concrete and vinyl-liner pools, garden pools, ponds, hot tubs, spas and buildings 9

2
PLANNING AN OUTDOOR
IN-GROUND CONCRETE POOL

Sizes; Shapes; Costs; Building restrictions; Landscaping; Water circulating and filtration systems 17

3
BUILDING AN IN-GROUND
CONCRETE POOL

Step-by-step construction of a rectangular pool from excavation to addition of coping and surround 31

4
INSTALLING
A VINYL LINER POOL

Cost and ease-of-installation advantages versus an in-ground concrete pool; Setup procedures 45

5
ADDING AN
INDOOR IN-GROUND POOL

Types of pool enclosures; Costs and other restrictions; Detailed design and construction information 57

6
HOME SPAS & HOT TUBS
Buying guidelines for spas and hot tubs; Indoor and outdoor installations; Health and safety tips   **76**

7
CREATING ORNAMENTAL GARDEN POOLS
Shallow saucer pools; Concrete and vinyl liner garden pools; Octagonal tiled pool; Sprays and fountains   **104**

8
ABOVE GROUND POOLS
Integrating an above-ground pool with the landscaping; Buying and setting up the pool system   **115**

9
MANMADE NATURAL PONDS
Geographic restrictions and requirements; Planning, excavating, filling and maintaining a manmade pond   **125**

10
POOLSIDE STRUCTURES: CABANA, LANAI, GAZEBOS, FENCING
Directions, drawings and materials lists for a 4-sided and 8-sided gazebo, a cabana, lanai, and fencing   **132**

Appendix **154**   Metric Charts **157**
Contributors **156**   Index **158**

A raised, separate pool area can experiment with shapes and styles, since it is not limited by the design of the rest of the landscape.

1
BACKYARD
WATER RECREATION

When possible, indoor in-ground pools should be designed to take advantage of solar heat and the beauty of natural surroundings.

Fencing that is placed around the pool for safety reasons can also dress up a vinyl liner pool and tie together the design of the house and yard.

CHOICES IN POOLS

Each of the in-ground and above-ground swimming pools now available has specific advantages and disadvantages to which the homeowner should be alerted before a final swimming pool selection is made. The type of pool chosen will depend upon your home's space or site limitations, budget, local zoning and building codes, and the pool's intended use.

Alternatives to In-ground Pools

Low-Budget Kits For a very limited budget, the answer to a swimming pool may be an above-ground pool that comes as a kit. The kit needs minimal ground preparation and frequently avoids the costly plumbing and maintenance of the larger in-ground pool. The pool can be moved, and poolside amenities such as ladders, diving boards and poolside surrounds, are available at a reasonable cost. In addition to the above-ground pool, poolside cabanas, protective covers and enclosures are available.

Moderately Priced Vinyl-liner Pools For the moderate budget, the vinyl liner in-ground pool is aváilable in a variety of sizes and shapes and is an economical type of pool construction. It has a rigid outside frame over which a heavy vinyl liner is draped.

The In-ground Concrete Pool

An in-ground pool, constructed of concrete, can take almost any form desired. Walkways of broomed concrete, brick, treated wood, or other materials, can tie the pool to the rest of the landscape. The pool can be partially or completely indoor, with retractable covers. This is the most expensive pool choice, but often is the most satisfying.

PLANNING CONSIDERATIONS

Whether you are planning an in-ground or above-ground pool, there are certain requirements that must be taken into consideration when planning the construction.

Accessories

Enclosures It is often necessary to enclose the swimming pool area for safety reasons, as well as personal privacy needs. Most state and local codes require that an enclosure be provided. You, as the owner, could be a prime target for a lawsuit if someone should be drowned or injured in your pool. Your current property insurance policy may require additional coverage, even if you do take the necessary precautions. The enclosures should encircle the entire recreational area.

The most common enclosure is a fence, which can range from very dense hedge to a metal chain fencing. Although the fence is a necessary part of the pool environment, it can be attractive and well integrated into your landscape. In the case of an above-ground pool, the need for fencing is somewhat alleviated by the height of the pool above the ground level. It is still wise, however, to provide some sort of protection to insure against uninvited guests.

Gates A gate is needed in the fence design for ready access to the swimming pool area. A gate that is constructed from opaque or transparent materials, depending on how you want it to be used, should provide a visual link to the exterior and the fence. Above all, a gate to a pool area should be able to be secured or locked.

Landscaping

Landscaping concerns the total yard area, going beyond your pool and the immediate area surrounding the pool. The overall landscaping scheme is important to insure the swimming pool areas work well and are easy to maintain. Plan the pools in relation to the house; with small children, you might want the pool to be close to the house.

The materials selected and the design that evolves should reflect the scale and charm of the immediate area. This might include your house or outbuildings. If your lot is long and narrow, with a minimal side yard around the house, select a pool shape that is in keeping with that form, so that the back part is not cut off by the pool itself. When the pool is placed in a backyard, try to maintain as much free access around it for maintenance purposes. It is frustrating to be cut off from the grass on the other side of the pool.

Location of Grass and Shrubs

Grassy areas should be kept at some distance from the pool if it is to be used on a regular basis. The grass and grass cuttings may fall into the pool and block the plumbing. Grass also tends to "burn out" if subjected to the chlorine that is used to maintain the pool water. The splash of the water could affect the roots of plants and trees in the immediate area. Another concern is the proximity of trees to the swimming pool area. Leaves, bugs, tree sap and refuse from the tree generally tend to collect on the bottom of the pool, causing an undue amount of work for the owner. Try to keep the plantings low, and select plant material that tends to be nonshedding. Keep the larger trees to the perimeter of your lot. If the wind direction can be predicted (consult your local Weather Bureau), try to locate all the trees downwind to minimize shedding into your pool.

Exposure to Sun Probably the most overlooked point, and yet important, in planning the pool is to situate the swimming pool and patio area in a place where it will get maximum sun exposure and minimum winds. A pool whose main axis runs east to west will get better exposure than one that runs North to South.

Slope An above-ground pool requires the same planning in the selection of the landscaping materials. Because it rises above the ground, it is often more difficult to integrate into the landscape unless there is a sloping site. In the case of a gently sloping site, the pool can be adjusted through the use of wood decking extending the slope of the hill to the rim of the pool. The use of steps then can be used as an accent for the downhill side.

Utilities

Electrical/Lighting Lighting in and around the pool increases the amount of use you can expect from a pool — a late night dip is then always possible — and adds to safety.

When selecting lighting that will be in the pool or in contact with water, the lighting fixture and outlet must meet all the code requirements of the National Electrical Code. Most underwater lighting is connected to a junction box that is located in the vicinity of the diving board, where it can be accessed for repair. Be sure to consult an experienced electrician to plan your underwater pool lighting. At the same time, you may want to discuss the placement of above-ground accent or mood lighting and the power outlets that should be located around the perimeter.

Above-ground pools can offer all the style, convenience, and accessories most often associated with in-ground installations.

A raised wooden deck becomes a practical, attractive surround for an above-ground pool, unifying the pool and yard levels.

Curved shapes provide unusual design possibilities, but are hard to build yourself unless you use a vinyl liner, as shown here.

For some above-ground pools, the wooden deck around the pool can be utilized as a backyard design feature in itself.

In addition to the power and lighting, the pumps and filtration equipment require an electrical connection. This may be supplied underground to the equipment to minimize the unsightly look of overhead wires in and around the pool area. Before you do any underground investigation, be sure that you have identified and located all the underground utilities that are within the planned swimming pool area. This can be done by consulting your local utility companies and building inspectors.

Plumbing A pool is little use without water. Therefore, a major consideration is the location of the water supply to the pool itself. This applies to above-ground as well as in-ground swimming pools. For example, an in-ground pool is almost always set up on a recirculating water system. The water is pulled through a drain or skimmer below the top edge of the pool. This removes the layer dirt particles and lint. Then the water circulates through a strainer and pump filter, where microscopic debris is eliminated as waste. Most of it is returned through a heater (if applicable to your climate) and then returned back to the pool.

To begin this cycle, the pool must first be filled. If the water source is the local water supply system that supplies your house, the pool hookup will simply be an extension of that supply system to the pool. However, the local water supply authority may prohibit pool filling due to the drain on the system. If this is the case, there are trucking firms or water-supply firms that specialize in filling pools with water. The charge is based on the capacity of the pool. In this way, the pool may be filled in a very short period of time, compared to filling it from your local water supply system. For pools that must be emptied for repairs or for winter, provision of waste disposal must be taken into account when selecting the pool's location. A higher spot in the landscape is more advantageous because it aids drainage of the pool. Many local codes prohibit the emptying of the pool and/or the pool filter into the local sewage system or a natural resource such as a pond or lake. In that case, a drywell is recommended. If waste provision cannot be made, some water supply firms will empty a swimming pool for a fee.

In addition to the plumbing and mechanical requirements necessary to support a swimming pool, poolside showers and toilets also require supply and waste piping. Surface drains located in the poolside surround must be connected to the waste piping. This will minimize burn-out of the nearby plants, and often is required by local and state building codes.

Poolside Facilities

Changing areas such as a cabana or a small outdoor structure outfitted with a shower, toilet, room for changing clothes, and room for some storage, add to enjoyment of a pool. The mechanical system for the pool can often be housed in this structure and accessed through its own door or panel. Storage for lounge chairs, umbrellas and pool equipment may be included. You might be surprised at the amount of equipment that is collected and the amount of storage space it calls for. The poolside area might also include an eating area, room for dishes and serving food, a BBQ pit, food preparation area and lounging area. You may want to include built-in seating in the deck or patio area or built-in planters. If protection from the elements is needed, an enclosure or shading device is easily constructed.

The poolside facilities for an above-ground pool are often less elaborate. This is primarily because many above-ground pools are just simply set on the ground, with minimal ground preparation and without any degree of permanence. It becomes more difficult to blend in a pool that might be temporary and ultimately moved to another area on the site or to another site altogether. The above-ground pool can, of course, have all the amenities of an in-ground pool if the owner wishes and is concerned with good planning practices.

Environmental Concerns: Site Selection and Location

There is seldom a site that is perfect; nearly every one will have some flaws. When selecting a location for your pool consider some of the following points.

Slope and Drainage Is the pool to be located on a flat area near the house? It is important that the site not only slope away from the house, but that the pool not be placed where it might become flooded from heavy rains or accumulated snow. Shape the land so water flows away from the house and pool. The large, hard surface area of the pool surround will increase the run-off potential; plan accordingly.

The pool should be at the high point of the site if at all possible. The refuse that can be picked up will cause the filtration system to be far less efficient in cleaning the water. Where the slope is so steep as to make the cut-and-fill a very expensive operation, a retaining wall on the low end of the pool is required.

Accessibility to Water Supply Locate the pool so that the main water supply source is accessible to it. The cost of providing a new water connection to the swimming pool mechanical equipment may be prohibitive if located some distance from the house water supply or the

This relaxation center has recessed lighting for night use, and is flanked by simple slat structures for shaded daytime enjoyment.

For a relatively low-cost but striking appearance, a brick deck around the pool often can be laid by the homeowner.

main supply in the street. If this is not possible, plan for access by a water truck or a hose to fill and drain the pool.

Exposure and Orientation to Sun and Wind For the fullest use and enjoyment of the pool, place the pool where it will have a southern and western exposure. This permits longer usage during the day. The location could also mean the elimination of pool heaters, or at least the feasibility of installing solar water heaters for the pool, which often reduces the amount of maintenance.

The pool location should include protection from the wind. A steady wind can often make a pool an unbearable experience. Can the pool be enclosed? Is the setback adequate for a wind break, such as a fence or other suitable barrier?

Soil suitability Is the soil of sufficient quality to support a swimming pool? There have been cases in which the swimming pool has been forced out of or crushed by the ground when the water has been drained from the pool. It is important to keep in mind that a swimming pool floats in the ground in much the same way that a boat floats in water. If the ground water table is high enough, it could cause the pool to rise when empty.

The quality of the soil is another important factor. In soil that is well graded and drained, few problems are encountered. In the case of clay or silt-like soil, settlement or movement could occur, causing cracking of the concrete or warping of the liner material. For an above-ground pool, pools can slip down a hillside if not properly anchored or grounded.

In addition, there may be an underlying strata of ground water that must be taken into consideration. Since the quality of the soil will determine the ease with which the pool can be constructed, the soil should be evaluated by a knowledgeable individual.

A sound base is necessary to minimize settlement and prolong the life of the pool. Sandy soils, fills, topsoils and clays are not desirable materials to build on. A mixture of gravel, sand and silt is best because the material is dense and quite stable. Clay tends to change in volume and cause heave of the pool unless it is consolidated by compaction.

If there is a high water table, the excavation may have to be dewatered until the forms, or sides and base are poured. It is better to build above the water table, since it is less expensive.

In the areas where the waste from the pool cannot be voided into the sewer system, a leaching field or septic tank is needed. A leaching field must be at a lower elevation than the pool and built into a gravelly area a minimum of twenty feet from the house. Topsoil should not be included in any excavation, since it is primarily organic and is decomposing. Try to keep all excavations free of refuse or topsoil.

Acoustical Privacy The question is not so much the amount of noise generated around the poolside area, as how much is transmitted to the neighbors or to the area surrounding the recreation area. While there is no way to eliminate the noise of people having fun, try to locate the pool so that there are physical barriers between the pool and the outside area. Keep in mind that while the pool might be protected from the house or another building, the noise will reflect off hard surfaces. There can be no one solution, but generally the introduction of very dense plantings and baffled fences should be considered as part of the swimming pool construction. Of course, this recommendation will not

The shape of the pool, which is drawn from the curves of the rocks, effectively contrasts with the rectangular wooden deck.

The effect of these natural materials and the jagged lines of the pool produce a good example of the "natural pool" look.

The natural look requires planning. This dramatic example of a modified natural look is the result of careful design and materials selection.

Instructions for this rough-timbered ornamental pool can be found in Chapter 7; details for the gazebo are in Chapter 10.

really apply in rural areas where homes are far apart.

ORNAMENTAL POOLS, FOUNTAINS, WATERFALLS AND HOT TUBS

Many families and individuals are enjoying the cool refreshing qualities of water without going to major expense and effort. They are installing decorative pools, water fountains and waterfalls, and hot tubs, to accent their gardens and landscaping. An ornamental pool, fountain or waterfall cannot only provide a tremendous amount of pleasure but can also become the centerpiece of the garden layout. It can be organized around very formal and geometric principles, or be very organic and natural. It can be as fancy or as restrained as you may desire. The sizes, shapes and materials that are available are numerous and vary from inexpensive to exhorbitant.

Ornamental Garden Pools

Evaluate the area under consideration and what type of pool is best for your needs and enjoyment. It is possible to form natural pools that are sculpted from the earth, free-form and lined with a vinyl liner and then edged with stones or rocks. Ornamental pools may be strict geometric squares that fit into a planting pattern or even rectangles and circles that are poured concrete over wire mesh and then edged in a variety of finish materials. Other ornamental or decorative pools are built from molded plastic or fiberglass, which are then sunk into the ground. They come fully prepared for hookup to the water source. These pools can house fish and water plants, such as water lilies, and should be at least 18 inches deep. To maintain water aeration balance, recirculating pumps are often recommended. Decorative or ornamental pools should be drained and cleaned periodically to remove any growth or bottom dirt. Try to orient the pool so it has at least 3 to 4 hours of direct sunlight each day. This will help keep the bacteria growth to an acceptable level. In the less expensive ornamental pools, recirculating pumps are not included. This means that the water must be changed and the pool cleaned on a regular basis.

Water Sprays and Fountains

Water fountains are easily added to a garden scheme, or even in the house. While there are many shapes, sizes and materials to choose from, the most important part of the fountain is the shape and type of fountain spray and the distance that the water travels in the air. The size and shape of the fountain spray are related to the size of the water pump and recirculation system. The fountain will have to be connected to a water supply system and electrical circuit. Since the water is moving continuously, less cleaning of the pool area is required. The fountain mechanism can be integrated into a decorative or ornamental pool.

Waterfalls

A waterfall is a decorative and natural device that can be integrated into a variety of decorative garden designs. If you are installing an ornamental pool, a vertical wall can be erected alongside the pool to serve as the platform for a waterfall. The water system can utilize the same pool recirculation system as in an ornamental pool, while the free fall of the water can provide the desired aeration of the water. The waterfall need not end in a pool but could be part of a small stream or brook arrangement that winds through the garden.

Another option is the waterfall that is built into the side of a hill or earth berm. This type of waterfall relies on the flow of water down the hill, over a series of carefully placed stones and splash pools, to accentuate the variety of sounds. Water plants can be incorporated as desired. If fish are living in the pool or stream, automatic feeders can be attached to the recirculation system. If you have a natural spring on your property, a natural waterfall could be a delightful accent to the garden landscape. The upper part of the waterfall can act as a miniature dam to control the flow of the water.

Hot Tubs and Spas

The current interest in hot tubs and spas goes along with our heightened interest in recreational fitness and better health. A hot tub or spa can provide some of the benefits of a swimming pool at a fraction of the cost and the space. In many parts of the United States, the tubs are installed outdoors surrounded by a wood deck or patio area of varying sizes and shapes. Most often the location of the tub or spa is in a secluded area to insure privacy. The size of the tub is designed to hold about six people, with a water temperature of 102 degrees F. The space required for a hot tub

or spa is far less than that required even for the smallest swimming pool, while still providing a similar healthful feeling and of social gathering.

A hot tub is normally constructed of redwood with a diameter of 4 to 7 feet. A hot tub is always built above ground. Some are available in molded plastic or fiberglass set into the ground with water jets acting as a whirlpool.

Spas are often bigger than a hot tub, measuring about 7 feet or wider, and are often built alongside a swimming pool. They are easier to install and operate than a hot tub, and can be installed indoors as well.

Both hot tubs and spas use water heaters, recirculating water pumps, and water filters to keep the water free from debris. In addition, their chlorine and PH level

Warm, bubbling water can be a luxurious extension to your pool, usually for a reasonable additional cost if built at the same time as the pool.

This shaded spa uses meticulous brick detail trim as part of the overall landscape theme.

As this basement installation shows, hot tubs need not be limited to outdoor locations if comfortable interior space is available.

Exterior hot tub arrangements are usually placed on grade, and can incorporate raised deck and seating for a complete leisure area.

must be controlled and they need cleaning on a regular basis. Both hot tubs and spas can be installed in almost any climate. In the more severe northern ones, winterization should be considered.

Hot tubs and spas seem like a relatively low-cost way to have fun and keep healthy. In fact, needed for therapeutic reasons and prescribed by your doctor, they sometimes can be tax deductible.

Drawbacks The primary concern is safety. The water temperature must be carefully regulated or overheating may occur. There have been several cases of individuals falling asleep in the hot tub and either suffering severe burns or death. In addition, if the pool is not in use, a cover of wood or similar material should be placed over the opening. Small children and hot tubs or spas are a dangerous combination unless properly supervised.

Check with your physician prior to using the tubs or spas to make sure that your physiology is capable of taking the heat. People with high blood pressure should not use them. The benefits of owning a hot tub or spa are numerous if these precautions are observed.

Due to the problems of abuse, some localities now include the installation of the hot tub and spa in the local building codes. Inquire if there are any special local or state requirements.

THE NATURAL POND

The natural pond is often a by-product of the landform or topography of your area. It is not something that can be easily installed as you would a decorative or a swimming pool. A natural pond requires a considerable amount of area, a soil that can support the amount of water involved, and a water source that is preferably a natural one. The depression in the landform must be near the water source.

If you can meet all of these requirements, you should be able to create a natural pond that will provide years of enjoyment with minimal maintenance. The possibilities of its being used by wild animals and waterfowl are obvious. Being a natural water container, many state Department of Natural Resources require that you consult them prior to undertaking the project. In some states, the Department will conduct a survey of the property with a soil and water analysis and assist you with the plannings and layout of the pond itself. Landowners have in some states, been awarded grants from the state specifically for the creation or preservation of the natural wetlands.

The pond itself is often built on a nonpermeable soil, which means a soil that does not drain well. This keeps the water contained. Once the basin of the pond is shaped, the area is compacted and a layer of clay is placed over the bottom. Clay is a good liner, since it fills all the voids of the base material. Once the pond is filled and the water level is maintained, nature will take over in the form of plant life and use by birds and animals.

Although a manmade pond must be created in accordance with the restrictions of the topography, it can still be designed to fulfill specific esthetic devices.

The relationship between this house and pool was worked out with an eye toward usability as well as beauty. The attached greenhouse offers living space with an extraordinary view of the pool.

2
PLANNING AN OUTDOOR
IN-GROUND CONCRETE POOL

PRACTICAL CONSIDERATIONS

Once you have decided to add an in-ground swimming pool, there are several planning considerations to which you must pay attention to avoid surprises or unforseen costs.

Contracting the Job

Always consult several reliable, reputable contractors. Generally, these contractors are associated with a dealer who, in some cases, are one and the same. When you discuss the options, make sure that they are willing to give you a contract that is not open-ended. The contract thus becomes a legal document, and should be thought of that way.

Setting Up Estimates and Contracts Soliciting an estimate for the construction of a swimming pool is probably the only way you can get an understanding of what the actual costs are going to be. Solicit at least three estimates. This will give you a better comparison of not only what is provided, but under what terms and for what duration. A low estimate on a comparison basis, or a verbal agreement on the part of the contractor to beat the opposition with a lower price, does not mean that you will get the same quality for less money. Do not be lured into accepting the low bid without making sure that the contractor is reputable and provides quality materials on a guaranteed delivery schedule. If you are in doubt, obtain legal counsel to make sure that everything you wanted is included in the price.

If you are contracting the entire package, make sure the contract stipulates a completion date. Often, contractors will promise a completion date that is not very realistic in order to get the work. To discourage this, a penalty clause should be inserted into the contract requiring the contractor to forfeit a certain dollar amount for each day beyond the completion date.

Doing Some or All of the Work Yourself

If you are ambitious enough and have enough time, you can be responsible for building your own swimming pool. The procedures outlined above are applicable, with some minor changes. If you rely on subcontractors, you will save money by assuming the responsibilities of a general contractor and subcontracting out those phases that you are unable to actually provide yourself.

For example, excavation would require a backhoe or bulldozer to dig to the necessary depths. While it is possible for you to rent the equipment and dig the hole, an excavation contractor is well versed and probably would be able to equal the price of doing it yourself. If you elect this option, a contract should be required stating all the requirements, the completion date and actual costs. Include the hauling of the excavated material away from the site unless you can use it for backfill. Many owners are stuck with a mound of dirt with no place to put it. The filling of the pool may also become part of a contractors requirement.

There are a number of contract forms available to the owner. The most respected one is that developed by the American Institute of Architects. It outlines the responsibilities of the owner and the contractor and is frequently used for contract-installed and the owner-installed arrangements.

Pool Operating Costs

Your budget should take into account expenses involved in ownership and operation of a pool. One often-overlooked cost

Concrete pools permit custom shapes and designs, and are often chosen when the pool must be tailored to fit specific or unusual site needs.

is the tax increase generated by your new improvement. The addition of an in-ground pool usually is regarded as a taxable improvement. Check with your local tax assessor to discover the tax assessment so you can add it into your annual operating budget.

Once you have decided to install an in-ground swimming pool, talk with the insurance agent handling your homeowners insurance policy. By the time the swimming pool is in operation, you should have in effect sufficient liability insurance. This kind of protection must be considered mandatory; you are protecting yourself from the unforseen.

Major annual operating costs over the lifespan of the pool will exceed the actual cost of the pool itself. Some of the operating expenses you must plan on include: electrical power demands; water-purification chemicals; replacement of worn equipment; plumbing repairs; insurance; finance charges and interest; regular maintenance; fuel charges; monthly payments.

THE WORKINGS OF AN IN-GROUND POOL

The overall operation of a swimming pool is very straight-forward. A swimming pool is a waterproof vessel large enough to accommodate a number of people and to hold water. While this definition is accurate, it says very little about how the pool stays rigid, how the water gets into the pool, or how the water is removed.

A swimming pool is composed of two main ingredients, each one dependent on the other.

The Container or Shell

This continuous form is watertight to contain a large volume of water. The shell is constructed from concrete, concrete block, steel or compacted earth, excavated to a depth that allows the user to stand. The base of the shell often is sloped.

The Basic Water System

The water system is composed of a number of elements, each one providing a certain function. At the bottom of the pool is a drain that connects to a pump through a gate valve. Another line to the pump, from a water filter, removes the impurities from the water. The pool water enters the filter through a skimmer, which is often part of the pool construction. A small water heater can be added for heat. A connection to a

When planning the location of your pool, take into account the surrounding scenery and the view from house windows; you can create a "picture window" effect.

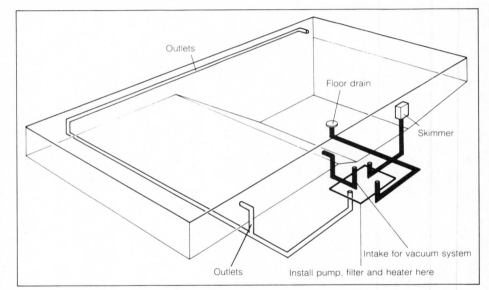

Shown are the basic layout and components of the water circulation and piping system.

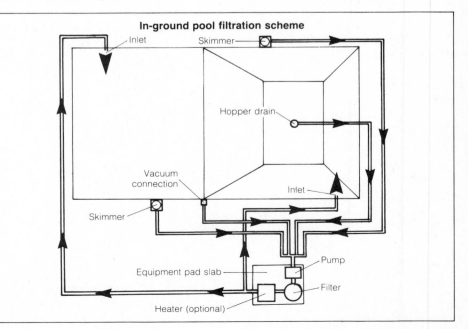

water main makes up for any amount of water that escapes the pool either through evaporation or through waste.

Water Circulation The pool water is recirculated through a system made up of a skimmer, filter, heater, lint trap, pump motor, valves and piping. These are all necessary to maintain the quality of the water. Without the recirculation system, the water would become cloudy with small dirt particles and organic elements that could cause the water to become cloudy; the water would become infested and infected; the water would stagnate and become a source of growing algae and bacteria.

No matter what size pool you have, it is recommended that you select a recirculation system that will recycle all the water once every eight to twelve hours. The maximum time permitted for a complete recycle is 18 hours. The reason is that during the daylight hours the sunlight promotes algae growth. Therefore, it is important that the water be recycled within that time period.

For example, if your pool is a 16x32 rectangular shape with an average depth of 5 ft., it has a capacity of 19,100 gallons of water. This would require that the 19,100 gallons of water be recirculated at a rate of 1600 gallons per hour to meet the 12-hour

The size of the pump you buy depends upon the size of the pool. This self-priming model needs priming only the first time.

Position a pump at least 24 in. above the ground. This will give you easy access to it when it needs to be drained.

recommendation, or 1065 gph to meet the 18 hour minimum requirement. To convert this rate to gallons per minute, you would divide by 60 for the "filter rate." The filter rate required for the 16x32 ft. pool would be 27 gpm for the 12-hour rate and 18 for the 18-hour cycle.

Selecting a Filter System The filter rate represents the capacity of the filter. The filter represents the main resistance to the normal flow of the water. When choosing a filter system, try not to select the smallest or the largest. The 8- to 12-hour cycle for water recirculation is considered the optimal time period. Some owners trying to conserve money will run their filter systems only 6 to 8 hours per day, although the pool filtration system was sized for the 18 hour cycle. This means that the water is changed every other day, which in most climates is not satisfactory. Do not be misled; if the wind is kicking up a lot of dust or the rain carries more dirt particles, you will need every bit of the 12-hour capacity or more. The shorter the cycle time, the greater the energy savings. If the pool you choose is to be enclosed, the longer cycle might be more appropriate. If you live in an area where there is a lot of windborne dust, the 8-hour cycle is definitely recommended.

Water Pump Requirements The size of the pump depends upon the number of gallons to be circulated through the filtration system. There are two types of pumps: self-priming and regular. The regular pump must be primed prior to every operation. If a regular pump is to be cycled every 8 to 12 hours, it would be necessary to prime it every time; a self-priming pump reduces this effort.

The pump itself should be placed 24 in. above the level of the ground. This way it is safe from puddling and can be easily accessed for draining. The motor attached to the pump should be protected from the weather and grounded according to the National Electrical Code requirements. The shelter for the pump and motor, and often the filtration system, should include ventilation.

Choosing a Water Filter

The water filter is the most important part of the recirculation system. There are many different filter types, sizes and price ranges available on the market. The variety makes the selection a somewhat difficult task. It is worth your time and effort to

familiarize yourself with the operation and types of water filters. Three types of filter systems available that are applicable to the residential and multi-family swimming pool include: sand filter systems; diatomaceous earth filter systems; and cartridge filter systems. Each one of these filter systems has certain unique qualities that make it attractive to the pool buyer.

Rapid-rate Sand Filter Systems The most commonly used filter system for residential use is the sand filter. The basic ingredient in this system is a tank filled with very fine sand that traps the particles to dirt that are retained in the swimming pool water. The water from the pool is drawn into the top of the sand filter tank by the pump, which is located on the outlet side of the tank. As the water is drawn down through the fine sand granules, the suspended dirt particles are trapped and suspended in the sand layers. As the sand filter removes more and more dirt from the pool water, the filter begins to close. The sand voids fill with dirt particles until a pressure difference exists between the inlet at the top and the filtered water outlet at the bottom. This is measured by the pressure gauge. To remove the dirt, the filter must be "backwashed". The filtered water is then circulated back to the pool by the pump and the cycle begins again.

Most sand filters are sized according to their filter rate. The filter rate is the number of gallons that can be filtered based on the filter area of the sand. A sand filter is known as a "rapid rate" filter since the filter operation uses the surface area of the sand to determine capacity.

In the previous example of a 16x32 ft. swimming pool, a total of 19,100 gallons of water required 25 gpm of water for a 12-hour cycle. A 30-in. diameter filter can process 25 gpm on a sand filter area of 4.90 sq. ft. The filter rate is the selection criteria; the flow rate is that rate by which the filter can effectively be backwashed. The "backwash flow rate" can range from 50 to 70 gpm. By reversing the flow of water at a controlled "flow rate", the particles are dislodged and flushed out of the sand layers into a waste pipe or receptacle, without serious disturbance to the sand layer. The amount of water necessary to backwash the system could be as high as 300 gallons. This process normally occurs only on a weekly basis.

The High-Rate Sand Filter This type of filter produces crystal clear water, but instead of basing the capacity of the filter on the surface area, the critical factor is the depth of the sand. The high-rate sand filter is a fiberglass or stainless steel spherical tank with a viewing ''lid'' that permits a view of the inside during the operation cycle, as well as allowing easy access to the inside. The tank can circulate between 20,000 to 65,000 gallons economically. This type of filter system can be purchased with a 6-way selector valve that will permit a vacuum attachment for pool cleaning purposes. Each manufacturer has certain variations. These filters are generally used on the larger pools. The amount of sand installed after the filter is in place can range from 100 to 800 pounds. The high-rate sand filter is moderately priced.

Diatomaceous Earth Filter Systems (D.E.) The diatomaceous earth filter system is composed of microscopic remains of marine plants called diatoms. These marine fossils are able to filter particles up to one micron in size. The system has the same components as the sand filter with one major difference: the D.E. filter does not require backwashing.

An injection molded tank contains a series of closely spaced plastic tubes that are suspended in the water. The unfiltered water enters through the bottom of the tank and flows upwards through the plastic tubes and returns to the pool via an outlet in the head of the tank. When the filter is initially started, the diatomite filter powder is fed into the system. This powder is lodged into the pores of the plastic tubes as a coating. The dirt particles in the water are stopped on the surface of the diatomite powder.

Eventually, when the accumulated dirt particles cause the filter pressure to rise and the water output to fall off, ''bumping'' takes place. Bumping is a mechanical process in which a lever is moved up and down several times, shaking the dirt and the powder off the tubes. The dirt drops to the bottom of the tank and the filter starts again. When the bumping process no longer restores normal water flow, about twice during a normal swimming season, a new diatomite filter powder coating is fed into the system.

The performance of a D.E. filter ranges from 25 gpm to 75 gpm which can circulate from 21,600 to 54,000 gallons based on the recommended 12 hour cycle. This filter type is often used in residential and multi-family swimming pool applications. Its cost, however, is higher than an equivalent capacity sand filter.

Cartridge Filter System The cartridge filter system operates in a similar manner to the D.E. filter. The major difference is that instead of a renewable powder that is placed into the system, a cartridge of polyester or cloth, or a paper filter, is placed in the tank either singly or in clusters. This filter must be removed periodically for cleaning. The filter performs the same function as the sand or diatomaceous earth. The filter must be removed from the tank and placed in a cleaning solution to float the microscopic dirt particles off the filter material. Since this takes as long as 24 hours, purchase of a second filter is recommended for continuous operation of the pool.

Maintenance of a cartridge filter is low compared to other filtration systems. No backwashing and no selector valves are required when cleaning is required. Some filters can be removed easily and hosed off.

The "Throw Away" Cartridge This is the least expensive of the cartridge filters, but requires frequent changing. The changes could become expensive if the swimming pool is large or subjected to large amounts of airborne pollution. In

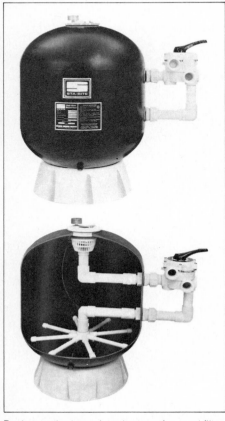

Pool water is drawn into the top of a sand filter: as it passes through the sand, the sand removes suspended dirt particles.

The skeletons of marine life form the main element in a diatomaceous earth filter and coat the filter's tubing.

When a D.E. filter is "full," it must be bumped. A level shakes the dirt off the tubing and onto the bottom of the housing.

some filtration systems, the filtration tank is large enough so that the cartridges can be stacked. In general, each cartridge filter contains 6 sq. ft. of filter area. In some models, the filters are placed in clusters of up to 21 in a tank. The larger model provides up to 126 sq. ft. of filter area with a 126 gallons per minute flow, which will handle up to a 60,000 gallon pool on an 8-hour cycle or a 90,000 gallon pool on a 12-hour cycle.

Filter Selection Guidelines All of the filtration systems discussed are excellent for in-ground swimming pools. The quality of the water and its particular mineral content could affect the selection of the filter. For example, where the available water is "hard", a diatomaceous earth filter would not be suitable because the calcium content in the water would block the filter in a short period of time. A better choice would be a sand filter, because it does not remove as many particles as the D.E. filter.

Check with your local building or plumbing inspector for water-quality sample information. If your water supply is from a drilled or artesian well, have your water sample tested prior to selecting the filtration system. Another point of investigation should be in the area of energy conservation. An undersized or oversized pump motor and filter could result in higher electrical charges.

Types of Sites

No two sites are identical. To say that a backyard is flat or sloping is not adequate information for placement of an in-ground swimming pool. Your plans must take into consideration the sun location, wind direction, plumbing, slope, drainage patterns, visibility, security, electrical and lighting and acoustical isolation. Some of these criteria are going to be more or less important, depending on your specific site location.

One aspect applicable to all types of locations is accessibility. If the machinery can move in and out of the site with relative ease, costs will be kept at a minimum. If the site is too constricting or is inaccessible, costs could increase considerably.

Urban Site Determine how the sunlight moves across your property. In an urban site, the height of nearby buildings can affect the pool location because shadows interfere with the location. Try to plot the movement of the sun; it is possible to

extend the number of hours of use by relocating the pool to a more southern orientation. If you keep the pool open to the sun, you will save on the use of a pool heater and lengthen the amount of time that the pool may be used.

Suburban Site The suburban site allows for more land space into which a swimming pool can be built. There may be local restrictions on distances from lot lines or adjacent property or hook ups to sewers that must be checked. Security is an important consideration in the suburban site, due to the number of children that might be attracted to the pool. Another concern may be utilities that are under the yard.

Rural Site A rural site offers possibilities without many of the restrictions imposed by the urban and suburban density. The most important considerations are location with respect to the house and the protection of the pool from animals and wind.

Building Code Requirements The first step after you have decided to build an in-ground swimming pool is to consult your local or county building inspector. Most communities and states have very specific requirements for the installation, security and maintenance of swimming pools in single and multiple family residences.

Take along your house and plot plans to

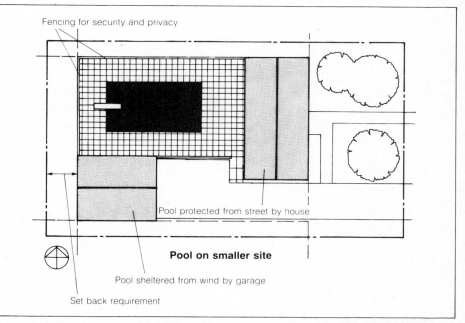

If possible, plan pool layout to shelter the pool between existing structures such as the house and the garage. Wall surface reflection also helps keep pool water warm.

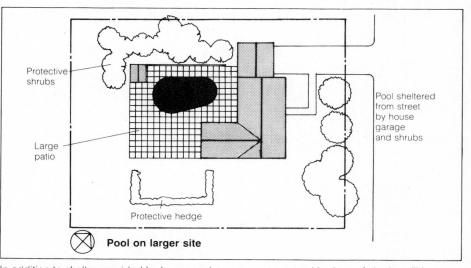

In addition to shelter provided by house and garage, screens and hedges of shrubs will increase privacy and serve as a windbreak.

show the inspector and to verify setback requirements, fence heights and easements. Most codes vary from locality to locality, but they do require that the public health and safety requirements be met. The points of major concern would be water, plumbing, waste, electrical and security. In some areas, side-yard pools are prohibited in favor of backyard locations. Also review the code requirements for detached buildings, such as cabanas or pool enclosures.

POOL DESIGN OPTIONS

Look carefully at all the types of pools available before selecting one. The sizes and shapes are varied and should be carefully considered before making the investment.

Types of Concrete In-ground Swimming Pools

The most durable and long lasting pool is the concrete pool. Concrete can be formed to a variety of shapes specifically tailored for your property or site requirements. This particular quality makes concrete the preferred choice for customized in-ground swimming pool installation. There are three types of concrete construction used for most in-ground swimming pools.

Poured-in-Place Pool Since it is liquid prior to the curing, poured-in-place concrete requires forms to hold the concrete. The forms, of reinforced fiberglass, steel or plywood, can be premade or customized depending on the design of the pool. They are often available on a rental basis. The forms interlock with pins and ties that maintain the shape of the pool.

Once the forms have been set, steel reinforcing rods are installed to maintain the structural integrity of the pool form. The pool will have vertical and horizontal reinforcing, especially in the areas where freezing and thawing might affect the pool's performance. The bars retard the cracking of the concrete and maintain the watertightness of the material. The minimum pool wall thickness is 8 to 10 in. The thickness is determined by the size and shape of the pool and by the siting of the pool.

Concrete is said to be watertight, but without the aid of a waterproofing agent or membrane, most concrete pools will leak. Therefore, once the forms are pulled from the concrete (after 3 to 7 days) and the concrete has cured for a total of 28 days, waterproofing is added.

Hand-packed Concrete Pool The use of hand-packed concrete, sometimes referred to as dry packing, does not require forms. A very stiff concrete mix is pushed into the reinforcing and then hand finished until the desired surface is achieved. While this method is less expensive in materials than the poured-in-placed method, it does require a lot of hand labor, which could be very expensive. Without skilled labor, the pool surface can end up wavy and uneven. If this method is selected, a skilled concrete mason should be retained for the work.

Gunite Pool The use of gunite is a popular alternative to poured-in-place construction. Gunite is a stiff concrete mix that is sprayed over concrete reinforcing under high pressure. The gunite has one quality that poured-in-place does not

have — it hardens upon contact with the reinforcing and thus it cannot be reworked.

Since gunite is a mixture of cement and sand, it performs very well in milder climates. It is not recommended for colder climates because it tends to spall when subjected to the freeze and thaw of winter.

It is important to have the gunite sprayed in uniform layers to achieve a constant thickness. If the thickness varies, the overall integrity of the pool is reduced considerably, shortening the life of the pool. The workmanship involved in a gunite pool is critical to its longevity.

Concrete Block for Pool Walls

Many pools are constructed using concrete masonry for the perimeter walls. The concrete block must be reinforced with steel rods that are set in both horizontally and vertically. This type of wall is less expensive than alternatives outlined above, and is suitable for the do-it-yourselfer. However, the wall height is limited to 36 inches because any greater height could cause cracking. If block is used in a colder climate, the freeze and thaw could result in spalling of the concrete. You should consult your local contractor before selecting this method of construction. The primary advantage is cost.

Pool Sizes and Shapes

Before you select an in-ground pool, examine what the intended use of the pool is to be. If your main goal is to provide Olympic training for teenagers and adults, you may have to select a large, rectangular pool, with at least one racing line and provision for the water buoy markers. A swimming pool for a family with many small youngsters might call for a shallow end pool tapering down to a deep end for adults.

Diving requires some additional depth so that the diver does not touch bottom diving from a 1.5 meter board. The depth of the diving end is determined by the height of the diving board, so plan well in determining diving activities. The average swimming depth is 42 to 72 in. and an average diving depth is between 96 to 110 in. When determining the proportions of the pool, allow about 100 sq. ft. of pool surface area per diver.

For a swimmer, the proportion is between 24 and 36 sq. ft. of pool surface per swimmer. A ''splasher'' (usually a child)

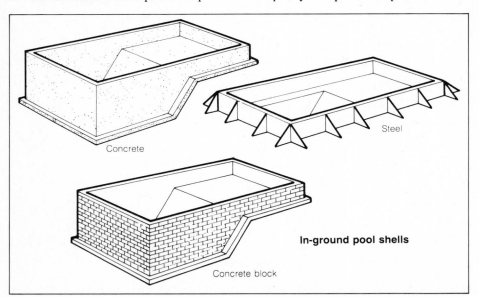

Concrete

Steel

Concrete block

In-ground pool shells

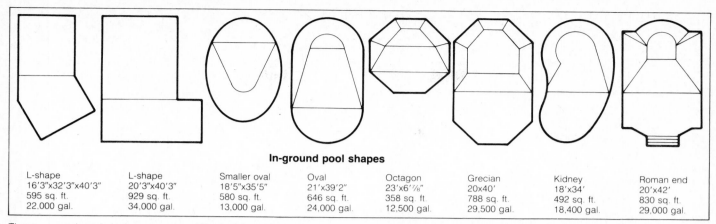

In-ground pool shapes

L-shape	L-shape	Smaller oval	Oval	Octagon	Grecian	Kidney	Roman end
16'3"x32'3"x40'3"	20'3"x40'3"	18'5"x35'5"	21'x39'2"	23'x6'⅞"	20'x40'	18'x34'	20'x42'
595 sq. ft.	929 sq. ft.	580 sq. ft.	646 sq. ft.	358 sq. ft.	788 sq. ft.	492 sq. ft.	830 sq. ft.
22,000 gal.	34,000 gal.	13,000 gal.	24,000 gal.	12,500 gal.	29,500 gal.	18,400 gal.	29,000 gal.

These unusual pool shapes are more difficult to form and to build than a standard shape, and should be hired out to a professional.

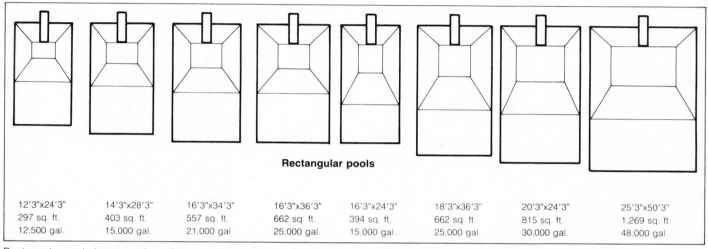

Rectangular pools

12'3"x24'3"	14'3"x28'3"	16'3"x34'3"	16'3"x36'3"	16'3"x24'3"	18'3"x36'3"	20'3"x24'3"	25'3"x50'3"
297 sq. ft.	403 sq. ft.	557 sq. ft.	662 sq. ft.	394 sq. ft.	662 sq. ft.	815 sq. ft.	1,269 sq. ft.
12,500 gal.	15,000 gal.	21,000 gal.	25,000 gal.	15,000 gal.	25,000 gal.	30,000 gal.	48,000 gal.

Rectangular pool shapes such as these are simpler to lay out and to construct than free-form or oddly shaped ones.

needs 10 sq. ft. Based on these averages, a family of 2 adults and 3 children, of which one is a splasher, might require a total pool area of 230 sq. ft. or a pool of 12x24 ft. For a smaller family, a 10x18 ft. pool would be satisfactory. There are certain minimum dimensions that should be kept in mind, since there is so little cost differential between the smallest pool and the next size up. Here are examples:

Ovals	10x18, 13x24, 15x30
Kidney	17x29
Reverse Kidney	17x29
Pear	17x29
Rectangular	10x18, 13x24, 15x30
	16x32 and larger

Other shapes that are available are dog leg, L-Shape, Grecian and Eliptical.

Integrating the Pool with the Site

A pool should be so much a part of the site that the two cannot be separated. The shape and size of your pool should reflect the shape and style of your house. A formal country French or Georgian house might call for a formal rectangular or gre-

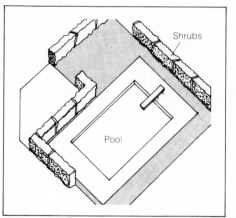

Plantings that frame the pool can spark an otherwise plain landscape and will contribute to pool enjoyment.

cian pool. A wood-sided residence might look best with a pool with a wood surround. A ranch house could adapt well to a free form pool or an oval-shaped one. The pool surround and/or patio area can act as the go-between the house and the pool, tying together all the materials and the scale of the house and pool.

Creating a Windbreak To utilize

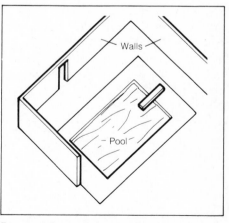

Free-standing wall panels of various materials and transparencies can be erected around the in-ground pool at a reasonable cost.

your site to its best advantage, select an area that is sheltered from the wind. If possible, use your house as part of the windbreak. Try to avoid creating a wind tunnel between the pool and the house. A windbreak can keep the pool water warmer for a longer period of time and save on the use of a pool heater. Shelter from the wind could extend use in fall and spring

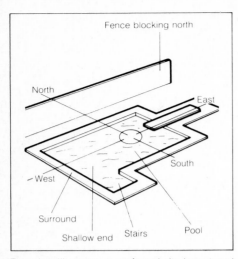

This view illustrates a preferred site layout and orientation for an in-ground pool, with the diving board facing east.

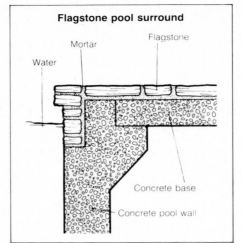

When flagstone is used as a pool surround, it must be laid in mortar, with a support below that extends into the ground.

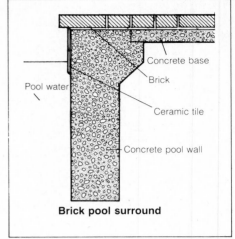

This brick pool surround is laid in mortar, but ceramic tile (also in mortar) is used as a facing for the pool walls.

swimming seasons. If you are in an area that is very open to the wind, you might add a pool enclosure. Fencing helps control the wind, as do shrubs and hedges. Free-standing windbreaks can be built of transparent panels, erected around the pool to shelter it from the wind.

Drawing a Site Plan

To aid in the planning of the in-ground pool, draw a site plan drawn to scale (¼ or ⅛ in. equals 1 ft.) indicating the location of all the trees, plants, house, property lines, etc. If your property was platted when you purchased it, you should have a property survey already in your possession. If not, contact your local Recorder of Deeds office for a property description and copy of your plat. Once you have located all of the objects, cut out some paper pool shapes and see how they fit in those areas that you have selected. Try to maintain simple geometric relationships between the house and the pool or the surrounding landform. Determine your best options before calling a contractor.

Planning the Pool Surround

The area immediately around the pool is very important. The surface must be durable, skid-resistant and attractive. Most surfaces are treated with a waterproofing or similar material to minimize maintenance. Popular materials include concrete, mixed aggregate, brick, redwood, flagstone, ceramic tile, outdoor carpeting and patio block.

Most pool surrounds are a minimum of 3 ft. This dimension is often regulated by local code. However, for an in-ground

pool, 6 to 8 ft. is recommended. This will protect most of the area around the pool from the treated pool water. Leave enough room for a diving board, ladder area and possibly a sunbathing area. A 10-ft. long diving board extends back into the surround a total of eight feet.

The surround also assists in the maintenance of the pool's water quality. If stone and grass were used as the pool surround, dirt tracks from the grass to the stone and the pool could result in dirt washed into the pool. This overloads the pool's filtration system and causes undue maintenance requirements. Try to keep the material selection to one major surface material. Use of many different materials could cause undue maintenance problems in the long run. It also is easier to try to replace one wearing material, rather than many.

Choosing Diving Boards, Ladders and Slides

If the size of the pool permits it, addition of a diving board, ladder or slide can make a pool even more enjoyable.

Diving Boards Diving boards for residential use are either of fiberglass or wood. Fiberglass and wood-core models normally are 18 in. wide, and length varies. A wood-core diving board tends to be more expensive than a fiberglass one, since the manufacturing process produces a more pliant board.

For most residential pools with a diving board, a minimum diving depth of 8 ft. is required. If the height of the board is increased, the depth must also be increased. A 3-meter board would require at least

Concrete is the most frequently used pool surround; it can be dressed up with redwood-strip expansion joints, as shown.

A redwood deck next to the pool is desirable but optional. A fence, however, is often required in order to prevent accidents.

12 ft. of diving depth to insure the safety of the diver. The diving board is installed into the surround using predrilled bolts. The support for the diving board is generally a thickened concrete slab or surround. The board must be anchored securely.

Slides Slides usually are fiberglass with aluminum steps. The height varies from 6 ft. to 9 ft. depending on the model and the length of the slide. The amount of surface area required for a slide varies from 3.5 ft. to 9.5 ft. for the largest model. It is preferred that the slide legs be anchored in a concrete base. If this option is not available, deck anchor flanges can be used. Since the slide is elevated above the pool, care should be taken to place it in an area where the danger of falling on surface objects is minimized.

Ladders Ladders used in residential swimming pools are generally made of stainless steel and have three stainless steel or plastic treads. The handrails are often made of stainless steel as well. In walk-up pools, the handrails are located along the side to assist the swimmer. The location of the ladders and handrails is important and must be assigned before excavation. Inserts into the concrete or coping should be embedded when the pool edge is poured. Usually ladders are located at the shallow end, with an additional one at the diving end. Some ladder models can be removed during the winter if necessary.

All pool equipment must be installed in accordance with the regulation and recommendations of the National Swimming Pool Institute. A copy of these standards is available from: National Swimming Pool Institute, 2000 K Street, N.W., Washington, D.C. 20006.

Adding Pool Enclosures

Pool enclosures come in a variety of sizes and shapes. Their primary function is to make the swimming pool a more pleasant area. In very windy areas, an enclosure can protect the swimmers and the pool area. There are two basic types of pool enclosure.

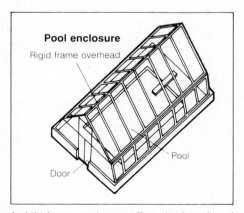

Pool enclosure
Rigid frame overhead
Pool
Door

A ridid-frame enclosure offers the benefits of solar heating, but suffers from the drawback of the "greenhouse effect."

The Rigid-frame Enclosure This type of enclosure has spanning members of aluminum or steel. Plexiglass or glass is inserted between the members, providing the shielding necessary. A few rigid-frame enclosure manufacturers furnish a modified greenhouse as a pool enclosure.

Some enclosures use a rigid frame that can roll back on tracks built into the pool surround, so that you may have both the open and the closed option.

The major limitation of the rigid enclosure is that, for economic reasons, the area around the pool is limited. The minimum distance between the pool and the wall of the enclosure should be no less than 4 ft. and preferably 6 ft., so that you can move around the pool freely. Also, adequate ventilation must be provided to minimize the "greenhouse effect". This effect causes considerable condensation over the interior surfaces and can cause serious mildew and rotting of wooden objects. However, with a rigid frame enclosure you can gain the benefit of solar heating in a cold climate.

The Inflatable Enclosure The second method of enclosing a pool uses a pneumatic type of structure. With the aid of a fan, the inflatable enclosure is able to span relatively large distances. The major problem is that the fan is drawing in outside air which, in colder climates, must be heated. Its main advantages are its roominess, the conditioned air, and its ability to withstand most climatic variables. Transparent panels come built in so that sunlight can penetrate through to the pool. This type of structure is seen most often over tennis courts or large playing areas.

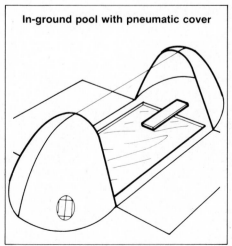

In-ground pool with pneumatic cover

The pneumatic (inflatable) enclosure is relatively inexpensive to install, but it can be costly to heat in cold regions.

ELECTRICITY FOR LIGHT AND POWER

There are three main areas of concern when planning outdoor electrical services: outdoor lighting (exterior and underwater), power and signal.

Lighting Needs

In warmer climates, exterior lighting can extend the use of the in-ground swimming pool far beyond the daylight hours. Exterior lighting can take many forms, such as accent, landscaping, in-pool and security. Probably the most important aspect is the lighting directly around the pool. This is for safety and security. The most direct method is to locate several spotlights above the pool level as task lighting. This is inexpensive, but could detract from the visual and spatial qualities of the pool at night. Another method, which can be used to great effect, is the introduction of lights into the coping of the swimming pool. Along with the pool's lights, plan a series of small garden lights throwing light over the pool surround area. This maintains security and safety and at the same time enhances the visual impact of the pool area.

Exterior Lighting The exterior area around the pool should be well lit, while still treating the area as a stage set. Patios next to the pools should be treated with accent lighting. The highlighting of physical features should be placed to eliminate any possible glare. An ideal position would be above the feature instead of to the side.

Many pool owners prefer to have the deep end of the pool away from the house in order to see the divers and swimmers move towards the shallow end. At night, a light that highlights the diving area might shine into the house, which is not desirable. To avoid this problem, locate the light high enough above the pool so that it does not shine in the diver's face, nor into the house.

The pool surround should also be well lit so that children or adults running around the pool will not slip or trip over pool related objects. The most effective type of lighting is the Malibu light, or a similar low-voltage type that sheds indirect light on the surround surface. These bulbs should not be visible to the viewer.

Backlighting for fences, hedges and other prominent features will accent the three-dimensional quality of the landscaped area and provide visual warning to the bathers who might be running around oblivious to the potential hazards. Try to avoid the use of colored lights. They often make the area appear distorted or warped. Try to balance light intensity. Where a more intense light is required, provide a lower light level elsewhere. This can be accomplished with dimmers.

No matter what type of lighting you may desire or require, consult a licensed electrician. The electrician can insure that your requirements are possible and will meet the local or state building codes. Do not attempt to wire an exterior fixture without expert advice unless you have had considerable previous electrical experience.

Underwater Lighting Underwater pool lights are a wonderful addition to an in-ground pool. They make swimming at night easier and safer. It is easier to do this installation during the construction of the pool than afterward. Most in-pool lighting, whether it is above or underwater, must conform to the National Electrical Code Requirements for fixture safety. The NEC requires that all installations be grounded and watertight, that waterproof wiring be used and all electrical connections be located above the pool water surface.

The first consideration in the selection of the in-pool light should be the type and amount of light that is needed. A rule of thumb is to have one light for each 24 to 30 linear ft. of pool side. For a 16x32 ft. pool, which has 96 linear ft. of pool side, 3 lights are recommended. You might also consider the addition of a light in the area of the pool stairs. The placement would be 1 on each side and one under the diving board or deep end.

Once you know the number of lights needed, select the voltage system to be used. A 110-volt or 12-volt system is available. The 12-volt system is called a low-voltage system. It uses 110v, which is fed to a transformer that in turn is connected to the underwater light. The low-voltage light is available in 300 watt lamps. The primary advantage of the low-voltage system is that if shorted, it is safe. A swimmer will not be aware of the shock. However, in a 110v system it would be very noticeable. The low voltage system is recommended for almost all installations. It is equal in cost to the 110v system.

"Wet" and "Dry" Niches The lamps are placed in either a "wet" or a "dry" niche. The niches are the housings that accommodate the lamp assembly. A wet niche is a waterproof housing with a chrome plated face plate that will fit all fiberglass, vinyl, steel, aluminum and structural polymer walled in-ground pools. Unlike the dry niche, the lamp assembly is sealed and can be changed underwater. In fact, the sealed lamp will only function under water. The lamp is then connected by waterproof wiring in a conduit to a junction box at the pool surround or coping level so it can be easily accessed. The dry niche requires that the pool level be dropped in order to change the lamp. Both systems are available in 110v and 12v.

Product suggestions Colored lenses for the underwater lamp assemblies are available and can be easily changed without having to change the lamp. Other types of underwater lights also are available, which require no in-pool installation. Several manufacturers offer a portable underwater light that can open up a whole new world of after-dark beauty for those pools built without underwater lighting. This lamp is safe, low-voltage, and it operates up to 6 hours on its own rechargeable battery. The lamp assembly hangs into the pool and will illuminate a pool up to 20x30 ft. This type of lamp is often chosen as an alternative to the underwater lighting previously discussed, since it is economical.

There are several types of pool lights that add decorative ambience rather than serve a functional purpose. These are strictly to enhance the visual quality of the pool and should not be used when the pool is in use. One example of this type of lamp is the Floating Blossom Light.

Other Power Needs for the Pool
Electrical needs should be planned ahead, not added after everything is completed. The running of power lines and lighting circuits is critical to the operation of the pool. All power outlets must be at least 18 inches above the level of the surround and be fully protected. The electrical service must have a circuit of its own. The electrical service to the pump and filtration equipment must be on its own circuit. Check with an electrician or swimming pool contractor to make sure that your current amperage capacity is adequate for the size pump. Keep in mind that the size of the pump is dependent on the size and type of pool you are to select.

Filtration System Recommendations The motor size on most filtration systems will vary between ½ to 2½ horse-

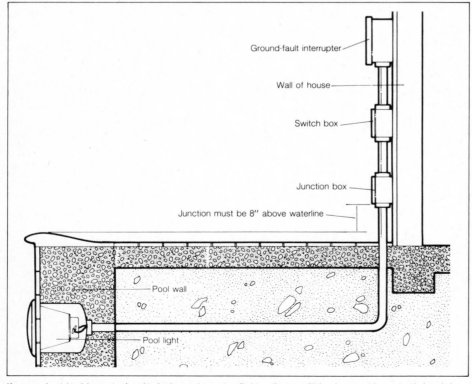

If your electrical layout plan include underwater lights, these will be housed in watertight niches. Power connections will be made above the waterline.

power. The general ratings, based on approximate pool size are as follows.

FILTRATION SYSTEM REQUIREMENTS

Horsepower	Size	Volts
½	16x32	115
¾	18x36	115/230
1	20x40	115/230
1.5	20x45	115/230
2	24x36	115/230
2.5	25x40	230

The pump horsepower is determined by the gpm, which in turn depends on the filtration cycle. A 3-wire connection to the motor junction box and disconnect switch will permit a 230 volt system for future use, if desired. All wiring should be grounded and, in most localities, codes will require installation by a licensed electrician.

When figuring out your power requirements, take into account provision of a pool heater or additional pumps for other parts of your recreational area. If you select an electric water heater, check your current electrical service before choosing the heater. Electric water heaters can service pools from 4,800 to 42,000 gallon capacity. Their power demand can require as much as 71 amperes on a 3-phase 480-volt connection. This type of service is not found in most residential situations.

Entertainment Areas Entertainment areas around the pool call for a number of outlets. Install underground conduit connected to a series of carefully placed outlets. In additon, if a gazebo or cabana is contemplated, provision for lighting or outlets should be made.

HEATING THE POOL WATER

If you live in a climate that will allow you to swim all year, this section does not really apply to you. The information that follows is for the less fortunate, who reside in climates that are more extreme. Most pool owners want to extend the swimming season as far as they can. The most common way to "stretch" the swimming season is to heat the swimming pool water. Depending on where you live, a pool water heater will enable you to start your swimming season earlier in the spring and later in the autumn. There are three primary methods for heating the pool water: solar heating systems, conventional heating and solar-blankets.

Solar Panel Heating Systems

In recent years, the advent of solar power has affected and changed attitudes about how we heat and cool homes. Technology that was developed for the house has been modified and adapted to the heating of swimming pool water. The investment in a solar pool-water heating system can pay for itself in a very short period of time.

To use solar energy efficiently, the geographic location must be considered. There are some regions in the United States where sufficient sun is not available, due to cloud cover. In some areas, the sunny days may account for only 36% in any one month. This means that 2 out of every 3 days will be overcast. Without the sunshine there is little solar energy transfer. To determine what your percentage of cloud cover is in any one month, contact your local weather bureau or television station weatherman. If over 50% of the days are to be overcast, a backup heating system may be required.

Systems Components and Operation Most installed solar heating systems utilize 4-ft.-wide unglazed flat plate collectors that are of a very dark color. The plate collectors range in length from 4 to 10 ft. In addition to the collector, stainless steel installation components and temperature-sensing controls are included to determine the rate of water flow through the panel. Most panels are manufactured of a propylene copolymer that is impervious to pool chemicals and resistant to exposure from sun, heat, pollution and oxidation. The number of solar collector panels is determined by orientation, roof faces, latitude and climate. Each one of these criteria must be carefully analyzed to figure the number of panels. In general, the number of solar panels should be equal in area to about one half of the surface of the swimming pool for a true-south orientation. This would be based on a water flow rate through the panel of 3.5 to 4 gpm (gallons per minute).

Safety lighting around the pool is always recommended for night use, but it can be arranged to serve as dramatic accent lighting as well.

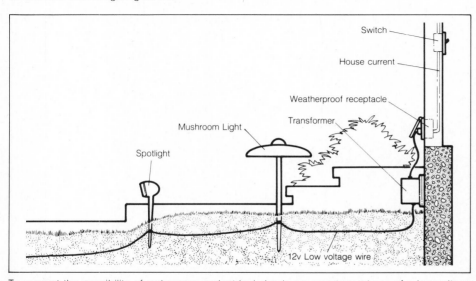

To prevent the possibility of a dangerous electrical shock, we recommend use of a low-voltage lighting system (stepped down to 12 volts) around the pool.

Most collectors operate as a "fully-whetted" collector. This means that the entire collector is composed of small tubes that allow the pool water to touch nearly every square inch of the collector's energy absorbing surface. The tubes are connected to piping that runs between the outlet side of the filter and the pool. This system uses the filter motor to pump the water through the solar collectors.

The solar panel(s) can be set up to work automatically. Once the desired pool temperature is set, the pump is activated and the pool water sensor signals that the temperature is below the selected setting. The system will automatically activate a valve that directs the water flow through the solar collector panel if the Solar Sensor finds that there is sufficient solar energy available. If there is not, a supplementary water heater is activated to make up the temperature difference. Once that has been made up the Pool Water Sensor closes the valve. If you live in a climate where winterization is required, most of the panels are self-draining when the pump stops. The piping is winterized as for standard pool piping.

Panel Location Most of the solar panels can be installed or mounted on a cabana, roof or on the ground and should face either due south or slightly east of south at an inclination equal to the latitude of the installation. While other solar face angles are workable, the ideal angle places the panel perpendicular to the sun.

Solar collectors are becoming more popular as swimming pool heat sources. The panels are placed on a roof near the pool.

Conventional Heating Methods

Gas, oil, electric or heat pump water heaters are the conventional heating systems for pools. Most pool water heaters are best installed during the construction of the pool. The output of a pool heater depends greatly upon your geographic location, the size of your pool and how much sun it receives on a daily basis. Usually, gas water heaters are the most efficient.

However, recent developments in heat pump technology have produced comparable efficiency for residential swimming pool use.

Gas-fired Water Heaters Although energy shortages in the past years have curtailed use of many gas-fired pool water heaters, the gas-fired hot water heater is an efficient unit. Most models are available with electronic ignition, which represents

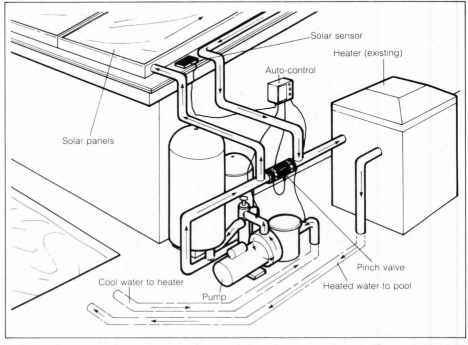

Solar panels can provide low-cost heating, especially in warmer climates. (For instructions on buying or building panels, see *Heating, Cooling & Ventilation* by Jay Hedden.)

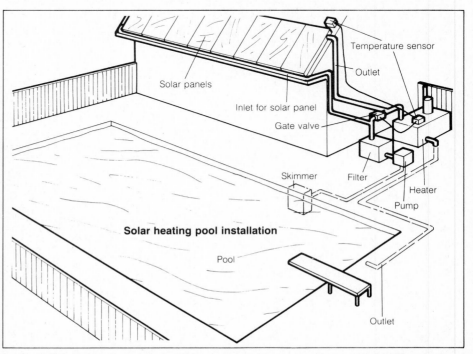

For cost efficiency, try to arrange the piping routes so they are as short as possible. The number of panels needed to heat a pool depends primarily on pool size.

a 10% savings per season over those without. In addition, newer combustion chamber designs and flue closure devices have boosted overall efficiency of the gas fired heater to 78%. Most heaters have a finned tube heat exchanger with a baffle system that channels the heat around a greater surface area. Many have electronic temperature thermostats to control temperature variation and energy consumption for at least a 10% savings over conventional thermostat arrangements.

To determine the size of the heating unit, first calculate the square footage of the pool. Then pinpoint the temperature rise desired (the temperature rise is the difference between the average outdoor air temperature and the desired pool water temperature during the coldest month of pool usage). Based on the results of these calculations, refer to the accompanying chart to determine the BTU/hr input capacity that the heater must provide.

BTU/HR INPUT CAPACITY

Temp Rise	Max. Square Footage of the Pool				
15F	367	513	734	954	1174
20F	275	385	550	715	880
25F	220	308	440	572	705
30F	183	256	367	477	587
35F	157	220	315	409	503
Total Heating Required in BTU/hr (MBH)	125	175	250	325	400

As an example, consider a 16x32 ft. pool with a surface area of 512 sq. ft. If the coldest outside air temperature during the swimming season is 56° F. and the desired pool temperature is 70° F., the temperature rise is equal to 14° F. Read down the chart to find 15° F. and match that with the closest larger value under pool size, which is 513. Drop to the bottom of the chart to find that a 175,000 BTU/hr unit is recommended. This chart is based on an average wind of 3.5 mph and an average pool depth of 5.5 ft. These charts are based on an intermittent heating cycle as a means of conserving energy and are designed to bring the pool water up to temperature within 36 hours.

A gas-fired water heater should be located near the pump and filter system to minimize the lengths of piping. Most gas-fired water heaters should be protected from the elements by an enclosure.

Heat Pump Water Heaters The heat pump is really a refrigerator in reverse. It takes heat from the air through a coil and transfers that heat to the pool water. As long as the outside air temperature is 55° F. or higher, the pool water will be heated to 80° F. or higher. Unlike the solar panel, sunlight is not required for the operation of the heat pump. The heat pump, if used properly, can be effective on almost all outdoor and indoor pool operations.

Most heat pumps require 240 volts. Their operation is affected by pool temperature, air temperature, wind factor and relative humidity. The sizing of a heat pump is based on the pool size and the current draw required to operate the pump. The heat pump represents a higher initial investment than an equivalent capacity gas heater. However, over the life span of the pool, the high cost heat pump may pay for itself quickly.

Oil-fired Water Heaters The oil-fired water heater operates in a similar

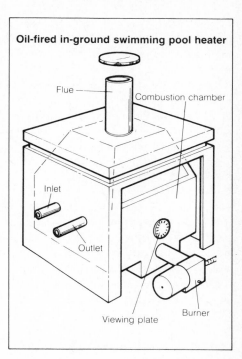

Oil-fired in-ground swimming pool heater

Flue — Combustion chamber
Inlet
Outlet
Viewing plate — Burner

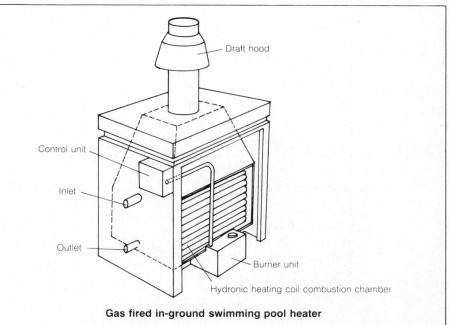

Draft hood
Control unit
Inlet
Outlet
Burner unit
Hydronic heating coil combustion chamber

Gas fired in-ground swimming pool heater

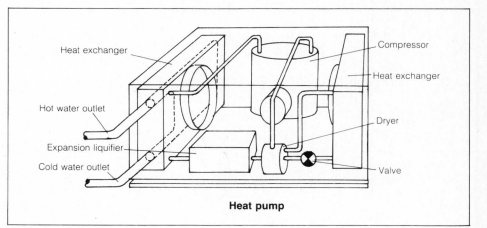

Heat exchanger — Compressor
Heat exchanger
Hot water outlet
Dryer
Expansion liquifier
Cold water outlet — Valve

Heat pump

fashion to the gas-fired unit, but with a different fuel. The main requirement is that an oil storage tank must be installed near the heating unit. The typical unit can use either #1 or #2 heating oil. The unit is capable of heating large quantities of water with an output of 350,000 BTU/hr. Refer to the gas-fired selection chart to determine the unit size required.

Solar Blankets

Covering the swimming pool with a solar blanket provides the owner with a twofold savings: savings in energy costs of heating the pool water, and savings due to reduced water evaporation. Whether a heater is added or not, the solar blanket can reduce the total energy demand by 70% compared to a noncovered one. In an unheated pool, the introduction of a solar blanket can raise the pool water temperature by 10° F. or more. This is dependent upon the number of sunny days in any one month.

During the day, when the pool is not in use, the blanket floats on the surface, transmitting the solar energy into the pool at all depths. Since the blanket reduces the evaporation of pool water, it lowers the demand for chemicals as well. During nonuse or night use, the blanket acts as a

very thin insulating shield, sealing in the heat trapped during the day. In many cases, the solar blanket will eliminate the need for a hot water heater. Buy a version that is installed with a track system.

Safety Another reason for using a pool blanket is safety; it can save lives.

The statistics show that two thirds of all drownings occur in unattended pools with the victims being children under the age of five. The reinforced vinyl fabric of the blanket is strong enough to support several adults when the edges are restrained. This feature can reduce potential accidents.

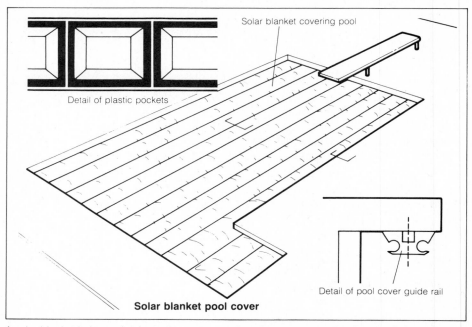

Detail of plastic pockets

Solar blanket covering pool

Detail of pool cover guide rail

Solar blanket pool cover

A solar blanket helps maintain pool temperature, but also acts as a safety lid to prevent accidents. For a secure fit, attach the blanket with a guide rail.

Solar blankets are increasing in popularity in most regions, even in colder climates, because they reduce pool heating costs.

3
BUILDING AN IN-GROUND CONCRETE POOL

The steps for building an in-ground swimming pool are complex and require a certain dedication. Not only will you save money (if it is properly done) but you will also have a vested interest in the pool, knowing the time and effort that was invested in it.

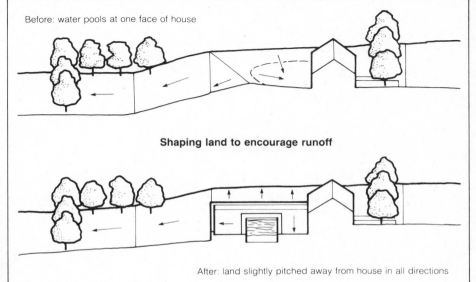

Shaping land to encourage runoff

Before: water pools at one face of house

After: land slightly pitched away from house in all directions

If land dips, regrade to encourage runoff and to prevent water from pooling.

Sliding glass doors connect this pool to the house entryway. The patio area provides space for both swimmers and onlookers.

Bathers should not remain too long in a heated spa. This layout permits movement from the spa to the pool's cooler water.

Even a small lot can hold a swimming pool. Here, the entire backyard has become the surround for a kidney-shaped pool.

PREPARING A PLOT PLAN FOR THE POOL

A plot plan is essential both for acquiring a permit and receiving accurate bids. Draw the plan on graph paper, using a scale of ⅛ in. equals 1 ft. To help you draw the plan, we suggest that you first stake the pool dimensions.

Tools Needed To stake the property you will need some wood stakes, string and a tape rule. To find the slope of the lot, use a carpenter's level or a line level.

Step 1: Staking the Area. Pinpoint the specific location of the pool on your property. Now locate the first stake. Once that first stake is in place, locate the next corner stake, along the short dimension. Position it and check the measurement, which will represent the outside dimension of the pool. Run string between the stakes. Keep the string as level as possible, using the line level or carpenter's level.

From one of the corner stakes, measure 12 ft. along the line toward the other corner stake. At 12 ft., place an intermediate stake between the two already in place. This new stake will be used to align the sides of the pool and to square the staking of the pool corners. From the stake that you used as a reference point for measuring out 12 ft., measure another 16 ft., but this time along the long side of the pool. Stake the point. Measure from the intermediate stake to the 16 ft. dimension along a diagonal line between them. If the corner is a perfect 90 degrees, as it should be, the diagonal will be 20 ft. If it is not, continue to adjust the 16 ft. dimension until the diagonal measures 20 ft. exactly. Then drive in a stake to complete the triangle. Now complete the dimension for the longer side by sighting along the 16 ft. line. Once this third stake is in place, place the last corner stake opposite it. Repeat the 12-16-20 ft. triangle procedure for the opposite corner in order to square all four corners for a rectangular pool.

Step 2: Checking the Vertical Level A string line that is connected from post to post usually will be adequate to check the ground slope. Make sure that all the lines are level from stake to stake. Measure from the string down to the ground level. This measurement should be checked against all four corners. A difference in dimension will indicate a slope, which is referred to in terms of "rise" and "run." Make sure that your pool is located in an area that slopes away from the pool, not toward it.

For a sloped-site pool location, try to arrange the pool so that the length or the long side of the pool runs parallel to the slope. This reduces the amount of slope, which is advantageous to your construction.

Step 3: Drawing the Plan Once the pool is staked out and the dimensions and location are set, transfer all the measurements to a plot plan.

CHOICES IN POOL EXCAVATION

There are a variety of opinions concerning the excavation of the pool. If you decided to build a 16x32 ft. pool with an average depth of 6 ft., that represents approximately 3000 cu. ft. or 120 cu. yds. of earth. If you armed yourself with a shovel

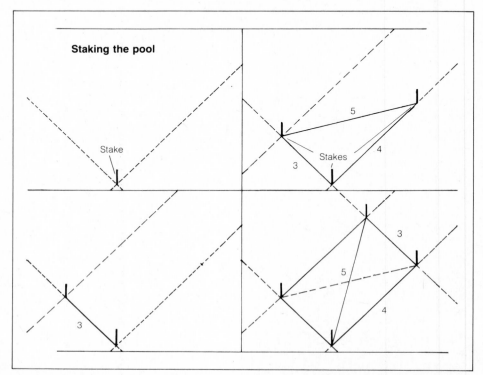

Using multiples of the 3-4-5 right triangle to lay out the pool (in this case, 12, 16 and 20 ft.) helps ensure perfectly square corners and exact dimensions.

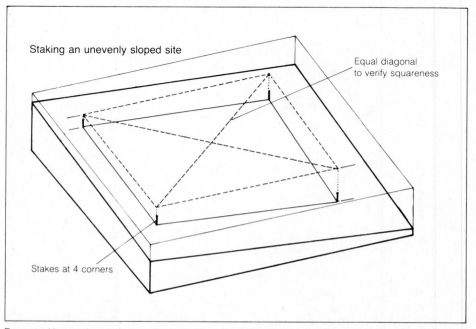

For a pool located on a slope, adjust markings on stakes to allow for changes in elevation. Note that the horizontal shape becomes skewed when placed on a slope.

it would take you several weeks to complete the task. While this is possible (and economical if you have the time), an experienced excavator with a backhoe or bulldozer could provide the same service in less than a day. In addition, a backhoe will accurately cut the hole to your layout requirements with a minimum amount of recutting. Considering the economics, subcontracting the excavation to an experienced contractor makes sense.

Another major concern in the excavation of the pool is the preparation of the soil under the floor of the pool, as well as the walls of the pool. In an in-ground pool, the preparation of the soil is critical to the continued life of the pool. A properly compacted and consolidated soil will minimize any movement or settlement of the pool. A bulldozer or backhoe provides the necessary pressure as it moves about in the excavation. The continued compaction of the soil will be further reduced if a mechanical tamper is used. Most contractors will finish the base and the walls using a mechanical tamper.

Whether you arrange for the excavation or perform it yourself, provide an area where the excavated soil will be placed. Most of the stored soil will be used as backfill, but there will be some soil that must be hauled away or used in another portion of your property. Locate the storage spot so that it is accessible to a truck or a backhoe. If possible, cover the excavated soil in case of rain.

HOW TO SET UP BATTER BOARDS

Before the actual excavation, the stakes that you located to indicate the inside corners for the pool must be relocated using batter boards, as illustrated. The boards are set back 4 to 6 ft. from the corner stakes, allowing room to work. Line is run from the boards to cross the exact tops of the corner stakes. The line will be used to align the concrete form boards and determine the proper depth for the base of the pool.

You can also mark onto the batter boards the vertical heights desired. When figuring the height of the pool, allow 6 inches above the highest ground elevation. Then the soil will be formed to meet that elevation.

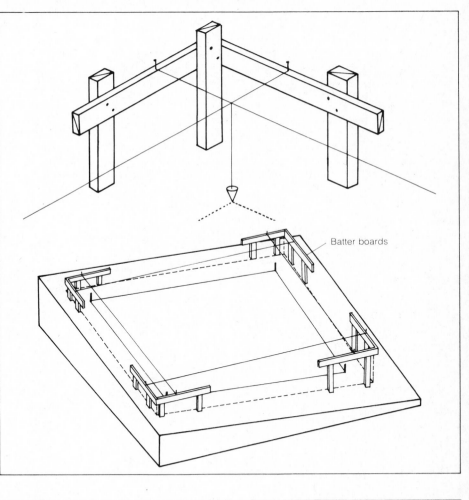

Batter boards

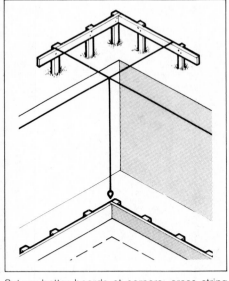

Set up batter boards at corners; cross string lines above corner stakes. Use a plumb bob to pinpoint exact stake positions.

CREATING THE WALL FOOTINGS FOR THE POOL

Wall footings are necessary not only to support the pool walls but to provide an adequate water stop between the walls and the pool bottom. For a pool of an average depth of 6 ft., the continuous footing should be no smaller than 10 in. deep x 24 in. wide. This footing will be able to support a wall up to 10 ft. high and 10 in. thick.

Step 1: Setting the Stakes Using the batter boards that were installed before the excavation, verify the vertical inside face of the pool wall by dropping a plumb line to the bottom of your excavation. Stake that corner and the remaining corners, if you have not already done so.

Stepped Footings If your pool is not of a constant depth, the elevation of the stakes relative to each other will not be equal. In this case, a stepped footing will be necessary. This "steps" down in equal increments from the shallower elevation to the deeper one. For example, if the shallower footing depth is 48 in. above the deeper one, four steps of 12 in. each could be used, or three steps of 16 in. each.

Step 2: Preparing the Soil Place several cubic yards of crushed gravel along the floor of the pool to a depth of 12 inches. Compact it to a 6-in. depth using a mechanical compactor or a tamper. After the gravel has been compacted, construct the forms.

Step 3: Constructing the Form To construct the form for the footing, you will require 2x12s and 2x4s. To find the amounts needed, determine the length of the perimeter of the footing and multiply by two (for outside and inside face) to approximate the length of the 2x12 material. Place the 2x12 on edge and then fix it in place by driving 2x4 stakes at 24-in. centers along the length. Where the pieces butt, double stake to prevent any shifting

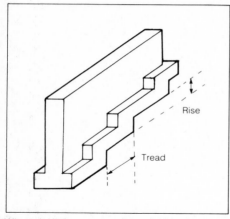

When building on a sloped site, install a stepped footing that rises continuously as it progresses up the incline.

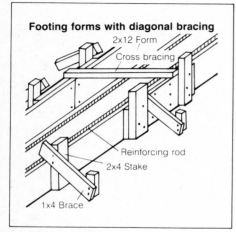

Footing forms with diagonal bracing

2x12 Form
Cross bracing
Reinforcing rod
2x4 Stake
1x4 Brace

Footing forms should be supported with 2x4 stakes and diagonal braces in order to withstand pressure from the poured concrete.

of the form. Oil the forms to aid stripping later.

Step 4: Placing the Reinforcing Once the form has been braced, insert steel reinforcing into the form. Make sure that the reinforcing is spliced together for at least 18 in. from either end. The steel rods can be suspended from the cross pieces that hold the sides of the form together, using wire that is tied to the cross support piece. The rod should be at least 3 in. above the bottom of the form.

Step 5: Pouring the Concrete Once the form is in place and checked for dimensional accuracy (check it several times), it is ready to receive the concrete. The concrete should be at least 3000 psi, or what is traditionally referred to as a six-bag mix. Always arrange for several people to assist you in placing the concrete; doing it alone is an almost impossible and very frustrating job.

Precautions As the concrete truck backs up to the excavation, make sure that it does not come too close to the pool edge. Have the driver add extensions to the concrete chute. Do not allow the concrete to free fall into the forms over 3 ft. If you do, the aggregate will separate and reduce the strength of the concrete.

Concrete Placement As the concrete is poured into the forms, move the material into the nooks and crannies of the form. Once the form is full, take a reinforcing rod and push it up and down into the concrete. Work along the entire length

of the form. This increases the density of the material. Never pour more than you can rod in 45 minutes to 1 hour.

Step 6: Inserting Reinforcing Dowels As the concrete begins to settle into the forms, insert reinforcing dowels, which tie together the wall and footing. As the forms are filled, rodded, and screeded, try to keep all the dowels in alignment along the length of the forms no more than 48 in. on center. The dowels should protrude 24 in. above the surfaces. In areas where there is a high water table, a neoprene water stop should be inserted along with the dowels. This will keep the ground water from moving up into the pool above.

It should take no more than a half a day to place a 16x32 ft. pool, which represents about 24 cu. yds. of concrete. After all the concrete has been placed, go back and check the dowels (and water stop, if applicable).

Step 7: Finishing the Surface Screed the surface of the form using a short piece of wood. Move the wood back and forth over the form until it is level and fairly smooth. You do not need to trowel the surface, since the footing will never be seen.

The forms and the concrete should be sprayed with water, starting the afternoon of the day the concrete was poured, to aid and produce stronger concrete. Continue to keep damp for 3 days.

Step 8: Stripping the Forms You can strip the footings at the end of the

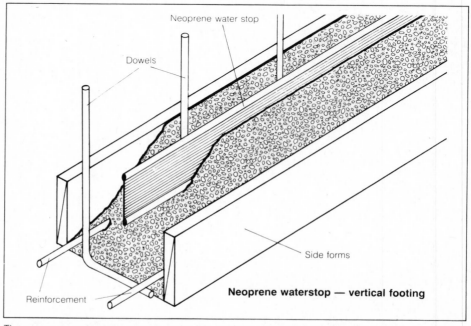

Neoprene water stop
Dowels
Side forms
Reinforcement
Neoprene waterstop — vertical footing

The neoprene waterstop prevents water penetration in the wall and footing joint. Center it vertically (half of it projecting out of the form) before pouring concrete.

second complete day of curing. The concrete will still be green (condition of curing and coloration).

Try not to hit the concrete with the sledge hammer while you remove the wood forms. If you are stripping the forms on a very hot day, keep the concrete wet at all times. In a colder climate, less than 50°F., cover the concrete footings with a tarp or polyethelene sheet to keep the heat and moisture in. Never pour concrete in freezing weather, unless you have ordered heated aggregate.

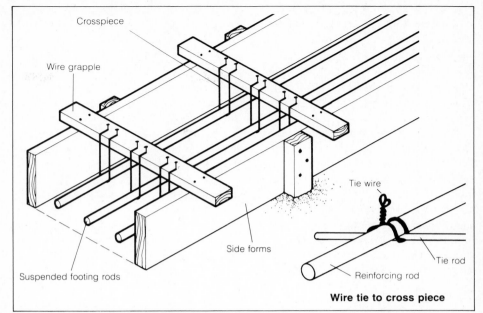

Wire tie to cross piece

In this reinforcing rod placement alternative, bars are suspended in galvanized wire cradles, tied to the form tie with tie wires. Wire is cut off after the concrete pour.

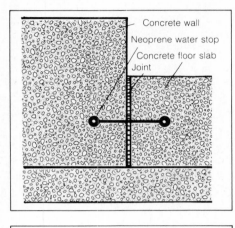

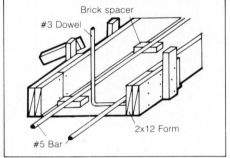

Footing reinforcing rods can be held up off the floor of the footing trench by brick spacers and bent dowels.

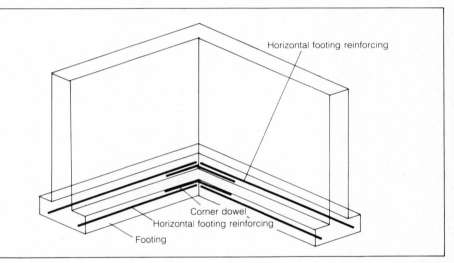

Shown are correct positions for: (above) footing reinforcement in poured-in-place wall; (below left) vertical dowels; (below right) horizontal plus vertical reinforcing.

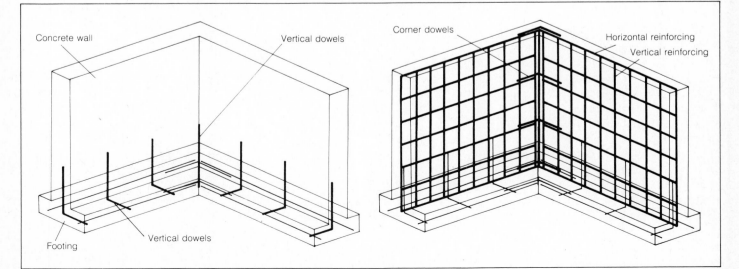

FORMING AND POURING THE POOL WALLS

If you decide not to subcontract the walls of the pool out, there are several sources that you may contact that not only rent the necessary forms (they are usually prefabricated), but deliver and erect them to your specifications.

Most wall forms are modular and can handle wall thicknesses ranging from 6 to 18 in. They come in "exterior wall plus interior wall" sets. The normal height of the form varies from 4 to 8 ft. since a typical panel is 4x8. Between the exterior and interior panel, a thin metal wall tie is installed. These ties are located every 2 to 4 ft. on center, and at least two per 8-ft. height.

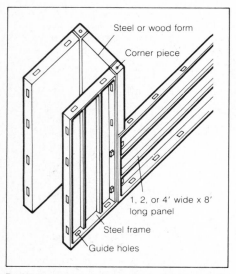

Prefabricated steel forms can be inexpensively rented and substituted for the homebuilt, wooden variety.

Step 1: Installing Exterior Forms

Place the exterior panels along the footing, flush to each other and interlocking. Most panels come equipped with interlocking devices that are a part of the panel construction. Complete the entire perimeter of the pool. Before installing the interior panels, check the alignment of the panels using the lines connected to the batter boards. You will require at least two helpers to lift and install the panels. As you erect the exterior panels going around the pool, incorporate any recessed stairs that extend beyond the edge of the pool face.

Step 2: Placing Reinforcement

After the exterior panels are in place and all the inserts are in their proper places, install the steel reinforcement. The reinforcement is an integral part of the con-

crete wall. It must be placed properly into the form, tying it to the dowels that extend from the footing.

A minimum requirement for an 8-in. concrete pool wall would be #4 reinforcing bars at 18 ins. on center, placed horizontally along the center of the wall. In addition, #5 bars would be needed at 12 in. on center, spaced vertically along the entire length of the wall. All corners must be further reinforced with #3 dowels every 6 in., placed horizontally. Where inserts are placed in the wall, additional reinforcing must be installed around the opening. In all concrete walls, the reinforcing should never be closer to the side of the wall than 3 in. This is to reduce the possibility of corrosion due to moisture penetration.

As you place the reinforcing into the form, tie it together using a medium sized wire. All the reinforcement should be tied

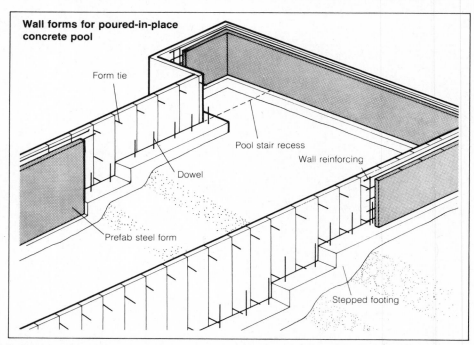

Wall forms for poured-in-place concrete pool

Prefabricated steel forms can be rented so you don't have to build them from wood. Detail of form structure is shown at left.

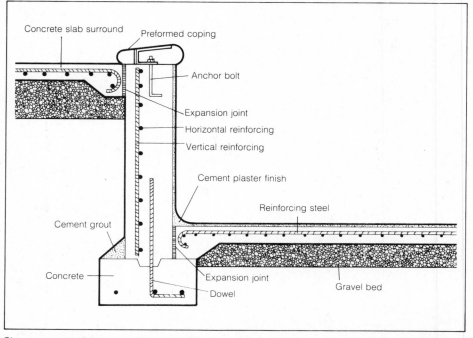

Shown are materials, components, positions and relationships for a poured-in-place concrete pool (view on facing page, top left, shows reinforcing placement).

together so that when the concrete is placed into the closed form, the rods will not lose their respective positions to each other; this would weaken the wall.

If you have any doubt about your ability to install the reinforcing as described

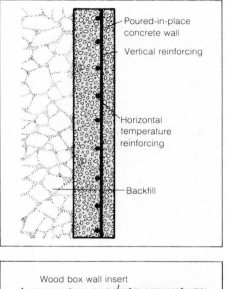

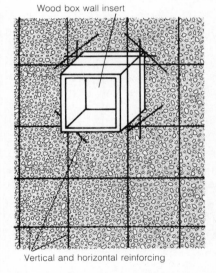

To leave space for openings for piping filtration system components, position wooden boxes as spacers before pouring concrete.

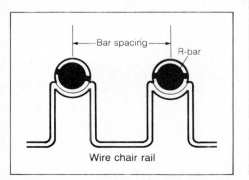

Reinforcing rods sit in steel chair supports. Spacing between bars can vary, since chair rails adjust by 3-in. increments.

above, consider hiring a reinforcing fabricator to install the reinforcing cage into the form. Another option is to have the reinforcing fabricator furnish all the necessary pieces and the directions for the proper installation.

Step 3: Installing Interior Forms Make sure that you have located all the openings in the wall for the skimmer, water inlets, underwater lights, etc. These generally consist of simple boxes built to the width of the form and placed so that the concrete will not fill in that space. Make sure that all inserts are well anchored so that they do not move. As the panels are interlocked with each other, the joints between the panels should align with the exterior wall joints. There is a provision for a metal tie that fits between the panels, holding the exterior to the interior. These normally occur every 2 to 4 ft. horizontally and at least twice over the height of an 8-ft. wall. The wall ties will be embedded in the concrete when the forms are stripped away.

Once all the interior forms are in place, check all the forms again for alignment and level. This is an important part of the entire procedure.

Step 4: Bracing the Panels Although the forms interlock, additional stabilizers will be required to brace the entire length of the pool wall. In smaller pools, horizontal braces can be used, reaching from side to side. In the larger pool, 45-degree braces must be utilized. Most from suppliers and contractors have rules of thumb as to proper bracing distances, such as 48 in. on center. Remember that it is better to overbrace than to underbrace. Generally, a formed panel wall must be braced on both sides. This might affect the area that must be excavated, to give enough room. Check with the panel sup-

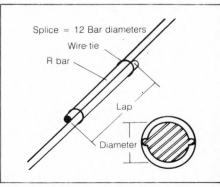

Shown is a cross-section of a deformed reinforcing rod. End laps of bars should equal at least 12 bar diameters.

plier for those particular requirements. Keep all the panels true (square).

Step 5: Oiling the Forms Apply an oil coating to the forms if recommended by the panel supplier. This coating reduces the adhesion between the concrete and the forms, making it easier to strip the forms after the curing period has elapsed.

Step 6: Pouring the Walls When pouring the walls of a 16x32 ft. swimming pool, you will be able to pour the wall all in one day. Plan the pouring schedule. Start early and make sure that where you end one pour, you begin the next. Never pour the full height of the wall all at once. Pour concrete in horizontal layers never exceeding two to three feet. Once the concrete had been poured into the form, use a mechanical or "pencil vibrator", or rod the concrete thoroughly with a ½ or ⅝ in. reinforcing bar every 12 in. to the full depth of the concrete wall to consolidate the concrete. This also ensures that all

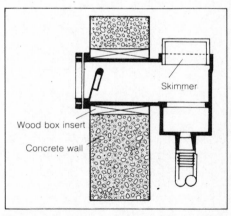

Box out the openings for the skimmer and similar items. After concrete has cured, remove the box and insert the skimmer.

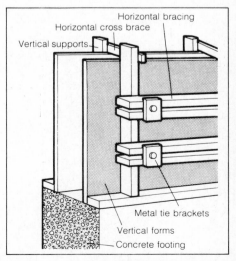

Home-built concrete wall forms are braced horizontally and supported vertically, with cross bars for additional stability.

parts of the form have concrete. Do not overvibrate or overrod, because segregation of the cement and the aggregate may take place. The recommended number varies from two to three good passes per linear foot of wall.

Never permit the driver of the concrete truck to add water to the mixture to make it more workable. The mix should be stiff. If the material coming down the chute is too sloppy or watery, it could deteriorate at a much faster rate than normal.

As the concrete is poured around the inserts, make sure that it flows all around the inserts. Several do-it-yourselfers have found gaping holes that had to be filled in because they did not make sure the concrete was properly placed in the form.

As the concrete is poured higher and higher into the form, greater pressure is exerted on the forms. This outward pressure is counteracted by the wall ties between the panels and by the bracing. Try to reduce the amount of contact with the forms so as to not dislodge them or move them.

Step 7: Finishing the Concrete

After the concrete has been poured, screed the top of the exposed concrete level and finish it with a steel trowel. Allow the concrete to cure for several days. During this period, keep the concrete moist or even wet in hot weather. If the concrete is allowed to cure too fast, the strength (and thus the watertightness) will be reduced.

Step 8: Stripping the Forms

After the third day, begin to strip the forms. As each panel is removed, the wall ties will stay in place. After all the panels are removed, the ties should be broken off on the interior of the pool. The exterior ones can remain in place, since they do not affect the operation of the pool. Keep the inserts boxes for the inlets in place until the units are to be installed. After all the forms have been removed, keep on watering the walls for another five to six days. Most concrete will achieve 80% of its maximum strength at the end of 7 or 8 days.

If there are areas that are honeycombed or incomplete due to improper concrete placement, now is the time to correct the flaw using a high quality epoxy or vinyl patching cement. Knock off any loose material prior to the placement of the patching material. Always patch one spot at a time. The patching cement dries at a very fast rate; never mix too much of it at one time. Always make sure that the patched surface is flush to the existing wall line. Generally, a trowel will do a creditable job.

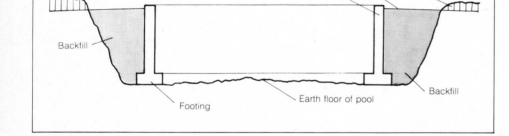

Once the footing and the side walls have cured, you are ready to backfill. Add the backfill in layers; tamp each firmly. Then you can pour the pool bottom.

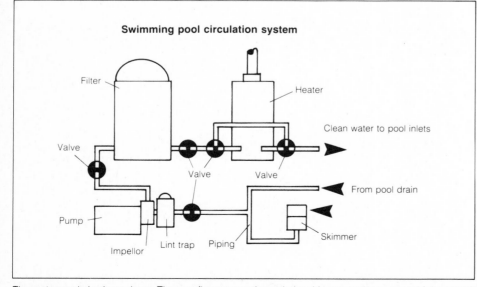

The water cycle is shown here. The overflow moves through the skimmer to the pump, which sends it to the filter. Finally, the water is heated and returned to the pool.

COATING AND BACKFILLING POOL WALLS

Once the pool wall forms have been stripped and the forms removed from the area (service provided by the panels supplier), install any electrical conduit and water piping that is to be located along the pool walls. If in doubt as to what should be included, consult a swimming pool dealer. A bituminous waterproof coating usually is applied to the outside of the concrete wall. Do not apply this asphaltic coating until the wall has been allowed to cure for at least one full week after the forms have been removed. The coating can be rolled on with

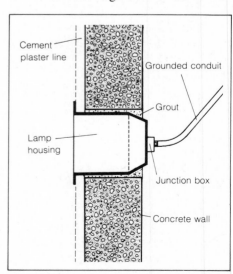

After curing, place underwater light housing in recess left by wooden spacer box in concrete; add finish grout and pool plaster.

a roller or troweled on depending on the manufacturer's recommendation. Once the coating has been applied and the piping, conduit and drain connections have been installed, the wall is ready to be backfilled.

The backfilling procedure is a delicate one. You should not just pour the dirt back into the excavation. In most cases, a crushed gravel is placed in the excavation to a height of 24 to 36 in. This allows the soil to drain properly along the base of the wall and footing.

After the crushed gravel has been laid, the excavated soil is placed along the outside portion of the wall until the level of the soil is equal to the level of the wall. If you are using a backhoe to place the backfill, make sure that you place the soil in equal layers. If not backfilled, uniformly, the wall could cave in due to the unequal pressure. Compact the soil gently as each layer is placed on the gravel base. Keep in mind that the level of the pool wall should be approximately 6 in. above grade, so that the grade slopes away from the edge of the pool. Place a 4 to 6 in. sand bed around the upper edge of the pool. This will form the base for the concrete surround.

FORMING THE FLOOR OF THE SWIMMING POOL

After completing the concrete walls of the pool, the next task is to build the bottom of the swimming pool. Since this is a poured-in-place construction, the shape of the pool floor must be achieved during the pouring of the base and not afterwards. For a pool with a sloping floor down to the diving end, the tapering that occurs must be built up using the existing soil base.

Step 1: Laying a Gravel Base After the soil base has been compacted sufficiently, place a 12-in. high crushed gravel base in the excavation. Compact the 12-in. gravel base down to 6 in. using a mechanical tamper. This will be the base for the pool floor. At this point, all the piping and the pool drain have been inserted in place. Make sure that the top of the drain will be slightly below the lowest surface of the pool floor. This will aid draining and cleaning.

Step 2: Adding Reinforcing The pool floor slab is generally 4 to 6 inches in thickness. It is reinforced with a welded wire fabric or ''mesh'' when the base is adequate to support the slab. However, in cases where the slab must span across soft spots or areas that are not able to support the full weight of the slab and the water, additional reinforcing must be included. The fabric is placed in the middle of the slab and performs two functions; temperature reinforcement, because it reduced the amount of expansion and contraction of the concrete due to temperature; tensile reinforcement, for the slab over minor soft spots. Refer to the chart for the correct size and dimension of welded wire fabric.

Step 3: Pouring the Floor Remove all excess material and check that the gravel is level. Start the pour at the deep end so that you will be moving out of the pool as you pour. The floor can only be poured after the wall forms are stripped, to give

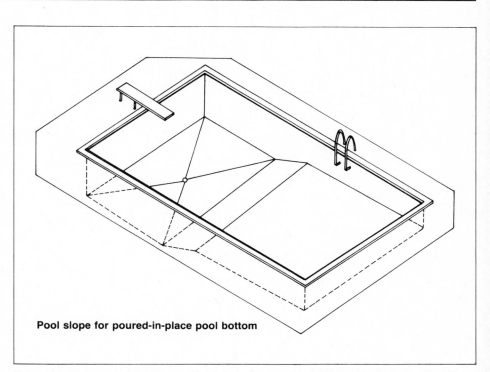

Pool slope for poured-in-place pool bottom

The pool bottom must slope down to the drain in the deep end of the pool. The floor will probably have to be poured in sections because of its size.

CORRECT PROPORTION OF STEEL PER SLAB THICKNESS

Concrete Slab Thickness	Area	Temperature reinforcement (WWF)
4 inch	.029 in2	6x6 #10/10 welded wire fabric
5 inch	.041 in2	6x6 #8/8 welded wire fabric
6 inch	.080 in2	6x6 #4/4 welded wire fabric
8 inch	.108 in2	6x6 #2/2 welded wire fabric

In the event that wire fabric is not available, straight deformed billet bars may be used. Select based on area indicated:

#3 Bar	.11 in2
#4 Bar	.20 in2
#5 Bar	.31 in2

The straight deformed billet bars can be substituted for the WWF.

---

you a reference line from which to work. A chalkline around the pool walls establishing the correct level is a great help. Another device is a screed, which is just a piece of wood that is placed along the wall. It acts as a guide to level the larger expanse of concrete. Once the larger slab has been leveled, the screed is removed and the void is then filled and leveled to the larger slab area.

Pour the slab in sections if necessary. Make sure each pour is well connected to the previous one. If in doubt, rough the edges to insure an effective bonding be-

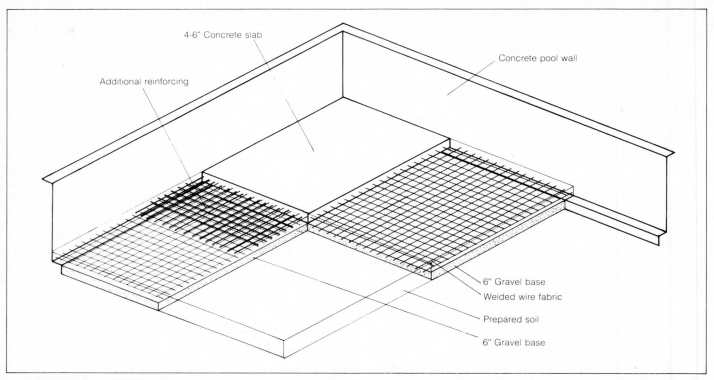

Lay welded wire fabric (WWF) on bricks or chair rails. Pour slab in sections. For more support, place #4 or #5 bars across the short direction of the slab, 6 in. o.c., over the WWF.

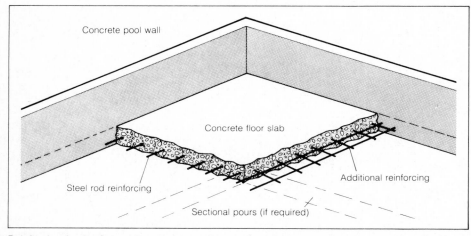

Reinforcing for the floor slab calls for regular spacing of the temperature bars in both directions.

tween the new and the old pours. Level each section to the previous one. Do not over-pour into the form. This could result in extra work shoveling the excess into the next pour area.

As the concrete is being worked into the form, use a stevedores hook or preinstalled chair rails to keep the welded wire fabric in the midway in the slab. A chair rail is a simple device that sits on the gravel subbase and suspends the reinforcing the correct distance above the gravel. These become useless if you walk all over the slab reinforcement, so some care is in order. As you move upwards to the high end of the pool, repeat the procedures for each section of slab that is poured. If the pool is small enough, the final section is generally finished by spanning boards from side to side and lying on them. Another method is to pour the middle section first and allow that to cure and then pouring either end. This method will allow you to be a little more flexible in the timing. Either method works very well. If you are not an experienced mason, the center pour is preferable.

Step 4: Finishing the Floor When pouring the concrete walls, the smoothness of the forms and the rodding or vibrating of the concrete provided a smooth surface to the wall. To achieve the same degree of finish in the slab, you must work the surface. There are several steps in the process, which can be time-consuming.

Screeding Screeding is the process of taking off any excess concrete from the poured concrete in the form. It must be done immediately after you have compacted the material in the form. It also gives a desired level to the concrete.

Select a very straight 2x4 or 2x6 of construction grade material, long enough to span from side to side of the largest pour. This could equal the pool width. Keep in mind that the larger the screed, the harder it will be to move it. This is a two- to three-person operation. Lay the screed from side to side, working the screed back and forth to skim the excess concrete to the next pour area. Level all high spots and fill in all low spots. Do not worry about how smooth the surface is at this point. The main thing is to keep it level.

When filling in the low areas, always screed the area again. Continue until the entire slab has been leveled.

Darbying The next step in finishing the slab is darbying the surface. This means that the slab is smoothed with a darby to level any raised spots and to fill depressions. A darby is a long-handled float of either wood or steel, which can be rented. This process sets the final surface level.

Floating After darbying has been completed, floating immediately follows. There are three main reasons why floating is necessary: to embed large aggregate just below the surface; to remove slight imperfections, and to consolidate the cement paste at the surface in preparation for troweling. Use an aluminum or magnesium float, working it back and forth across the poured section of the slab. Work within the poured sections. The larger the poured area, the more difficult to maintain the level. Work toward the next area to be poured. All excess water or aggregate can then be cleared into that area.

Troweling The final surface on the concrete results from troweling the surface. A steel trowel is moved back and forth over the slab, bringing the cement paste to the surface. You are floating the trowel on the surface of the cement and water paste; therefore, the trowel must be kept level at all times. If it is tilted, a noticeable washboard effect will be produced. After the first pass, take a 10-minute break and then start the procedure again. This time the paste will be harder to bring to the surface. Each successive pass will increase the hardness of the surface and the watertightness of the slab. We rec-ommend at least two or three passes of the trowel.

Step 5: Curing the Slab After the troweling has been completed for each section, it should be allowed to cure. The curing procedure is what gives the concrete its strength. When concrete cures, it gives off heat. If too much heat is generated, the concrete loses too much moisture and becomes weak. To prevent this, sprinkle the surface every two or three hours with water, for three days. This will keep the slab from curing too rapidly. If the day is very hot when you are pouring, protect the slab from direct sunlight. For this, a tent fly is most often used. The better the curing process for the first three days, the stronger the concrete and the longer it will last. All the work will be for nothing if the concrete is not properly cured.

Step 6: Adding the Final Finish The concrete should be allowed to dry for at least another two weeks after the first three days of curing. Ideally, a total of 28 days should elapse between the pouring of the concrete and the final surface application. This is because concrete does not achieve its full strength until the 28 days, which means it is releasing moisture that might reduce the effectiveness of the pool finish.

You may cover the pool with one or two of several finishes. If you paint the pool with rubber-based enamel, epoxy pool enamel or a ceramic glazed finish, cover the imperfect surfaces of the walls and floor with a very fine cement plaster, similar to a cement-sand mixture. This is hand troweled in place for complete watertightness and uniformity. If you cover the pool with ceramic tile, do not surface plaster the pool.

Rubber Based Enamel An easy to apply rubberized paint, this does not lose its color in contact with the pool chemicals. If the pool has been properly constructed, the paint will last about 2 to 3 swimming seasons. It is the least expensive of all the surface finish options. It comes in a variety of colors and is applied with a roller.

Epoxy Pool Enamels The epoxy enamels provide excellent performance at a very expensive price. It is a very durable surface finish that should last 4 to 5 swimming seasons. On a new pool wall, a primer must be used to seal the concrete before the epoxy enamel can be added. It is most often applied with a roller, although a brush will provide a glossier finish. It is available in a limited number of colors.

Ceramic Glazed Finish This is a specialty finish that is most often used on gunite pools. When properly applied, it produces a surface finish resembling porcelain. It is the most expensive of all the pool finishes but should also last 4 to 5 years without any deterioration. It is applied by brush and is available in white only. If it is to be applied over new concrete, first prime the concrete with a suitable epoxy primer.

Helpful Hints No matter which surface finish you select, follow the manufacturer's recommendations. Spend the additional time necessary to read the labels.

Tiling a Pool Most people tile only the coping of the pool, since the entire job is so extensive. However, you can tile the whole pool. Cover the coping first, then the sides, and finally the walls. Work on one section at a time.

Apply a scratch coat and then a thick bed of mortar. Usually, the mixture for

Screed the tamped concrete surface. Fill in any low areas. One or two more screedings will be necessary to level the slab.

An edger slices a rounded edge in the slab to prevent later chipping. As you work, do not dig into the plastic concrete.

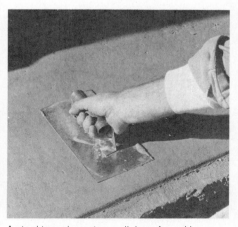

A steel trowel creates a slick surface. Use curving strokes. The more you trowel, the slicker the surface will become.

both is 1 part portland cement, ½ part lime, and 4 parts of dry sand (5 parts damp sand). Mix with water according to the directions on the mortar package. As always, check the instructions on your particular product; manufacturers' instructions vary. Let the mixture set for at least fifteen minutes so it homogenizes completely.

Then lay the scratch coat of the mortar to seal off the concrete. Using a mortar trowel, lay a rough coat, about ¼ to ½ inch thick. Once this scratch coat has set, trowel on a bed of mortar that is at least 1½ inches thick. The purpose of this bed is to level the concrete surface, fill in any depressions, seams or other variations in the surface of the concrete tank. Hold the trowel as flat as possible to achieve a flat surface and to prevent what is called the "washboard effect" — ridges in the surface of the mortar.

Once the mortar is laid, install the tiles into the mortar bed before the bed has set. (At this stage, the mortar is said to be "plastic.") Soak the tiles for approximately one half hour before you place the tiles in the mortar. Otherwise, they will draw water from the mortar, which weakens the bond. Plan horizontal and vertical working lines as you would for any other project. Cut tiles should fall along the wall edges and near the top of the pool rim. Place the tiles on the mortar; their weight will settle them into the mortar surface. Once you have covered the entire pool, grout the installation.

A second method for setting the tile is to allow the mortar bed to damp cure for seven days. At that time, apply a bond coat of portland cement or dry-set adhesive. This installation does not require that the tiles be soaked before they are laid.

Always select a high quality grout that will last underwater. The standard residential grouts are not made for this type of installation. Consult a supplier of tile products.

Step 7: Installing a Pool Coping

The coping connects the upper area of the pool wall and the pool surround. The surface should be rounded and the corners properly mitered or rounded. The coping attaches to the top of the concrete wall using ½-in. expansion shield and anchors on 24 in. centers. It can be a prefabricated extrusion or form into which the concrete is poured. The coping can include the receptor for the pool water as well. This,

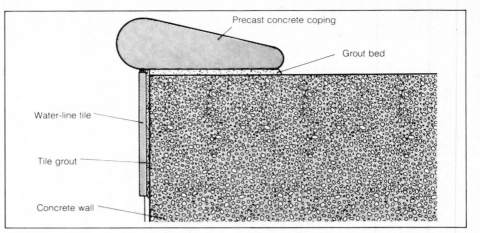

A precast coping set on a grout bed has a tile facing, placed after the coping installation, to insure watertightness.

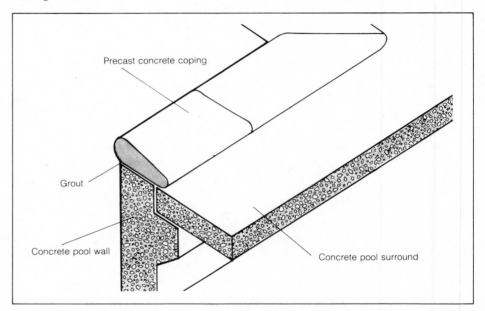

The precast concrete coping has corners that are mitered on a 45 degree angle to maintain the shape of the pool.

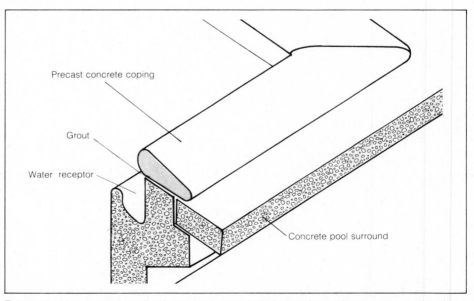

This pool with a precast coping is set on a grout bed, but an integral water receptor has been substituted for the tile facing.

however, must be determined prior to the pouring of the pool walls, because, the height must be shortened to accommodate the additional depth.

The main alternative to the poured-in-place coping is the precast concrete coping. This coping is set into a grout bed. Most pool supply dealers can furnish precast copings for most pool shapes. Some of the copings can be sawn to accommodate dimensional errors. Where the pool finish abuts at the underside of the precast coping, a water-line tile usually 6 inches square is placed flush to the underside of the coping. The tile is easier to clean than the painted side of the pool. In the water receptor, the electrostatically painted part of the form performs the same function as the water-line tile.

Once the coping is in place, lay a bead of silicone caulk around the underside of the coping, using a caulking gun. This keeps water from entering between the precast or poured coping and the wall. It is better to use the silicone caulk than the butyl or latex because of the life of the material. Be generous with the application. Make sure that the joint is free of dust and/or dirt particles.

Step 8: Placing Pool Accessories

At this time, the pool is ready for the diving board, underwater lights and ladders.

Diving Boards The diving board generally arrives at the site in a knock-down condition. Most manufacturers include a complete step-by-step description of what is required for the installation, as well as base hardware and mounting template. A typical installation requires a ½-in. masonry drill bit in order to set the anchor sleeves for the bolts that restrain the base. All diving boards and slides must be installed according to the National Swimming Pool Institute (NSPI) "Suggested Minimum Standards". Most pool equipment manufacturers adhere to the requirements of the NSPI.

Pool Ladders and Rails Most swimming pool ladders and rails come equipped with coping sockets or the anchor sleeves and base necessary surface mounting. In cases where you desire to have all the connection invisible or recessed, the inserts must be installed in the desired location before the pouring of the concrete walls. All of the anchor sockets or inserts that are to be embedded in concrete have grounding screws as required by the National Electrical Code.

This connection is critical, since it acts as a lightning arrestor when properly installed. Most ladders and rails are fabricated from 1.90 in. x .049 in. stainless steel rails with rubber bumpers. These are also delivered knock-down and should be assembled and installed according to the manufacturer's instructions.

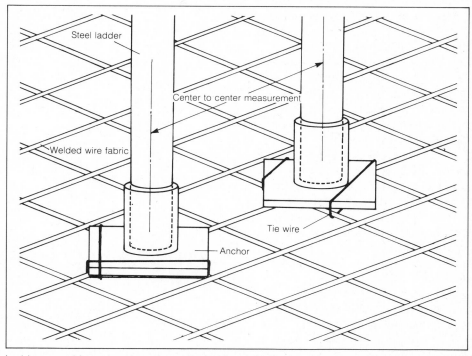

Ladder assembly anchor sleeves are wired to the reinforcing in order to minimize displacement and movement during the pour.

The usual source of the water supply for a pool is your local system. If local ordinances forbid this, you may have to hire a water tanker to bring in what you need.

Creating a Pool Surround

This represents the last part of the construction of an in-ground concrete pool. After the surface electrical wiring is in place and all the electrical junction boxes are stubbed or installed in the concrete surround, and the inserts or sockets for the slides, diving board and ladders are in place, you are ready to pour the concrete pool surround.

Refer to the section on pouring the pool floor slab for recommended reinforcement thicknesses. Place a 2-in. layer of sand, then a bed of gravel at least 6 in. deep, and a 4-in. concrete slab. Since the slab rests on the ground, not in it, you would excavate 8 in. from the highest ground elevation.

Lay out the pool surround in regular patterns, using 2x4s or 2x6s to build the forms. Pour each section and screed according to the recommended procedures previously outlined. After each section is poured, finish the concrete by darbying, floating and edging. The edger rounds off the perimeter edges against the form and the coping to eliminate chipping and give a smooth look. After the edging is completed, float to consolidate the cement paste at the surface.

The Best Surface A rough surface such as a broom surface is not recommended, due to possible abrasions. A smooth surface, on the other hand , could cause skids. The best surface is one with a nonabrasive, nonskid finish such as a nonslip paint. There are a number of manufacturers who offer a paint that gives a safe and durable wearing surface. To provide the finish for a painted surface, the concrete should be troweled (refer to the section on finishing the pool floor slab). After the surface has been troweled, let cure before painting.

Alternative Materials You may choose brick, treated wood, or modular wood sections for the surround instead of concrete. This is feasible if the pool is rectangular, but these other materials will be harder to use around a curved pool.

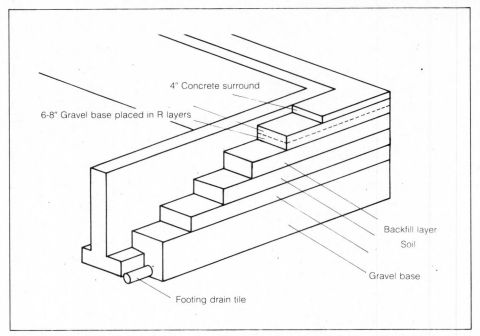

Place backfill in layers; then add the gravel base for the concrete pool surround. Drain tile is not mandatory, but is recommended.

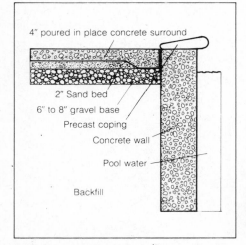

Before pouring the concrete surround, place sand and gravel layers for drainage.

The temperature at which you maintain your pool is a matter of personal preference. To heat the water, you may use any one of a number of heater systems or a solar blanket.

4
INSTALLING
A VINYL LINER POOL

Vinyl liner pools have developed in response to the high cost of a concrete pool. Their big advantages are quick construction time and a lower unit cost than an equivalent-sized concrete pool. The excavation requirements are the same as for concrete pools, but the framework that forms the outline of the pool is a prefabricated unit of either aluminum, steel or pressure-treated wood. Once excavation has taken place, a sand base is placed on the bottom of the excavated area. This base is then compacted and finished smooth. The prefabricated perimeter form is then placed in the excavation. The sides of the pool are, on an average, 40 in. high.

With the form in place, a heavy-gauge vinyl liner is draped over the forms. The vinyl liner is laid flat along the bottom of the pool and contoured to the walls. It is then anchored in place at the top of the wall and finished off with a coping that conceals the top edge of the liner and side form. Once the pool is filled with water, the weight of the water maintains the liner firmly in place. The vinyl liner pool, if kept partially filled, can be installed in the colder climates without any damage to the liner or the pool structure.

The vinyl liner pool is a complete prefabricated system that arrives at the site ready to install and takes several days from start to finish. The pool has other advantages than just its cost. It has a soft pool bottom, so that there are a minimal number of scrapes possible. The liner will suffer no chipping or cracking. There will be no seepage, and the pool requires minimal maintenance. One of the major advantages of the vinyl liner pool is that it can be easily repaired at minimal cost and time. Generally the water maintenance program is somewhat easier due to the smooth sur-

Vinyl liner in-ground pools offer not only substantial cost reductions but also considerable time savings, as compared to a conventional concrete pool.

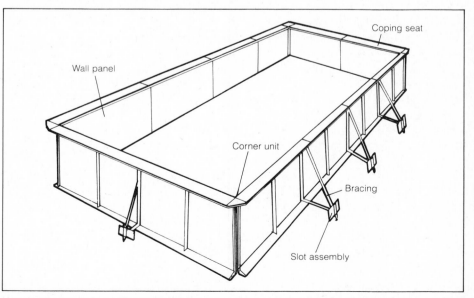

Here is an overall view of the assembly of a vinyl liner pool. The diagonal bracing, which provides necessary rigidity, varies according to the model and manufacturer.

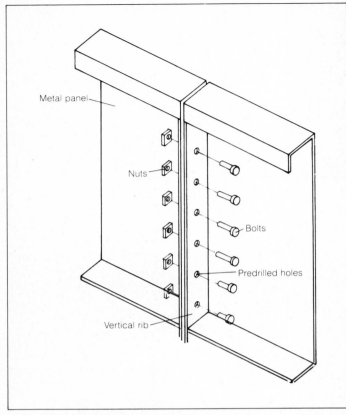

Each metal panel comes with the necessary number of machined bolts and nuts in order to connect the panels.

The money saved by installing a vinyl liner in-ground pool may enable you to undertake other desirable backyard projects.

face that does not pick up the particles as might a rough-surfaced pool.

POOL COMPONENTS
Structural Framework

The structural panels are built either from steel, aluminum, reinforced fiberglass or structural polymer. Each one has a particular advantage over the other. For example, the steel-panel model does not include a receptor along the side walls, whereas the fiberglass and polymer pools offer it at little or no extra cost. Another advantage of the polymer type pool wall is that it is not susceptible to rust or corrosion underground. However, the steel-panel pool is completely galvanized, and the aluminum one also is free from corrosion as long as it is properly installed.

All panels are modular and interlock. They are self-aligning and easily assembled with hand tools. They come with 45° bracing for stability. The panels are fitted with a coping receptor at the top and generally are available in 36-in. depths. Some manufacturers offer a variety of panel depths, but the one most often used is the 42-in. panel. Panels bolt together to form a semi-rigid pool enclosure, sitting on an earth shelf shaped during excavation.

Vinyl Liners

All vinyl liners are large, impervious sheets of vinyl material that is fiber reinforced and shaped to conform to a standard range of pool forms. The liners are available in a variety of colors. Most come with a water-line design ranging from 6 to 36 in. in depth below the coping. Most vinyl liners are available in thicknesses of 0.6 mm to the heavier models of 0.7 mm.

EQUIPMENT, MATERIALS AND TOOLS REQUIRED

One concern of most potential pool builders is the hidden costs in the form of materials and tools required to build the pool. The vinyl liner pool is far less complex in its requirements than its concrete counterpart. If you do not plan to subcontract the excavation to an experienced contractor, here is a list of tools, equipment and materials the job will require.

Tools for Ground Forming

Heavy Equipment To form the ground, the equipment is similar to that used for a concrete pool. A front end loader or backhoe with a 14- to 16-ft. reach is used, beginning at the deep end and moving to the shallow part of the pool. A backhoe will dig the most accurate hole and disturb the least amount of earth. This equipment saves time and efficiently levels the earth around the pool excavation. Exact cutting of the soil is required to meet the dimensions of the pool. A 24-in. shelf is cut around the entire pool for the panels previously discussed. This shelf must be carefully cut and stabilized because the earth must be as undisturbed as possible.

Once the panels are in place, the bottom is further smoothed out. The two methods of shaping the pool bottom are the Soft Bottom method, which uses sand, and the Hard Bottom method, which uses a cement/sand or cement/vermiculite mixture. The Hard Bottom method is most often used when some ground water is present. A mixture of concrete and vermiculite or other insulating material is carefully placed over the soil base and shaped to the contours of the pool. It is this base that becomes the form for the liner, since the liner has no structural capability whatsoever.

Hand Tools These include tools such as shovels, rakes, picks, axes, tamps and rollers, as required. If you have assistance (which is recommended) the number of tools may vary. Most of the tools are available from rental agencies. Measuring rules, yardsticks, string, chalk, and transit and 100-ft. metal or cloth tape are additional standard tools.

Steel hand trowels of several sizes are used to form the pool bottom. A pool trowel, which is a little larger, is recommended. Hand tampers and a garden roller also are needed to form the pool base and the shelf.

To bolt the panels, use a ratchet wrench with a variety of sockets, in addition to an equally matched set of open end wrenches. Buy a pipe wrench for pool fittings.

Screw drivers, both flat blade and large Phillips head type, a very large pair of pliers, a crescent wrench, needle nose pliers, plus all the usual pencils, stakes and flags, complete the necessary tools.

A vacuum cleaner, industrial-sized (or several canister household types) also is suggested.

Materials

The first requirement is a complete 16x32 ft. vinyl liner steel panel pool kit, delivered to the site.

Sufficient cement and vermiculite will be needed to provide a hard bottom pool for a permanent installation. Specific requirements will be outlined in each part of the construction sequence.

You will also need concrete ready-mix or transit concrete. This will be used to pour the surround or collar. For the plumbing, buy plastic piping and appropriate teflon tape, or thread compound for the piping. This may vary according to the type of piping used. Generally, all pool water piping will be plastic.

SETTING UP A VINYL-LINED POOL   The most crucial part of the pool installation is the pool layout. The outer dimensions of the pool must be 48 in. larger than the actual size of the pool. For example, the 16 ft. width would be 20 ft. and the 32 ft. length would become 36 ft. Then, to each dimension, add 3 in. to all dimensions to account for the corner radius. The extra 4 feet accommodates the installation of the wall panels.

STEP 1: STAKING OUT THE POOL

Place a stake in each corner, until they approximate the actual dimensions required. Then square the stakes so that a perfect rectangle will be formed, as described in Chapter 3. Make sure that at least two of the adjacent corner stakes are not moved, since they represent the corner set.

Once the layout has been squared and checked several more times for accuracy, attach string around the corner stakes to outline the shape of the pool. Be sure to account for the difference in elevation between the stakes. This could affect the depth of the pool or how much you must build up around the low end of the pool. After the string has been attached, pour lime over it. This line will help cut the most accurate excavation. Always check your dimensions, since once the cut has been made, it becomes increasingly difficult to rectify a dimensional error.

STEP 2: PREPARING FOR EXCAVATION

Stake the four corner posts. The finished surface of the surround should be at least 6 in. above the high point of the pool level.

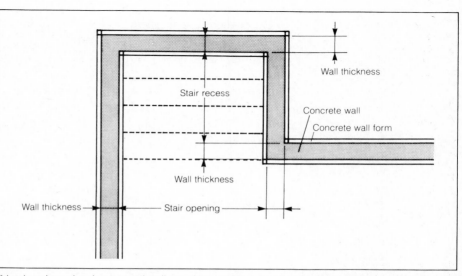

This plan view, showing a metal wall panel layout around a recessed metal stair unit, indicates the importance of careful pool planning.

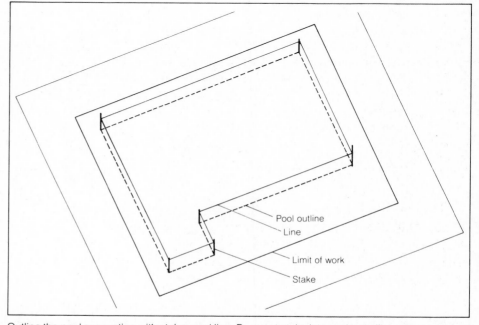

Outline the pool excavation with stakes and line. Be sure to take into account all recesses and pool accessory openings.

Preliminary excavation utilizes a transit to check elevations. Note the large rocks, which were not planned for by the homeowner.

Once the top surface has been cleared and leveled, lay out the diagonal measurements to verify that the pool corners are square and even.

The shelf is laid out by measuring in 24 in. from exterior string line, which outlines overall exterior dimensions. Pour lime over string to mark string line.

There should be a slope of 1 to 2 ft. below the lowest ground level. This will allow the grade to pitch away from the pool for drainage.

Mark the finished height on the highest corner post. This will be the benchmark used and should be transferred to to the other stakes where possible. Mark a 1x2 or use the transit pole to set a 36 in. depth below the highest point. This will be the guide to the excavator for the depth. The 36 in. will give the depth needed to level the wall panels and, thus, the height to the top of the pool. Always measure this excavated hole with the 1x2 or transit pole. Do not make the excavation less than the 36 in. suggested; if the pool is too shallow, the vinyl liner will not fit properly.

STEP 3: EXCAVATION PROCEDURES
Digging the Shelf

Always start the excavation at the deep, or hopper, end of the pool. It is easier to dig the pool from that end. As the excavation progresses, check the depth constantly, as well as the level. This is where the transit or level will be of use. Once the 36-in. depth has been achieved, the excavation should look like a very shallow and level pit. The shelf on which the panels will sit must be absolutely level and the earth must not be disturbed. Use shovels as the 36-in. mark is approached; skim the excess dirt away from the shelf area. This will allow the underlying soil to be free from any movement or change. An undisturbed soil is far more stable, and thus less susceptible to settlement.

There can be no doubt that an experienced swimming pool excavator should be employed for this operation. However, even though you may elect to subcontract the excavation, the contractor should be helped as much as possible to get the shelf and bottom dimensions as accurate as possible. This will save hours of hand labor and cost. The hopper bottom should be indicated by using lime guidemarks originally laid down over the string on the working ledge. The experienced excavator will be able to adjust the depths of the hopper more efficiently, because as the shelf is being dug, so is the hopper.

Digging the Hopper

The excavated depth of the hopper should be at least 4 to 6 in. deeper than the required pool depth. This will be the thick-

STEP 4: POOL WALL ERECTION AND ASSEMBLY

Locate the braces or "A frames" at each panel point. All the frames should be level with respect to each other. Before lowering the wall sections onto the shelf area, mark each panel along its entire length with a straight crayon line that is 2 in.

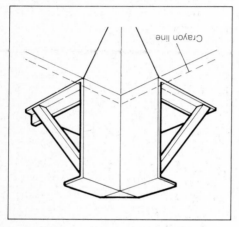

The dotted crayon line along the bottom of the panel should be marked onto the panels, to rest 2 in. above the pool bottom.

from the bottom of the panel. Then lower the panels onto the shelf of the excavation. You may lean the panels against the earth wall in order to space them properly along the supporting A frames.

Arranging the Panels

Most pools are supplied with specialty water-inlet and skimmer-outlet panels. These panels must be properly located in the panel arrangement. In the North American hemisphere, when you drain a pool of water, the water goes down the drain in a counterclockwise direction. The inlets should be located so as to encourage the counterclockwise movement of the water. This helps flush out dirt and suspended

are well fused and well supported by the earth. This will reduce any future breakage of the pipe.

Use a transit to guide the excavation. In the case of the 16x32 ft. pool, the overall depth from the top of the panels to the bottom of the hopper should be 8 ft. With the additional 4 in. for gravel/sand base, the total depth would be 8 ft 4 in. Hand trimming and shaping will be required for the last finishing touches. The hand work will reduce further shaping time when the pool bottom surface is installed. Trim the hopper end and the shallow end so as to disturb the least amount of finished earth.

minimize any possible side movement and the piping should be laid according to the location of the filtration equipment. To do this, set the drain and the necessary piping in position. Gently place concrete around the base of the drain and over the piping, sufficient to cover the drain and surround the drain. Finish the concrete around the drain collar. Make sure that the pipe connections

ness of the sand or concrete/aggregate base for surfacing the bottom. If a main drain is to be used, this is the time it should be installed. Most main drains are equipped with a cover plate to protect the drain during the construction. The drain should be located with the finish surface set slightly above the surface of the pool bottom. It should be concreted in place to

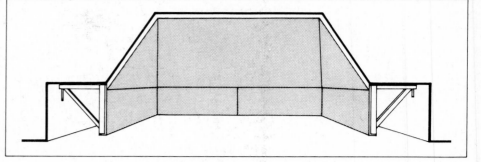

The braces and the metal pool panels rest on the excavated shelf that rims the pool. The liner then extends downward to form a smooth, continuous surface.

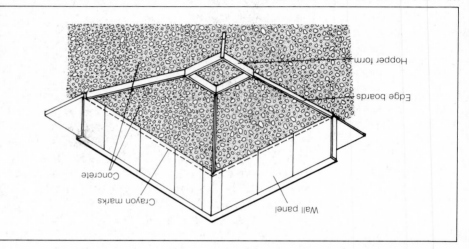

When laying out the hopper bottom of the pool, side boards are positioned with horizontal markings to aid in determining the final elevation of the pool floor.

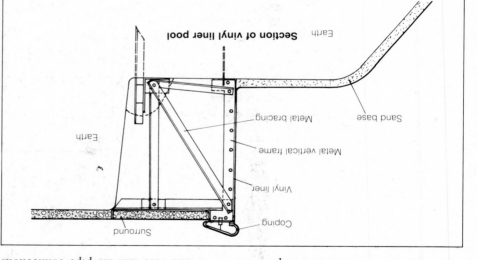

This cross-section of the vinyl liner pool installation indicates the assembly components and their relative positions.

The large opening shown in the hopper end wall panel is for an underwater light. Panel joints are ready to be taped.

To hold the panels firmly in place, drive reinforc-ing rods or spikes into the side wall plates, as shown.

materials when the pool is drained. Most manufacturers recommend that the skim-mer panel be placed in the middle of the wall to increase the efficiency of the filtra-tion cycle.

Bolting the Panels

Start bolting the panels together at a corner of the hopper end of the pool. Use the excavation stakes as the reference marks for the assembly. Work out from the cor-ner in both directions to give stability to the panel without additional support.

Once you have erected several panels in each direction, use the transit to verify the panels are square. Make sure that square is main-tained. It is difficult to keep the panels aligned, but not impossible. Once all the panels are joined, check each panel joint in relation to the first corner elevation.

There should be an anchoring A-frame installed at each panel joint. As each panel is leveled and the inside face surfaces are trued to each other, tighten the bolts. Do not tighten the bolts before leveling.

Checking the Alignment

After the pool is enclosed, and all the bolts are tight-ened, check the square by taking two diag-onal measurements from opposite corners. The dimensions should be the same. If they are not, adjust the alignment until the diagonal measurements are equal or with-in a 1/4 in. of each other. Then take the steel stakes that are provided with the kit and stake all four corners. Do not move the panel assembly in the process. After you have staked the panels, check the lev-el and the diagonal measurements again. Once the corners are staked, check the alignment of the bottom panels. The pan-els should be seated steadily on the shelf.

Making Final Adjustments

Alignment of the top of the panel is ac-complished by raising or lowering the A frame until the top of the panel lines are straight. The procedure results in the tilt-ing the top of the panel in or out as re-quired. If the A frame base plate requires shifting, shim it with a suitable material, such as a brick or shingle. Never shim with dirt. If the base plate needs to be lowered because the wall tilts inward, the ground under the plate should be carefully shaved away until the desired elevation is attained. When the base plates have all been set, the pool wall should be plumb all around and the top edge will form a straight edge on all four sides.

Check all dimensions and the level again for plumb and squareness. Once you have done this, drive a steel stake through the slotted opening in the A frame base plate. Generally each kit comes with a suf-ficient number of stakes. These stakes will hold the pool walls in position during the final phases of pool construction. Once the stakes are driven, walk around the out-side ledge to see that all voids under the wall sections are filled in. Use a cement grout to fill the voids. Do not use dirt or any excavated material for this purpose.

Bolt together steel wall panels (left). If pool wall is restrained by earth, some manufacturers do not include diagonal bracing. Prefabricated stair unit (right) bolts in place. Top of panel wall rises slightly above the soil level of the excavation.

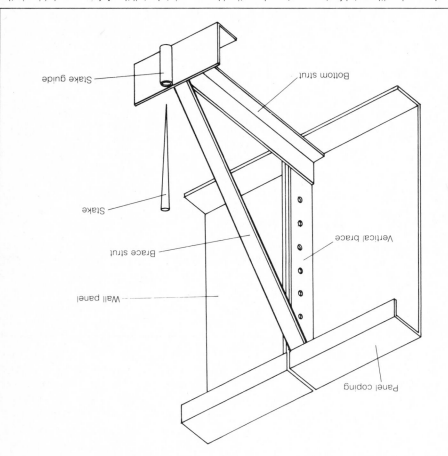

Attach panels with metal fasteners at each vertical brace point. Install the A-frame and drive in the stakes for permanent alignment.

Stake guide

Bottom strut

Stake

Brace strut

Vertical brace

Wall panel

Panel coping

In-ground pool walls on the downhill side of a sloping site must be supported with diagonal bracing at the panel joints.

STEP 5: TAPING THE JOINTS

After the panels are set, staked and re-checked for level, all the vertical panel joints should be taped with a 2-in.-wide grey duct tape. This is usually provided with the kit. Taping the joints gives the inside face of the panel a smooth finish.

STEP 6: INSTALLING THE ACCESSORIES

Once the taping of the joints is completed, install the skimmer, skimmer support and ladder mounts. Follow the directions given by the manufacturer of the pool. The methods vary considerably from type to type. However, do not forget to check that the vinyl skimmer gasket is properly mounted. Install inlets by inserting the in-let fitting through the inlet hole in the pan-el with the washer, mounting spacer, locknut and nut properly located. After the liner is installed, another gasket and the inlet cap will be installed. If there will be a diving board that requires a connection to the top of the panel or a concrete pad, that should be placed at this time. In the event that you have selected a pool with a pre-fabricated deck as well as the pool, the

Placement of panels on the uphill side of a slope does not require stabilizing bracing to support the perimeter of the pool surround.

INSTALLING THE PLUMBING AND RELATED SYSTEMS

Let the concrete set for 24 hours. Then you can install the plumbing connections that connect the pool to the filtration system. As the pipes are connected to the inlets, skimmer and outlets, they should be run down to the top of the concrete collar and supported on a sand bed to cushion the pipe. This will increase the longevity of the pipe and the usefulness of the pool.

If an automatic pool cleaner is to be used or planned for in the future, an additional return fitting must be installed at this time. It should be located on the wall opposite the position of the skimmer. Cap it until it is ready to be used. The additional return should be positioned so that it is closer to the filter system than the skimmer.

The plastic piping is easy to cut and install; it requires only a hacksaw, a file and a container of solvent/glue. The steps are: (1) cut the pipe (cut off more pipe than you think you need); (2) smooth the ends so that they will fit the joint properly and be well seated; (3) apply the solvent/glue and slip the pieces together.

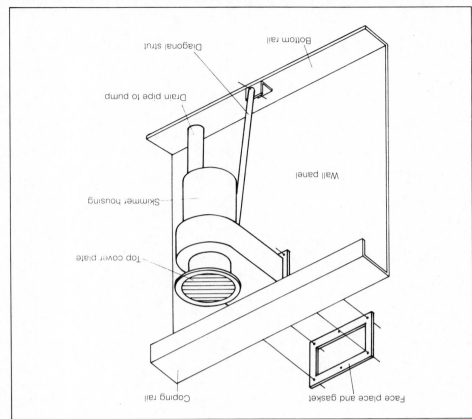

The outside gasket and faceplate provide a watertight connection to the skimmer housing, which is supported by a diagonal strut.

Labels: Bottom rail, Diagonal strut, Drain pipe to pump, Wall panel, Skimmer housing, Top cover plate, Coping rail, Face plate and gasket

---

STEP 7: CONCRETING THE FRAME

All the accessories should now be installed and the positions checked for accuracy. Go back and read the installation instructions supplied with each part to verify the completeness of the installation. Once you have done this, the A frame base plates are ready for concreting.

Place the concrete so that it mounds over the stake and the base plate area of the frame. Cover the entire frame and stake. After you have covered each stake and base plate, install a concrete collar around the entire base perimeter of the pool wall. This will assure that each panel is properly set and secure, so that it will not move during the next phases of the construction. For the 16x32 ft. pool, approximately 5 yds. of concrete are required.

deck supports should be installed at this point, one at each A frame panel joint. This produces the stiffest connection possible between the deck and the panels.

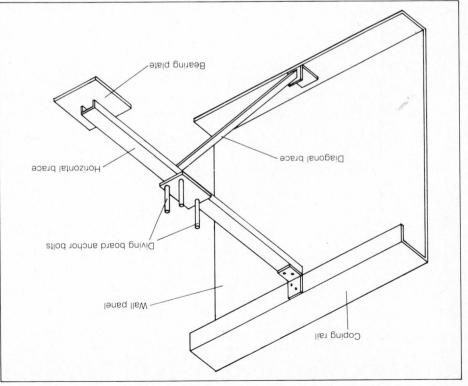

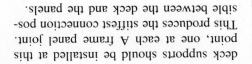

The diving board is supported on a braced frame. The bearing frame must rest on undisturbed earth and be covered with concrete when the pool surround is poured.

Labels: Bearing plate, Diagonal brace, Horizontal brace, Diving board anchor bolts, Wall panel, Coping rail

INSTALLING THE POOL COPING When you chose the vinyl-liner pool, you also selected a coping. The coping is the piece that connects to the top of the wall panel and the concrete surround or collar.

Rim Lock Coping This type of coping acts as a form for the concrete, which is poured into the area behind the coping. It reduces the upper edge of the material to a minimum. The rim lock coping can be installed at this time, but no concrete can be poured until adequate backfilling has been undertaken.

Prefabricated Coping At the corner of the hopper end of the pool, start attaching the coping. Sufficient hardware should be provided. Make sure that 2 bolts are set at the ends of every piece of coping. On a 12-ft. coping section, set 2 bolts at each end and space an additional 4 bolts over the 12 ft. This will anchor the coping to the wall panel.

Standard Coping In the Standard Coping, there is a continuous threaded section that runs the entire length of the coping piece. When the coping is placed on the top of the wall, this threaded section will align with the holes in the top flange of the wall panel. The long bolts with washer are inserted from the underside of the flange into the threaded section of the coping. A flat washer should be used with each bolt.

Do not tighten the bolts until the coping is placed on the top of the wall; this threaded section will align with the holes in the top flange of the wall panel. The long bolts with washer are inserted from the underside of the flange into the threaded section of the coping. A flat washer should be used with each bolt. Do not tighten the bolts until the coping has been placed in position and aligned. Always leave one section out until the bottom has been finished, to prevent the coping from being damaged. Leave about an 1/8 in. space between each piece of coping. Special coping clips provided with the kit will be snapped into this space. The best way to insure uniform openings is to get a piece of wood 1/8 in. thick and use that to space the coping sections. After you have aligned the coping, tighten the bolts. Do not overtighten, or it will cause noticeable surface variation.

Next, place the coping clips. Put the nose of the clip over the nose of the coping and hit the back of the clip. It should snap

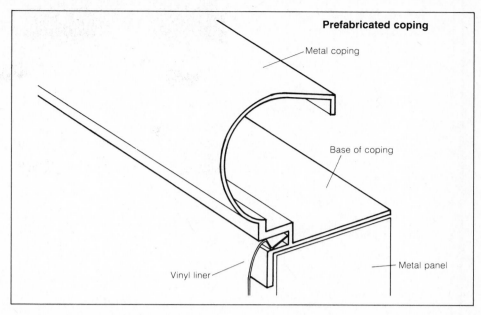

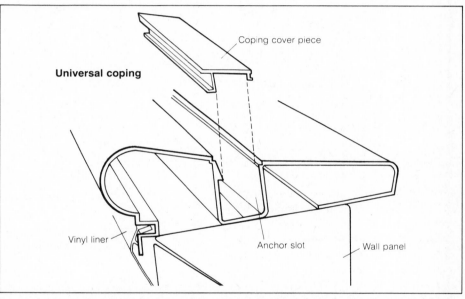

The universal coping has a removable top piece that is used to connect the coping to different types of wall panels and baseplates.

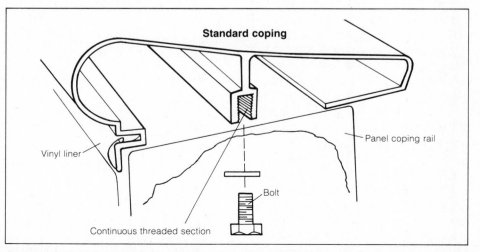

A standard coping attaches to the panel coping rail with bolts that come with the coping and that usually are spaced every 24 or 48 in.

in place. If it does not or is loose, pull the spring clips apart slightly.

When the coping has been installed, use duct tape to tape underneath the liner bead that is a part of the coping. This will close the joint between the coping and the panel wall, making it easier to draw out the air between the liner and the panel. When the pool bottom is finished (see next set of instructions), install the extra piece of coping and tape it to match either side.

PREPARING THE BOTTOM OF THE POOL

The pool bottom must be finished and shaped before the liner can be positioned. Take some preliminary elevations from various parts of the pool bottom. They should be accurate, since little has been done to change them from the initial excavation. The pool floor should be very near its exact depth, with only a small amount of hand trimming required. The hopper depth may be a few inches deeper than the specified 8 ft. from the top of the wall, but may not be less than the 8 ft. 4 in. specified.

Check the main floor drain, which is already set into a concrete block. If you have not piped the drain, do so now. Pipe it 3 in. below the surface of the side and the wall panel. The actual elevation of the drain should be 1 in. below the projected finish surface of the bottom to allow debris to run down the drain. Allow at least 2 in. of concrete/aggregate over the concrete main drain pad.

Refer to the drawing on hopper bottom pools and locate the position of the hopper area. There are two guide methods that can be used for bottom surfacing.

String Line Method This is the simpler of the two methods. By referring to the drawings, stake the 8 points of the hopper area and string a line 2 in. above the desired floor surface level. Use the horizontal lines you marked on the wall panels as guides in this process. The string line method is generally used to form sand pool bottoms as well as hard bottom pools.

Guide Board Method To square the hopper apex, construct a jig of 1x3s to form a hopper form. The next step is to set the side boards in each corner of the hopper side walls. These four boards should be 1x3s and their length set according to the accompanying chart. For a 16x32 ft. pool, those dimensions would be 14 ft. 9 in. The side boards are placed between the hopper form and the wall panels, up the pool sides. The 14 ft.9 in. center boards are placed at the corners of the hopper form, diagonally to the pool sides. The top of the boards should be even with the 2 in. crayon marking.

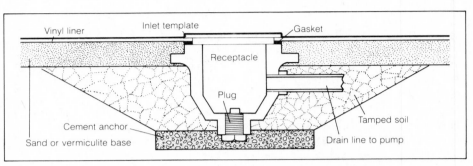

Hopper drain lies in concrete; liner connects to drain via gasket and template.

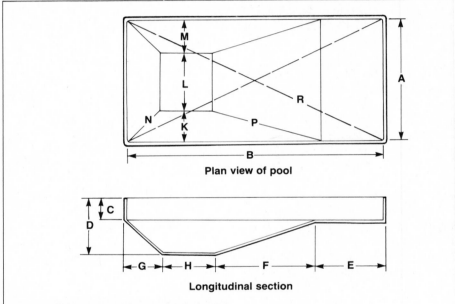

Plan view of pool

Longitudinal section

POOL DIMENSIONS AND HOPPER SIZES

Pool Size	12'x24'	16'x24'	16'x32'	18'x36'	20'x40'
Gallons	8500	13,900	17,800	21,300	27,700
Dimensions					
A	12'3"	16'3"	16'3"	18'3"	20'3"
B	24'3"	24'3"	32'3"	36'3"	40'3"
C	3'6"	3'6"	3'6"	3'6"	3'6"
D	6'	7'	8'	8'	8'
E	6'	6'	8'6"	10'6"	12'6"
F	8'	8'	13'6"	13'6"	13'6"
G	6'3"	6'3"	6'3"	8'3"	10'3"
H	4'	4'	4'	4'	4'
K	4'	4'	4'	4'	4'
L	4'3"	8'3"	8'3"	10'3"	12'3"
M	4'	4'	4'	4'	4'
N	6'2¼"	6'7⅞"	7'2¾"	7'2¾"	7'2¾"
P	9'3½"	9'7¼"	14'9⅜"	14'9⅜"	14'9⅜"
R	27'2"	29'2⁵⁄₁₆"	36'1⅜"	40'7"	45'11⁄₁₆"

Diagram and chart adapted from material supplied by Heldor Pools.

Soft vs. Hard Bottom Finishes

Soft Bottom Procedure Washed sand should be placed carefully into the shallow end of the pool. The sand should be at least 4 in. deep, which was the allowance made in the excavation. This can be reduced to 2 in. in case the previous depth was reduced by an additional 2 in. Shovel the sand by hand to the side walls and bottom of the hopper. Spread the sand even with the tops of the 1x3 boards or string and the 2-in. line on the panels. Work from the bottom upwards on the sloping sides of the hopper to produce a more compact base. If the sand begins to fall or slide as you are troweling it in place, sprinkle some water on the area. As you complete each section, sprinkle water over it so that it will continue to stay in place. Tamp the sand and add additional sand in depressed areas. Use a wooden or steel trowel to finish the surface of the sand.

Hard Bottom Procedures If a ground water condition exists, if a water table could present a future problem for the pool, or if you simply desire a permanent base for the pool (free from foot-

Smooth the sand floor slowly and carefully. Employ a semicircular motion, moving the trowel back and forth. Repeat several times.

prints), a hardbottom pool surface should be chosen. The two materials most commonly used are the cement/sand combination or the vermiculite/cement mixture, which has certain advantages over the sand mixture in colder climates.

Using the sand mixture After the lines have been strung, a cement/sand mixture of 3 parts sand to 1 part cement is mixed in the pool bottom. Proceed according to the instructions outlined for the soft bottom sand surface. Once the dry mixture has been placed and tamped, remove all imperfections, and the corner boards or the string. Clean the sides of the pool. Then, wet the dry cement/sand mixture, using a very fine sprinkler. It is very important that puddling of the water does not occur, since this will cause depressions in the finished bottom. Apply several sprays over the day. Always make sure that the mist is evenly sprayed over the entire surface. Allow the mixture to harden for at least 6 hours before placing the liner.

Using the vermiculite mixture The vermiculite method combines vermiculite, an inert insulating material, with cement. The two are mixed outside of the pool in a cement mixer, with a ratio of 1 bag of cement to 2 bags of vermiculite. Vermiculite normally comes in 40 lb. bags and a bag of cement weighs 94 lbs. The material is mixed and then hand placed into the forms. Make sure that the desired levels are reached and are in alignment with the 2 in. mark on the panel walls.

INSTALLATION OF THE VINYL LINER

At this point almost all of the work is completed, except for the finishing touches. The most important final step is the installation of the vinyl liner. The skimmer sandwich gasket, skimmer, inlets and returns also should be mounted now, if they have not previously been installed.

Step 1: Checking the Base Before the liner is even removed from the box, check to make sure that the pool bottom is clean and the immediate area is free of debris and objects that could rip the liner. Many a project has come to a halt because of a torn liner. Make sure that the area is free of debris.

Step 2: Preparing the Liner If possible, install the vinyl liner in warm weather, because the material is far more pliable and easier to work. If you must install the liner during colder weather, place the liner in a heated space or basement several days before installation.

Step 3: Positioning the Liner Remove the liner while standing near the shallow end of the pool. Note, the liner arrows all point in the same direction.

Place the liner in the center of the end wall with the arrows pointing to the deep end of the pool. Unfold the liner toward the sides of the pool, ending at the corners. Carry the liner toward the center of the pool or where the transition between the shallow and the deep end occurs. Rest the liner on the pool bottom. Do not drag the liner as you are moving it! Now grab the corners of the exposed top flap. The liner is shipped in a fan-folded condition. As a result, when the corner top flaps are pulled toward the shallow end, the liner opens like an accordian. Line up the bottom corners of the liner at the shallow end wall. Position and adjust the liner by shifting it back and forth until all points in the shallow end are aligned.

To prevent any movement of the positioned liner, secure the corners with help or with sand bags. While those shallow-end corners are being held, grasp the corners of the deep end wall and unfold them as you did at the shallow end. Eliminate as many wrinkles as possible by pulling and positioning the liner. When pulling the liner, always grasp a heavy fold of material with two hands. The heavy gauge of the

material will withstand a lot of pull without damage. Shift the liner back and forth until the deep end appears to fit. Once this is done, the corners should be pulled into position and held firmly. Check all the alignments of the liner. This is a critical time; all corners must be aligned and fit snugly.

Step 4: Snapping and Smoothing the Liner Once the liner is in position, insert the liner bead into the bead receptor channel of the coping. Start to snap the bead into the coping, putting 1½ ft. in on either side of the corners. Once the corners are snapped into place, the centers can be inserted to relieve the pressure. Working toward the corners, snap in the remaining materials.

When the liner bead has been completely inserted into the channel, place the vacuum hose through the top of the skimmer. Make sure all inlet openings are taped outside the pool. If you do not plan to use a skimmer, unsnap the liner and insert the end of the vacuum hose into the void between the liner and the wall. Tape the liner around the vacuum hose to make it airtight. Now you may start the vacuum.

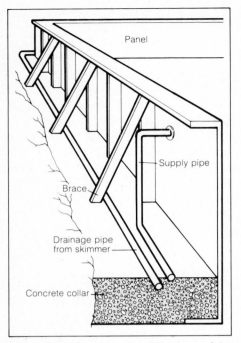

A concrete collar runs around the base of the metal panels. Piping for inlets and skimmers are attached to pool and then are supported by the collar.

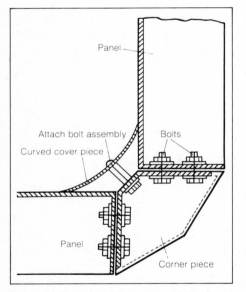

The curved cove at the corner, which relieves tension in the liner, is installed after panels are assembled and aligned.

You will notice that the wrinkles begin to disappear. If your vacuum is not strong enough, you might start adding water into the pool to assist the process. Wrinkles will not damage the functioning of the pool, but they will be unsightly. If your vacuum is strong enough, a majority of the wrinkles should be gone. At this point, fill the pool, using a garden hose. Lay the hose on the bottom of the pool; you do not want the water to splash into the pool bottom. Do not allow the pool to fill faster than you can remove the wrinkles. If you are going to use the main drain that was installed, fill the hopper about 8 in. deep so the liner will form itself to the bottom.

Step 5: Installing the Drain Plate
To install the main drain cover plate, you will require a 36-in. square piece of plywood that has been carpeted on the bottom side. In the center of the square, cut a 10-in. diameter hole. This will be used as a work platform while cutting the liner material away from the main drain opening. The platform prevents possible damage to the bottom of the pool and allows you to move about to install the pool drain cover and gasket.

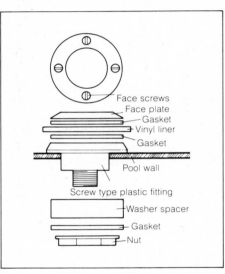

Pool water inlet fitting pieces join to form the inlet assembly.

Lower a ladder onto the 36-in. square platform. Once you are on the platform, place the secondary gasket on the outside of the liner. Alignment of the outside and the inside gaskets must be done by feel. Screw the self-tapping screws provided with the drain into position by screwing through the liner. When all the screws are in place, use a razor knife or sharp blade to cut the liner material within the circle of the main drain face plate. Install the grate cover inside the face plate. Check again to make sure that everything is tightened and that you have not mistakenly cut the pool liner in the wrong place. Climb out of the pool and remove the ladder and the work platform.

Step 6: Backfilling the Excavation
Continue to fill the pool, removing the wrinkles with the vacuum. Keep this up until the water has risen to just below the wall panels. It is now time to backfill the excavated area around the metal walls.

This must be done before the pool has been completely filled so that there is little stress placed on the panels by the water pressure, which pushes outward. The bottom layer of the backfill should be composed of 8 to 12 in. of gravel for good drainage. Try to keep clay from being used as a backfill material. It could cause continued settlement of the poured concrete surround. The backfill may be wetted and tamped to insure a good compaction.

If pouring a concrete surround, wait at least several weeks. If utilizing a deck support system, the decking may be poured immediately after the backfill has been placed. Although the pool walls are self-supporting, it is recommended that the backfilling progress keep pace with the rising pool-water level to equalize pressures.

Step 7: Final Installation Procedures Continue filling the pool until the water level reaches to about 2 in. below the inlets and skimmer. Screw in the inlet face plate and cut the liner material away from the opening. Do not cut the liner until the installation of the plumbing has been completed. Repeat the installation procedure for the skimmer face plate and the return face plate (if applicable). Fill the pool until the shallow end is covered with 12 in. of water. Remove the vacuum. If you have been vacuuming through the liner, replace the liner.

Step 8: Pouring a Concrete Surround If you had planned to install a deck support system, it would have been installed when the wall panels were being bolted together. Having done that you would now be in the position, having backfilled, to pour the concrete pool surround or deck.

Install 2x4 lumber to conform to the desired shape of the pool. Anything wider than the width of the pool support will be poured later. Make sure that you have sectioned the entire area before you begin pouring. Install the welded wire fabric to support arms to reinforce the concrete slab. Finish the concrete as outlined under the in-ground concrete pool section, in Chapter 3.

5
ADDING AN
INDOOR IN-GROUND POOL

If you want to be able to swim all year around in your own pool, you probably will need an indoor pool. There are numerous advantages: you are guaranteed maximum privacy and security; there are no season limits imposed on your swimming activities, and you can exercise through swimming all year. A swimming pool located indoors can be an extension of your house, providing a recreational zone as a part of the other house functions.

An indoor pool can receive both light and heat from a skylight installation. The solar gain during the day will offset heating costs all through the year.

ATTACHED VS. DETACHED

It is possible to construct an indoor pool and its surrounding structure either as part of new house construction or as a later addition. Each approach must be planned differently. The primary options available to the owner are the indoor pool attached enclosure and the detached swimming pool. The latter is somewhat less expensive to construct. On the other hand, a detached indoor in-ground swimming pools will be more expensive to heat and somewhat more difficult to get to in the winter from the house. Since the main reason for having an indoor pool in a colder region seems to be for protection against weather, most indoor pools in these areas are in attached enclosures.

PLANNING THE SITE
Choosing the Exposure

In considering an indoor swimming pool, whether attached or detached, the site must be evaluated and planned. Normally, it is preferable to select a southern exposure or southwestern exposure. This provides natural sunlight into the pool area (if there are enough properly placed windows) and helps keep down the cost of heating the water and the enclosed space.

On a south-facing site, the prevailing winds present fewer problems than on other exposures. An addition or the enclosure on the south face usually suffers less heat loss and gain. The additional thickness that the pool enclosure represents will reduce the overall heat loss during the winter season and reduce the overall heat gain during the summer.

The southern exposure requirement often dictates the placement of the pool and enclosure with respect to an existing house. This could cause some difficulties in the meshing of the existing with the new. For example, if your existing house has all the bedrooms on the south face of the house, the addition of a pool might not be as gracious as if it were off the family room or main living area. While there are no absolutes about the location of the pool to the house proper, a southern-facing exposure is recommended.

Structural Notes If the pool and enclosure are to be integrated into the overall house plan, the foundation could become a determining factor for the depth of the pool and its specific location. Placement of the plumbing and electrical connections also must be coordinated. The better integrated the pool, the more economical the construction will be. An attached enclosure will share a common wall with the existing house or new construction; this represents potential savings in construction and energy costs.

Soil Conditions and Types Review the discussion in Chapter 2 regarding the various soil types. The soil should always be well graded and compacted.

When building next to an existing foundation, which usually is about 8 ft. below grade, take care that the soil pressures that act on the wall and the wall acts upon are not disturbed. This could cause settlement problems in the main house. If you are in doubt, consult with an architect or engineer or excavation contractor about the potential problem.

Slope A level site for the pool and the enclosure usually are the most desirable. Drainage should always pitch away from the pool enclosure and the house. The problem with water drainage is not as large a problem with an enclosed pool as with an open one. If your site is a steeply sloped one, the only alternative you may have is to build the pool and enclosure right up to the lowest part of the house. Make sure that the enclosure does not cut off the vision of the upper windows. In some cases, the pool enclosure is simply an extension of the current roof.

Where the site is less severe but still requires a retaining wall to stabilize one edge, the pool may be recessed to the north to reduce the northern exposure. Try to imagine the pool in the slope of the hill or adjacent to the house in order to visualize what type of additional foundations will be required. A rural or suburban site may provide more siting options for you based on slope. Try to select a site with the least pitch since it will need the least foundation, and thus be more economical.

DESIGN CONSIDERATIONS: Pools Built Into New Houses

Of all the many options that are available to you, the pool that is built at the time of the original house construction can best incorporate all your design ideas. Since the new house will be designed to accommodate the pool, the enclosure can be located almost anywhere within the house plan. However, few homeowners have the budget to consider a total design package.

The most important planning consideration should be to orient the pool and the house so the pool has a southern exposure. This uses the sun's energy to heat the pool water as well as to reduces the total energy consumed by your dwelling. During the summer months, an enclosure that opens to the outdoors and has the potential of flow-through ventilation will use the water to cool the space. This reduces summer air conditioning costs.

There are several types of plans that use the indoor enclosed space to advantage. The atrium plan places the pool centrally to all spaces, which in turn can either face the pool or not. The "L" system uses the pool and its enclosure as an extension of the basic house plan. This allows a better tie between the family room and the pool. The "T" arrangement allows you to zone the pool to its own area without separating it from the dwelling unit. This plan also allows for a good relationship between the family room and the pool.

Energy Savings In addition to lowered costs of pool construction and the enclosure because they are being built along with the house, savings can be increased by taking advantage of shared en-

An attached pool enclosure shares a common wall with the house, making the enclosure less costly to build. Usually the design and materials are the same in both structures.

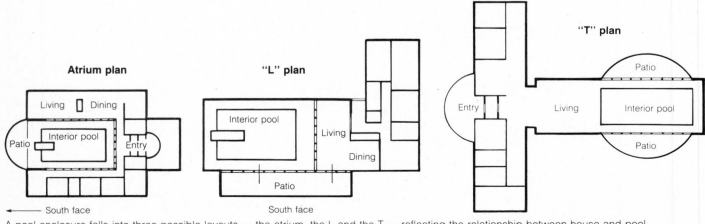

A pool enclosure falls into three possible layouts — the atrium, the L and the T — reflecting the relationship between house and pool.

ergy benefits. Some energy-conscious plans have been awarded a tax credit because the inclusion of the pool represents a renewable energy resource.

Indoor Pool Built Into Addition

Inclusion of an indoor pool in an addition can be a very wise decision, but the design of the pool and enclosure must be planned so that they blend with the ''look'' of the house and the site. One of the main downfalls of an ''added-on'' pool enclosure is that the structure bears no similarity to the character and design of the house to which it attaches. This also is reflected in the lack of effective landscaping.

Of main concern is the land available for the addition, taking setbacks and yard requirements into consideration. A location off the bedrooms is not as desirable as placement next to the family room, kitchen or bathrooms for better circulation. Try as many combinations as possible before deciding on the location.

Connection to the House Depending on whether the pool and enclosure will be directly attached, the foundation and excavation could present a problem. If you are excavating next to an existing foundation wall, take great care not to disturb the soil under the foundation. This could cause settlement and some internal cracking of plaster walls and ceilings. To reduce this problem, place a greater distance between the pool and the house proper by expanding the size of the pool

surround. Consider 8 ft. as a minimum distance, with 12 ft. preferred.

As the pool moves further away from the existing house, the pool enclosure must span longer distances. Depending on the type of enclosure selected, the span may be limited and thus reduce the size of the pool. Have an architect, engineer or qualified builder look at the existing structure to determine how much additional load it must carry. If a self-supporting structure is selected, this is not a problem. If the enclosure is using the house as a framing point, the roof of the enclosure

must be integrated in such a way to reduce rain water leakage in the valley between the two. This makes the integration more difficult between the enclosure and the house. When deciding about the type of structure, consider how the roof lines should meet with each other and whether one roof should dominate the other.

A DETACHED ENCLOSURE

The same ventilation requirements and orientation are recommended as for the attached pool structure. Refer to the previous section for more information. Plan

This attached enclosure is unusual because the materials and construction do not match those of the house. The enclosure still will have lower energy costs than a detached one.

A detached pool is often feasible only if your lot is large enough to house it. Water heating and plumbing must be extended.

to have the bathrooms in the vicinity of the pool or provide for one in the new space.

POOL AND ENCLOSURE OPTIONS
Vinyl Liner vs. Concrete Pools

The range of options that are available to you are similar to those offered for the in-ground pool. These fall into two major categories; the vinyl liner pool and the concrete pool. An in-ground concrete pool, generally gunite for an interior job, would result in a greater freedom of shapes, depths and sizes than are traditionally available in the vinyl liner pool. If you desire to swim under a wall from the inside to the outside of the pool, this might require a concrete or a custom vinyl liner application. On the other hand, a vinyl liner pool can be modified to meet most of your form requirements.

Where you are installing a new pool and enclosure next to or near an existing residence, the most logical selection would be a vinyl liner pool. It requires far less ground preparation, is most economical and is more adaptable to a variety of terrain conditions. The machinery for a concrete pool may be difficult to manuever next to an existing house without causing serious damage to your property. Select the option best for you.

Types of Enclosures

In selecting a pool enclosure, consider these questions: should the enclosure be heated? How open should the enclosure be to the outside? What kind of security will it require? Should the form and materials be compatible with the existing house? What is the best accessibility from the house? Answers to these questions should help you determine the type of structure needed. For example, if your pool is to be heated during the coldest season, you may have to limit the number of window or door openings, and add the same insulation values as new house construction.

The Greenhouse Enclosure The greenhouse enclosure, one of the more popular pool enclosures, is available as a freestanding structure or as a leanto. It may be purchased as a kit that comes complete with instructions and all the pieces, including the glass and ventilation system. The variety of sizes and shapes, and the economical nature of the greenhouse, make it a desirable choice.

The typical greenhouse is composed of three main elements: the foundation or pe-

rimeter support, the structural ribbing that will span across the pool, and the ventilation system which is part of the rib system. The ribs are generally made of high strength aluminum extrusions that are all preformed or shaped to the desired configuration. Each rib is placed about 24 to 30 in. on center, held laterally by horizontal bracing. Once the ribs are in place and bolted to the foundation, the glazing is placed. The glazing can be either single, double or triple strength glass and plexiglass. There are some insulated panels available, but at greater cost. Once the glazing is in place, the entire structure becomes quite stable and able to withstand relatively high wind loads. If you live in

an area subject to hail or have a vandalism problem, the plexiglass alternative might be a better and less expensive solution to glass replacement.

The "Greenhouse Effect" The greenhouse, being mainly glass, allows 80% of the radiated energy to pass through the glass, enter the water and warm the concrete surround. During the winter, this is desirable and necessary. During the summer, this benefit turns into a liability. The buildup of the heat and the moisture content of the air produce what is called the "greenhouse effect" when the dew point of the air vapor is reached; this results in condensation or even rain.

This effect may be overcome by effec-

A greenhouse enclosure is a popular choice for an indoor pool. Light waves pass into the enclosure and are transformed into long wave heat energy, which is trapped inside.

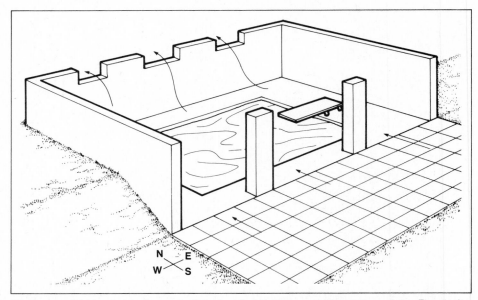

It takes careful planning to have a satisfactory installation on a hilly or steep slope. The design shown assures adequate ventilation with a separate vent system.

tive and immediate ventilation. The ventilation takes two forms — natural and mechanical. Natural ventilation requires that the ridge line vents of the greenhouse be opened in order to allow the hot moisture-saturated air to escape. In the winter, this may not be possible because of the need to maintain the temperature. Introduction of mechanical ventilation can reduce the ''greenhouse effect'' while at the same time controlling the amount of fresh air that is allowed into the pool area. This type of control filters about 90% of the inside air and adds an additional 10% fresh air to the mixture. The moisture is removed through refrigerated coils or a heat pump.

Another means of controlling the heat and moisture buildup during the summer months is provision of shade. Many manufacturers offer a light aluminum rolling screen that drops down the outside of the greenhouse, reflecting the energy back into the air. The screen gets hot but the interior temperature is greatly reduced. Some ventilation must still be provided, however.

Insulating Enclosures The insulated enclosure should be given serious thought by anyone living in a cold climate. The enclosed pool that uses an insulated wall, similar to standard house construction, with a limited number of openings, is the most cost-effective when designing a year-round swimming pool enclosure. The main ingredients are as follows: typical insulated perimeter foundation; insulated walls; insulated glass; a clear span roof structure that is well insulated; and a ventilation system that allows for a percentage of outside fresh air to be mixed with the recycled interior air.

This type of structure can be easily made into a extension of your house, with walls that match the existing ones. The major difference is in the choice of material you plan to use in the pool area; all interior finish materials should be moisture protected.

Pneumatic Enclosures One of the more recent developments in pool enclosures is the inflatable structure. These are economical in terms of material costs, but expensive to run on a year-round basis. Where your plans call for true outdoor living during the summer and complete enclosure during the colder seasons, the pneumatic enclosure is an excellent choice in that it can be dismantled with little effort during the summer and reinstalled during the fall. The major components are: a perimeter insulated foundation, a fan/ventilation system and the inflatable itself. The inflatable stays up because of a difference in atmospheric pressure between the inside and the outside.

The major drawback to the pneumatic is its energy usage. The air that enters the enclosure must be heated in order to maintain a comfortable swimming environment. The cost of the heat and the electricity to power the ventilation system could be prohibitive. The fan cannot be shut off without deflating the entire system.

Material Strength

The selection of materials should be based on the compatability with your decor or with the existing structure, and on the ability of the materials to withstand the moisture and temperature changes. Select materials that will not crack due to expansion and contraction. If the walls are not properly insulated and are without a vapor barrier, ice lenses can form in the walls, causing serious damage to the exterior finish and to the stability of the wall.

Always select materials that either you are familiar with or that a qualified contractor can recommend. If in doubt, consult for another opinion.

Ventilation and the "Greenhouse Effect"

There can be no doubt that effective and economical indoor pool ventilation is critical to the enjoyment of the pool. The greenhouse or hothouse effect, often a by-product of an enclosed pool area, can render the pool area almost unusable. The design of the ventilation system should be left to a heating and ventilation engineer or a qualified heating/ventilation contractor, who can help figure out the number of air changes needed for your specific size pool and enclosure. Also ask him to select the most appropriate fan and motor combination. Fees will be minimal compared to the savings you will gain.

A typical ventilation system uses a forced air fan or wall mounted ventilator, galvanized metal ductwork, fresh air intake, supply registers, return air grilles and a thermostat. To minimize the ''greenhouse effect,'' the air must be changed a certain number of times during the day. This means that the entire volume of air contained within the enclosure must be changed. Most local codes specify the number of changes required. For a house, the normal air change would be about .5 to 1.0 air change per day. This would prevent the air from becoming stagnant. For the pool enclosure, the range of air

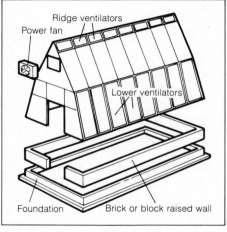

A greenhouse enclosure has three main elements: a foundation, structural ribbing for the glass and provisions for ventilation.

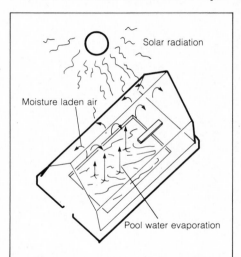

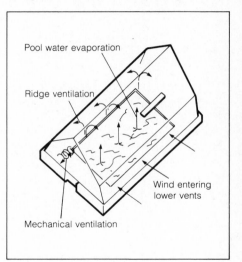

changes is from 2 to 6 complete air changes per day. This range is affected by outdoor humidity, climate and temperature, and should be verified for your specific condition.

The ventilation system for the pool should be separate from that of the main house because the influence of the pool environment on the house atmosphere could be a problem. If a ventilator is to be used alone, it can be mounted directly on an exterior wall. Make sure that it contains an automatic damper and insect screening.

The Pool Surround

The pool surround options are like those available for an in-ground pool. The possibility of using an indoor/outdoor carpet is often an option, since it provides a softer surface for walking. You can use it to differentiate the various zones inside the enclosure. One very effective way to do this is to use several surface materials, one for each zone. Always place some materials that will absorb the water from the swimmers before they enter the house. The chemicals in the water could bleach a rug or disfigure a wood floor. Thick pads or mats often work quite well. Another alternative is the installation of a poolside shower to remove pool water from the body.

Diving Boards, Ladders and Slides

The same range of options of pool accessories is available for the enclosed pool as for an outdoor one. You may not want to have an Olympic-sized diving board because of the height required to enclose it. The one major consideration should be in the area of clear room about the slides, ladders and diving board. Always allow enough height and side clearance from the house so that if someone falls they will not hit the enclosure.

Indoor Lighting

The installation of indoor lights in the pool enclosure is necessary for evening swimming and for accent. These two types of task lighting require two interactive approaches to poolside lighting. The general utility lighting for the pool can be a combination of overhead HID (high intensity discharge) lamps, underwater lights and spots on high activity areas. Several well-placed sodium lamps overhead will light the area so that all parts of the pool are equally illuminated. The intensity of the light varies, but 30 to 50 footcandles is often adequate for the indoor pool area. Take care to make sure the coloration of the overhead lamp selected is warm and not cold, and locate the lamps to minimize any glare. The effect of glare could be uncomfortable for swimmers and viewers.

In addition to the overhead lights, the installation of underwater pool lights is the same as for in-ground pools. The lights must meet or exceed the requirements of the National Electrical Code. Before selecting utility lighting, determine how the pool is to be used and the type of activities planned for it. A large pool with serious swimmers may require a higher level of brightness than needed by those with a casual or informal approach. Based on the size and height of the enclosure and the number of openings, figure out if utility lighting will be needed on just overcast days, or sunny ones as well.

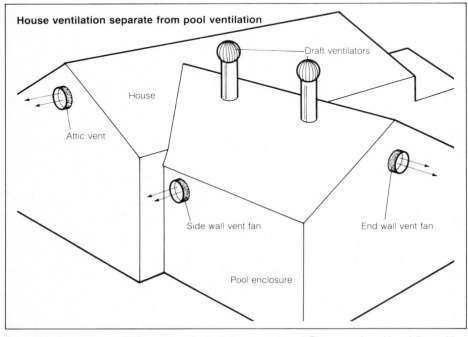

House ventilation separate from pool ventilation

Draft ventilators

House

Attic vent

Side wall vent fan

End wall vent fan

Pool enclosure

Do not use the same ventilation system for both house and pool. Because of pool humidity, neither area will be well served. Mount the pool ventilation fan on an exterior wall.

For both the pleasure and the safety of swimmers and onlookers, a pool area must be adequately lighted. Use waterproof fixtures to illuminate both the pool and surround.

Accent lighting is turned on when the pool is not being used. It is decorative in nature and can enhance the character of the pool. Indoor poolside parties or buffet dinners require mood lighting that the overhead utility lights cannot provide — arrange for a combination of indirect and spot lighting.

Heating and Cooling

Depending on your outside climate, you may require heating as well as cooling. If you are in an area where the outdoor temperature rarely drops below freezing, a heat pump may be best. If the heat pump option is used, the condensing coil should fit into the furnace so it can be used for both heating and cooling. If heating of the air is required using more traditional means, a gas- or oil-fired furnace is generally used. Electric forced-air furnaces are available as well. The specific size of the furnace, heat pump, condensing unit and ductwork should be determined by a qualified engineer or contractor. Do not select a unit unless you know the specifications you need; it may not do the job effectively.

Water Supply and Drainage

The systems for water supply, drainage and filtration are those outlined in Chapter 2 on in-ground outdoor pools. The main difference might be in the location of the filtration system. Most owners prefer to have the filtration system located in the basement next to a floor drain. This consolidates all mechanical equipment in one place and could be cheaper to run.

When draining the pool, the resulting waste (whether through backwashing or emptying the pool) will normally be placed into the house waste water system rather than into a separate drainage facility. This may differ by locale, since most state and local building codes specify how the waste is to be disposed of. A vinyl liner pool is never entirely emptied of water unless the liner is to be changed. In an indoor concrete pool, which is seldom exposed to freeze/thaw cycles, the frequency of repair and the need to drain the pool are reduced.

Since the pool is to be enclosed, it may not require the same filtration cycle that an exposed pool would undergo. This is due to a reduction in the airborne pollutants and debris. As a result, the filtration cycle, depending on use, could be under 8 hours.

In addition, the frequency of addition of chemicals may be reduced since the pool will not be in direct sunlight. Always check the pH balances (see appendix).

If you wish the filtration equipment in the pool area, it should be placed in a closet or in a built-in space. One very interesting method is to place the entire filtration system in a recessed vault near the pool. A wood cover over it makes it safe and quite accessible.

Electrical System Needs

A separate circuit breaker panel is recommended for the pool operation and enclosure. This will eliminate any confusion between the house and the pool service. Your local utility may require that you install a complete service just for the pool enclosure if the pool is to be installed next to an existing house. Recess the meter and breaker panel or enclose both in a recess with doors.

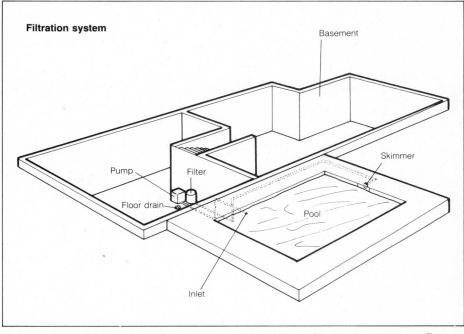

An indoor pool receives less debris but still requires adequate filtration and drainage. To save space, consider running the pipelines into the adjoining basement area.

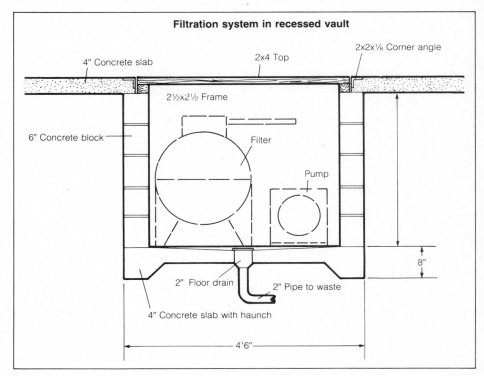

The breaker panel should be divided in five major zones, lighting, power, ventilation, pool lighting and filtration pump. The separate circuitry will help in the wiring and provide better service over the life span of the pool enclosure. By doing it this way, the pump amperage rating can be changed without having to rewire the rest of the circuits. If underwater low voltage lights or standard underwater lights are to be used, they should have their own place on the panel.

Select electrical fixtures and accessories that are waterproof or at least moistureproof. A licensed electrician will be able to assist you with the proper selection of components.

If you are planning to use the enclosed pool area for entertainment, you will require power outlets for the various poolside accessories. The outlets should be located in walls. All the outlets should be exterior waterproof type. This will prevent moisture from entering the receptacle and causing corrosion. These receptacles will be connected to the breaker panel and fully grounded. In some regions, all pool circuitry must be connected to a GFIC (ground fault interruptor circuit), which prevents possible shock. We suggest this even if not required by code. Always consult your local or state codes before installing electrical power circuitry.

If the pump is to be located in the basement of the house, it should be mounted on isolation pads to minimize the sound transmission problem. The ventilation system should have its own circuit and should be rated for peak power demand. In the case of a fire or other emergency, the entire system should be able to be shut down from a wall-mounted junction box in the pool area. This box is something like a fire alarm box in that it just turns the power off to the entire enclosed area. Make sure that it is accessible, but out of the reach of children.

Design Factors

Pool Shape and Size The pool form and size will shape the enclosing structure. In our example (a 16x32 ft. pool) a minimum clear space between the pool and the enclosure wall, for the surround and access to the house or outdoors, should be 4 to 6 ft. around all sides. This would make the enclosure a minimum of 28x44 ft. If you include a diving board, it must be at least 12 ft. from the edge of the pool to the wall.

Increasing Space of Activity Areas From the preceding discussion, you can see that the pool enclosure is roughly 28x44 ft. If you deduct the area of the pool proper, you are left with an open space that includes the 6 ft. pool surround. If you are planning to use the pool for activities other than swimming, you will probably require additional room to accommodate a crowd. One way to increase the available space is to reposition the pool so that one side has a minimum 4 ft. surround and the other increases to 8 ft. This may not satisfy your needs, since a lawn or pool lounger is at least 6 ft. long.

Another way to add space is to increase the length of the enclosure at one end by 10 or 12 ft. If you are unable to extend the building any further, an increase in the width of 2 ft., still maintaining a minimum surround, would offer a clear space of 10 ft. along the side of the pool.

Height Clearance for a Diving Board Many manufacturers recommend 10 ft. between the top of the diving board and the underside of the overhead structure. This would require a space that is 30x48x12 ft. high as a volume to accommodate a 16x32 ft. swimming pool.

Vehicular Access Make sure that the spot that you have chosen can accommodate a backhoe, gradeall and a cement truck; otherwise, costs of hand carrying the materials could be quite high.

ENCLOSURE SPECIFICATIONS
Excavation

The construction steps for an indoor inground pool are no different than for an outdoor pool. The same excavation requirements must be met for both. Since the pool will be enclosed, a perimeter foundation must now be considered as part of the excavation requirement. When excavating next to an existing structure, take great care to reduce the possibility of undermining the existing foundation. Since the existing house is all hooked up to the

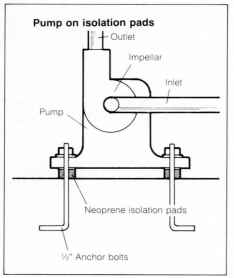

Pump on isolation pads

Outlet

Impellar

Inlet

Pump

Neoprene isolation pads

½" Anchor bolts

A pump in a basement can transmit sound into the house. An isolation pad placed beneath the pump prevents this type of a problem.

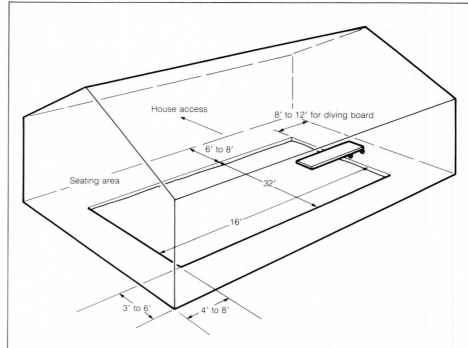

House access

8' to 12' for diving board

6' to 8'

Seating area

32'

16'

3' to 6'

4' to 8'

waste and water lines, check locations of all underground utilities.

Connecting to an Existing Structure

Connection of a pool enclosure to an existing house must be handled with respect. You cannot simply push an addition next to a house and expect everything to work. Here are the major components, which must mesh properly.

Foundation If your existing house has a poured-in-place concrete or concrete block foundation, the addition should have one too. If the basement of your house is about 8 ft. below the anticipated level of the pool, the pool foundation need not extend the full 8 ft., but should be at a level below the frost line. This depth ranges from 12 in. in southern areas to 48 in. in the northern climates. The foundation walls should be separated from each other with a piece of insulation placed between the existing foundation and the concrete form for the perimeter wall. In the excavation, try not to disturb any of the soil below the level at which the perimeter footing will sit. The disturbed soil will require that a grout bed be placed before installation of the footing form. If this is not done, undue settlement may occur.

Walls If the existing walls are brick construction, it might make sense to have brick walls in the covered pool area. If you

desire a contrast in walls, standard stud construction is the least expensive of all the alternatives. When building a new wall perpendicular to an existing one, there should be room for movement allowed. This is often called an "expansion" joint. Since the existing structure has already settled, the newer one must be allowed to do this. If they were permanently connected, the possibility of cracking could occur at the connection or elsewhere in the structure. To compensate for this problem, an expandable gasket material will be added to the joint to make it more flexible. Some contractors will simply nail one stud against the existing wall and then proceed to tie the entire structure together; this method works but is not recommended.

Roof The roof is the most difficult connection to make. It requires that everything be sealed so rain or insects cannot penetrate into the interior. The best method is to have the roof of the enclosure lap the existing roof or vice-versa. This eliminates the valley between the roofs, and avoids flashing and drainage problems. The pitch of the old roof should reflect the pitch of the new roof and eave line. This will blend the two together more effectively.

Before tying into an existing roof, make sure that it is capable of supporting the

additional load. If not, the existing roof will have to be strengthened, which is expensive.

If the structure is to be supported by an existing wall, verify that that wall is strong enough to assume the additional burden. Have a building inspector or contractor survey your wall and roof structure to determine its adequacy; a structural engineer will also perform the investigation for a nominal fee. The direction of the roof framing also will be a determinant.

If roof trusses are to be used for the new construction and are to bear on the existing wall, the existing rafters should be rein-

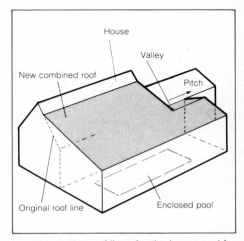

Incorporate the roof lines for the house and for the pool to prevent water buildup and leakage between the two structures.

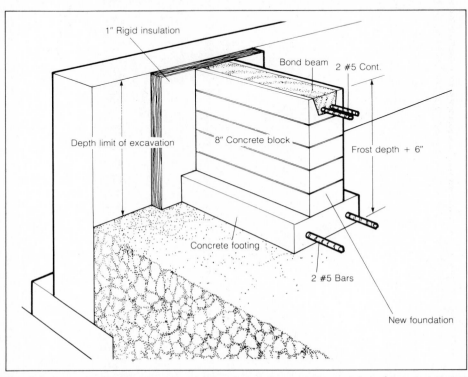

To allow for contraction between the existing foundation and the pool foundation, install rigid insulation between the two.

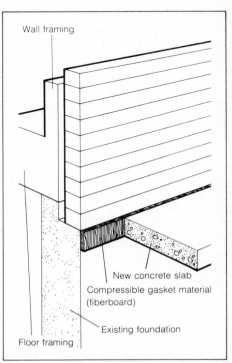

The joint between the two foundations must be flexible to prevent cracking due to frost heave. Use a compressible fiberboard gasket.

forced as well as the wall. This could be done by doubling up, placing a new truss next to the old one. When a valley between roofs exists, plan for the flashing to extend 48 in. up from the valley on either side. This should be increased in colder climates. Roofing materials should be compatible with each other. If you have thought of getting a new roof for the house, it would be better if you had the entire thing done now, at one time.

Mechanical/Electrical/Plumbing

When placing the pool enclosure next to the existing structure, be careful lest you disrupt existing service to the house. Extension of the utilities from the existing house to the pool addition requires planning. Consider the easiest places in which to break through the existing foundation wall. Allow sufficient area so that ductwork, if used, will pass easily through the opening with insulation. In some locales, when the addition is installed, the rest of the utilities and electric must be brought up to code. Plumbing is another concern, in that the lines to the pool, which should

be installed before the perimeter foundation, must be capped before actual hookup. A below-grade connection box might be used to simplify the construction procedures. Always run conduit under the floor for electrical connections to junction boxes. Make sure that additional wires can be run for future requirements.

Building Permits If you have retained a contractor for the purpose of building the pool enclosure, the contractor should be responsible for obtaining building permits. However, the plans and specifications will be required to demonstrate that the new pool enclosure meets all of the latest code requirements. In the event that the existing house is quite old, you may be asked to change certain portions of it to meet the present code. For example, where new electrical wiring and panel will be required for the addition, if the code requires a central source for all electricity, your older fuse box or bare fuse arrangement may have to be replaced. In some areas, special permits for electrical, plumbing and mechanical might be required in addition to the building permit. There is a fee attached to acquiring a building permit. This fee is generally based on a percentage of the total construction costs and does vary from state to state. If you are acting as your own general contractor, it is advisable to

seek assistance when preparing the necessary forms.

HEATING THE POOL WATER

The heating of pool water in an enclosed space is not as critical as heating the water in an outdoor pool. In most cases, the water will absorb some of the heat that is being pushed into the enclosed pool space. If you desire warmer water, the selection of the size and type of heater can be similar to those discussed in the outdoor in-ground pool. The major difference will be in the capacity of the heating unit. There are several types that you can select from.

MAINTENANCE

The maintenance for an indoor pool (see Appendix) is identical to that for the in-ground outdoor pool. The major difference is that pool cleaning will be reduced because of fewer particles trapped in the water. Thus the pool will need smaller quantities of chemicals also. In the pool a germicide or disinfectant is also required. The chemicals that are suspended in the air moisure could cause discoloration of cloth material.

Every couple of weeks or sooner, go over all the surface materials with a disinfectant to eliminate any possible bacteria. Mop the pool surround on a regular basis to reduce the smell of chlorine.

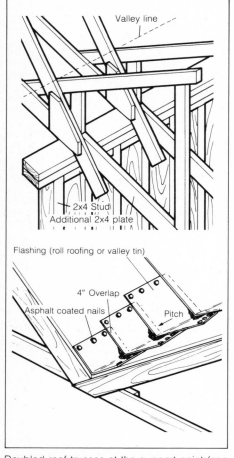

Doubled roof trusses at the support point (see above) add strength. Flashing (see below) prevents water leakage at the roof joint.

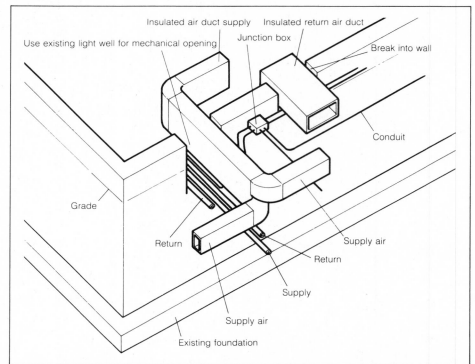

Most ductwork, plumbing and electrical connections must be run before the perimeter foundation is poured. Cap plumbing lines and make electrical hookups as required by code.

HOW TO BUILD A POOL ENCLOSURE

This section covers the actual step-by-step construction of a detached pool enclosure. The detached has been selected for discussion since it includes all the variations that might be encountered in an attached structure to the main house. Differences between the methods for attached and detached units are discussed as they arise. The selection of materials is all based on a finished pool size of 16x32 ft.

The construction for a swimming pool enclosure begins with the construction of the swimming pool itself. Whether you have selected a concrete or vinyl liner pool, the pool is the first step in the construction process. Before building the enclosure, most of the pool excavation must be completed, all the walls in place, plumbing installed as well as all conduit to the pool.

The procedures that were outlined for an in-ground pool are very much the same as those for an enclosed pool. For the purposes of demonstration, a vinyl liner pool will be the basis for our subsequent demonstration. The rectangular shape of the pool will dictate the shape and height of the pool enclosure, which will be a detached version. (In the attached op-tion, the height of the structure would be partly determined by the existing roof pitch of the house.)

The swimming pool enclosure to be described is mainly intended for a colder climate and will include passive solar detailing. These same principles can apply to many different climatic conditions; the principles are the same. The method of construction will be light frame with a modified rafter system.

CONSTRUCTION MATERIALS

The example pool enclosure will be a 30x48 ft. building that requires a 12-ft. height clearance over the diving board and window and/or door openings to the south. The existing house construction in the example is wood frame with an asphalt shingled roof oriented on an east-west axis. The existing house has a poured-in-place concrete foundation.

We suggest you prepare a materials list and then go around to several lumberyards to receive quotations. This will help you determine the actual costs of material. A sample materials list for the structure is given below. Materials for building forms are not includ-ed, but are found under "Construction Procedures, Step 2."

Materials List

Framing for Walls, Roof

Light Framing for Walls:	2x6 Construction Grade No. 1 S4S
Joists and Planking:	2x12 Construction Grade No. 1 S4S
Rafters and Beams:	4x12 Construction Grade No. 1 S4S
Sills:	2x6 Foundation Grade or Treated
Bridging:	1x4 Construction Grade No. 2 S4S
Plywood Sheathing:	C-D Exterior ½ inch
Building Paper:	15 lb felt for walls, 30 lb for roof
Insulation:	R-19 Walls R-38 Roof
Vapor barrier:	4 mil polyethylene sheeting

Foundation for Perimeter Walls
Concrete: 3000 psi or 6 bag mixture

Interior Finishes
Concrete: 3000 psi or 6 bag mix — Steel trowel finish with hardener
Glazed Ceramic Tile — 4x4 or 6x6 quarry tile
Wall board — Moisture-resistant gypsum
Wood paneling

Windows Fenestration
Sliding Patio Doors: 6 ft. 8 in. high x 8 ft. wide

Exterior Finishes
Hardboard siding, narrow clapboard (4 in. weather) or to suit

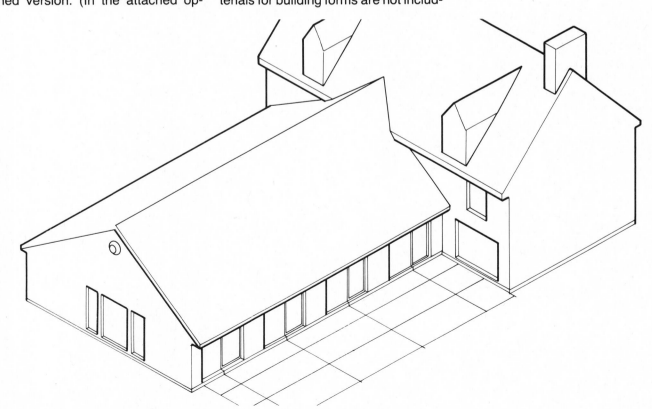

Project continued on next page

CONSTRUCTION PROCEDURES
Step 1: Excavation

The excavation for the perimeter foundation wall should not be started until after the vinyl liner pool bottom has been dug, the shelf cut out and the panels installed and bolted. In addition, place the concrete edging along the outside of the panels. All plumbing connections should be installed and the area backfilled around the pool. Once this has been completed, the perimeter foundation trench can be dug.

Setting Up Batter Boards Stake out the overall dimensions of the building as shown. This requires foundation dimensions of 30x48 ft. To do this, locate the correct dimensions of the side walls from the edge of the pool wall already installed: 4 ft. to the north and 10 ft. to the south. This establishes the proportion between the building and the pool.

Now that you have staked out the corner points, construct batter boards, 6 to 8 ft. back from the staked lines, at each corner. The batter boards may be constructed of 2x4s. The boards do not need to be carefully aligned, but should be in a similar relationship with each other. Drive nails into the previously installed corner stakes and string a light line between them.

Between the batter boards, string another line that crosses the corners of the stakes, as shown. Complete all four sides to outline the overall shape of the pool enclosure. Now align the corners so all dimensions are true and the building square. Use a 3-4-5 right triangle, as in Chapter 3.

Checking for Square and Level Starting at one corner stake, measure along the short side by a distance of 9 ft.; drive another stake. Along the long side of the perimeter wall, measure 12 ft. and drive another stake. Make sure the stakes are vertical. Check the dimensions again. Now measure between the two stakes on the diagonal. The measurement should be 15 ft. If it is not, adjust the long-side stake back and forth until the dimension is met. Once that has been done, adjust the line between the batter boards to reflect the changes. Now move to the next adjacent corner and repeat the procedure. Each time a change occurs, adjust the line between the batter boards. Once all dimensions are checked and rechecked, the building should be square. To check again, measure from the intersection of the lines, checking one diagonal dimension against the other diagonal. They should be equal; a slight variation of ¼ in. can be allowed.

Use the transit or line level to make sure that every line is level and true. If you measure down from the intersection of the lines to the top of the soil, you will see at that point what the grade elevation will be between the four corners of the building.

Variation: attached plan You will be using the existing house as one reference point. Follow the same procedures except that one side will already be determined.

Digging the Excavation The foundation walls will be 10 in. wide and require excavation to a depth of 4 ft. (or frost requirement) below grade. Place the excavated material on either side of the hole. This will be used as backfill later on. Make sure that the bottom of the excavation is level and free of any loose debris.

Step 2: Installing the Wall Forms
For the forms you have two options

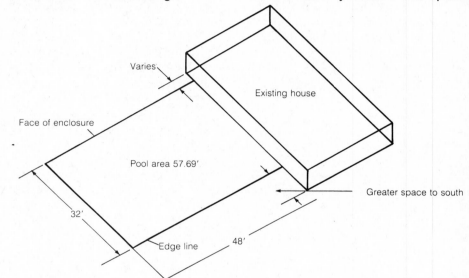

To lay out the perimeter foundation lines, first stake the building location. Then erect batterboards, 6 to 8 ft. back from the staked lines, as discussed in Chap. 3.

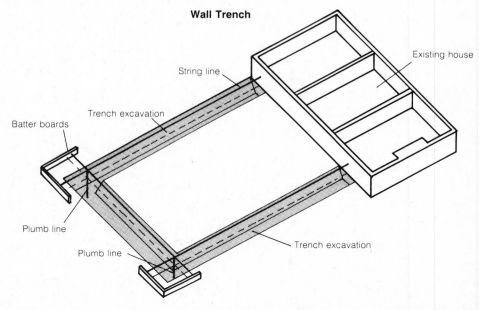

available: renting prefabricated reusable forms or building your own. Since building a form for our simple structure is not very difficult, here are the basic procedures.

Building the Forms Purchase enough sheets of ¾ in. 4x8 ft. plywood to complete one side of the perimeter. This will be the exterior form for the foundation, which serves as the base for the wood wall. Since the length is 48 ft., it would call for 6 sheets. You may also desire to form a short side at the same time, which would require an additional 4 sheets. Using 2x4s attached to the outside face of the plywood, locate the panels so the inside face of the panel is in alignment with the string. Stabilize all the panels and make sure that they are level and plumb. Provide as much bracing as needed to stabilize the entire wall. For later ease of removal, duplex nails are recommended.

After the long and short side have been formed, the interior face of the excavation must be formed. Pack the earth sufficiently up the side of the excavation to make a 12 to 16 in. tapered earth wall, the top of which should be approximately 8 in. below the level of the exterior form. Complete the entire perimeter in this fashion. If the soil is too dry, add a little water.

Place a 2x8 form board along the entire length of the top of the inside edge of the earth wall. This should align with the level of the exterior form, and be braced along its entire length. To maintain the 16 in. distance between this interior form board and the exterior form, use 2x6 braces (with duplex nails) to span between the interior and exterior form boards. Coat the inside faces of the forms with oil.

Place one brick every 48 in. along the length of the excavation. On top of this, place two ⅝ in. reinforcing bars to the bottom of the excavated trench. The bars should overlap by at least 2 ft. Tie them together with wire.

Step 3: Pouring the Perimeter Wall
Check the cleanliness of the forms. Examine the bracing of the forms so they will not move when the concrete is poured. Verify that the top of the forms

is at least 6 in. above the highest grade point.

We suggest you buy your concrete from a ready-mix supplier. The concrete will arrive on the site in a cement mixer. The mixer should be provided clear access to the forms; otherwise, the concrete will have to be barrowed in.

Place the concrete into the forms in uniform layers. Never drop concrete from higher than 2 to 3 ft. because it will segregate and be weaker. Cover all the reinforcing bars and compact well. To do this, take a ⅝ in. rod and push it up and down into the concrete (this is known as "rodding").

Rod the entire pour until the forms are filled and the concrete reaches the top of the forms. Smooth each section after pouring, using a screed and then a steel trowel. When that section of the wall has been completed, insert ½ in. anchor bolts 2 in. from the outside plywood faces. These should be placed 2 ft. from each corner and at least 4 ft. on center the entire length of the wall. Make sure that all walls have them, and that they are vertical. They should extend 3 to 4 in. above the wall.

Once the walls have been poured and the anchor bolts inserted, let the

concrete to cure for at least three days before removing the forms.

Step 4: Removing the Forms
After 3 days (or up to 7) remove the forms. Form removal is simplified if you have coated the inside face with an oil substance to reduce the adherence of the concrete. As you strip the forms, make sure that no unplanned openings exist. Check the level of the wall. If patching must be done along the exposed part of the foundation, use a vinyl patching cement.

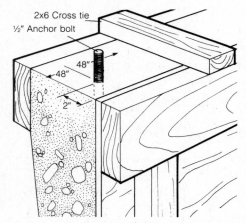

Once the concrete is poured and leveled, install ½ in. anchor bolts 2 ft. in from the corners and 4 ft. on center along the wall.

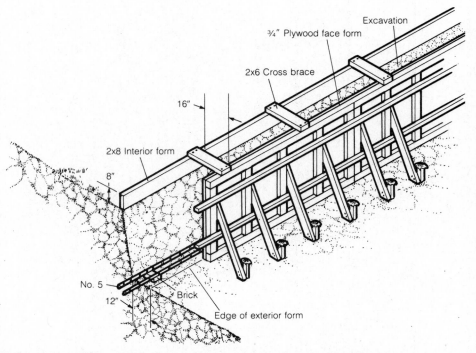

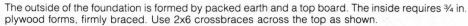

The outside of the foundation is formed by packed earth and a top board. The inside requires ¾ in. plywood forms, firmly braced. Use 2x6 crossbraces across the top as shown.

Project continued on next page

Step 5: Installing Perimeter Insulation

Generally, 2-in. rigid insulation blue board is used. This is available in 2 or 4 ft. widths up to 10 ft. long. This will be

Perimeter insulation and sills

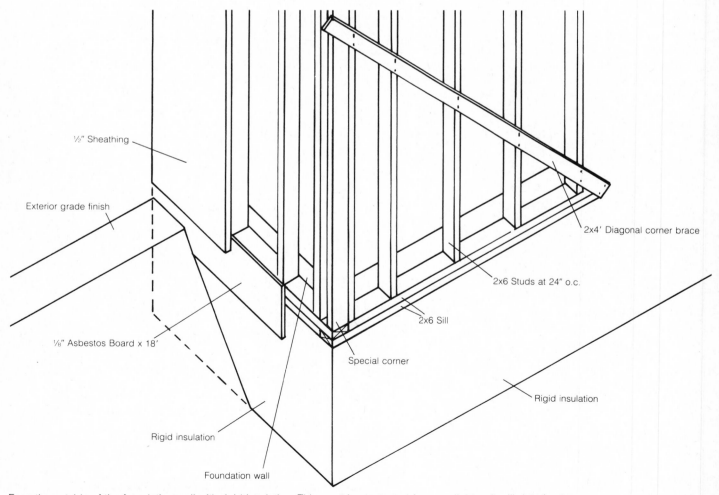

½" Anchor bolts, washers and nuts

2x6 Sill

8" Interior grade

4"

2"

2" Rigid insulation

Perimeter wall

placed along the exterior face of the poured wall. Where the pool enclosure is to abut against an existing house, the insulation may be eliminated. The top of the insulation should be level with the top of the wall; it should not extend over.

Lay the perimeter insulation, using some of the excavated soil to hold it against the foundation wall. Once the insulation is in place, backfill to keep it firmly in position.

Step 6: Installing the Sills

The 2x6 sill attaches to the top of the foundation wall with the previously installed anchor bolts. Correct placement of the sill is critical to the accuracy of the wall above. The outside edge of the sill should overhang the foundation wall by 2 in. so it will be flush with the rigid insulation.

Since the anchor bolts are in the way, drill holes in the sill before placing

it. Lay the sill along the edge until it lines up 2 in. beyond the foundation wall. Bolt the sill down using large washers to compress the member to the foundation. Complete this for the entire perimeter.

Step 7: Framing the Walls

The wall studs used are 2x6s less than 8 ft. long. This size maintains the 8-ft. vertical height of the wall from the bottom of the sill to the top of the double plate.

Start pool enclosure walls by temporarily fastening top and bottom plates together and marking them for the location of the studs and headers. This helps align the studs. Mark off the studs at 24 in. centers. Separate the top and bottom plates and nail in the studs. Each stud should line up in the middle of each mark on the top and bottom plate. In addition, indicate any additional openings such as rough

½" Sheathing

Exterior grade finish

⅛" Asbestos Board x 18'

Rigid insulation

Foundation wall

Special corner

2x6 Sill

2x6 Studs at 24" o.c.

2x4' Diagonal corner brace

Rigid insulation

Face the outside of the foundation wall with rigid insulation. This must be protected from sunlight or it will deteriorate.

openings for windows and doors. When all the walls are in place, an additional top plate will be added.

When all the studs are in place and the openings located with headers and additional studs as shown, a temporary diagonal brace on the corners so that the frame is stabilized. Since the pool surround has not yet been poured, the wall will have to be fabricated on the ground and then lifted up from the outside. Once the wall is in place and the plate has been located and flushed to the sill, nail the wall in place and brace it for stability.

Complete procedure must be completed for all four walls. Tie the corners together by adding another 2x6 top plate.

Some of the wall panels will be heavy. Lifting them up in place will require strength, or a wall jack. This device, when cranked, raises the wall up high enough so it can be maneuvered into place.

Variation: Attached Enclosure If the enclosure is an addition to the main house, certain modifications are required. The most important one is that the top of the plate should be placed so the eaves will line up. To do this,

shorter or longer studs may be required. Where the new wall connects with the existing one, the existing siding should be removed so that the sheathing is exposed. The corner studs should be doubled on the new wall and the entire wall assembly lifted into place and nailed.

Step 8: Finishing the Foundation
A protection layer must be installed between the blue board and the earth. This is normally a sheet of asbestos board. It comes in ⅛ in. thickness and nails to the sill and plate, extending down over the insulation by 24 to 36 in. The top of the board should be flush with the level of the plate. The entire perimeter should be done this way.

This both protects against damage to the insulation and offers a visual coverup.

Step 9: Sheathing the Walls
Now install the ½ in. plywood sheathing. This should be placed with care and be well nailed along each vertical stud. Use a chalkline to help with the placement of the nails. One method calls for sheathing the entire wall and then cutting the openings with a saw. The other method involves simply patching around the openings, which reduces the amount of waste. On the corners, the sheathing should be double nailed as well as along the sill. The sheathing should overlap the asbestos protection.

To connect the new wall to the old, remove the permanent siding at the joint. Add a doubled stud at the corner, by the sheathing.

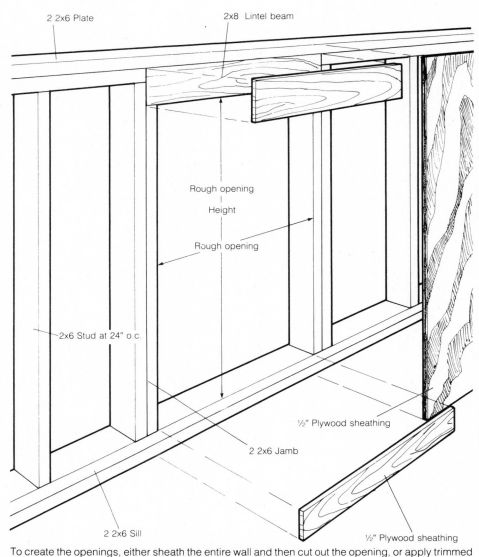

To create the openings, either sheath the entire wall and then cut out the opening, or apply trimmed paneling to fit around the opening. The second method reduces waste.

Project continued on next page

Step 10: Framing the Roof

To span the 30 ft., a series of modified 2x12 rafters and collar ties will be used. The premise behind this type of construction is that the 2x12 rests against the ridge beam, which will be a 4x12. To stabilize the entire structure, a horizontal 2x6 collar beam will be used at a point slightly higher than the 12 ft. above the finish pool floor. The proper design of the roof is critical to the success of the pool enclosure. It must be able to withstand the live loads and be watertight. It must also be able to accommodate enough insulation value for the pool to be economically heated and cooled.

Roof Pitch The pitch of the new roof is critical. It should correspond to the shape of the existing house and at the same time be high enough to clear the minimum diving board clearance requirement. In this demonstration the ridge of the roof, which will be located in the middle of the 30 ft. dimension, will rise a total of 8 ft. above the wall. This will produce a pitch of approximately 2 horizontal ft. for 1 vertical ft., which approximates many roof pitches. The figure could be adjusted either way to meet your specific requirements.

Roof Structure

To start the actual framing, support the roof ridge beam along the entire length of the pool (48 ft.) with wood braces until the 2x12 framing is installed.

Brace all the exterior walls down to the ground until the rafters have the collar beams in place. This eliminates any sagging of the 4x12 ridge beam along its length. Another way to install the

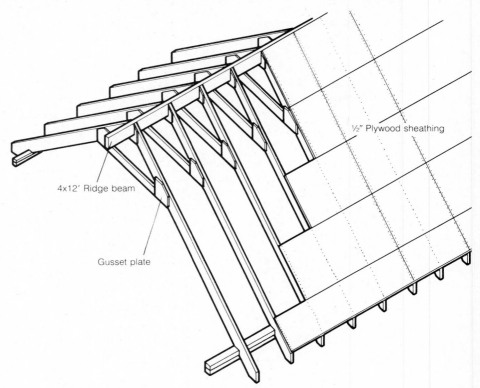

½" Plywood sheathing

4x12' Ridge beam

Gusset plate

Rafters run between the top plate and are supported by the ridge pole. Collar ties secure the rafters' positions; a sheathing of ½ in. CD plywood is nailed to rafters.

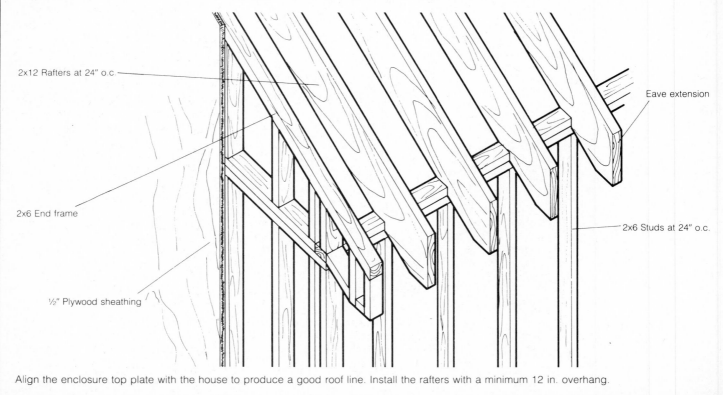

2x12 Rafters at 24" o.c.

2x6 End frame

½" Plywood sheathing

Eave extension

2x6 Studs at 24" o.c.

Align the enclosure top plate with the house to produce a good roof line. Install the rafters with a minimum 12 in. overhang.

roof framing is to fabricate it all in a jig on the ground, installing the collar beam but leaving a space for the ridge beam. This may prove to be the fastest method if you do not have many helpers.

The 2x12 framing is at 24 in. centers and the ends are notched so that they rest on and are nailed to the top of the wall plate. The overhang should be at least 12 in. all the way around. As each section is placed, brace it to the pre-ceding one with 1x4 bracing and roof sheathing. Note that all dimensions are based on multiples of 48 in. This allows all the sheathing to be framed over the centerline of a rafter or stud.

Once the rafter sections are all in place, the ridge beam can be installed. This is actually dropped into the notched opening provided.

Step 11: Sheathing the Roof

Once the ridge is in place and nailed, the roof sheathing can be installed. Allow room for ridge vents. If there are skylights to be installed, they should be framed out at this time. At this stage you should have a completely enclosed structure. All the openings should be present and the entire structure self-supporting and free-standing.

Step 12: Covering the Roof

Once the roof sheathing has been installed, you must install the eaves and fascia board along the four sides. In an attached situation, the profile should match the existing fascia piece and eave profile. Normally, this procedure entails a 1x12 finish piece on the underside for the soffit and 1x8 fascia which abuts the ½ in. roof sheathing. Before laying the roofing felts, standard aluminum or galvanized sheet flashings should be placed at the ridge and the eaves line. This keeps water from entering.

Laying the Felt Roofing felt comes in rolls and is marked along its length with white stripes that indicate the necessary spacing for the asphalt roofing. It also has provision for a wood shake or shingle roof.

Placing the Shingles Many shingle manufacturers provide detailed instructions, which should be carefully followed. Always use a galvanized roofing nails; maintain the horizontal alignment of the shingles. Start on one end at the eave corner. Move horizontally across the roof, working up toward the ridge. Make sure the shingles along the roof edges are properly nailed. As you approach the ridge, install any vent pipes or roof-mounted ventilators before laying the shingles around the vent flanges.

Finish the roof by capping the ridge with the ridge vent and the roof cap. Hang gutters from the eave line and place soffit vents.

Step 13: Placing Doors and Windows

Procedures for installing the doors and windows vary according to the manufacturer. Many furnish installation manuals with their product; others assume you are having a contractor install them. A typical window will be one

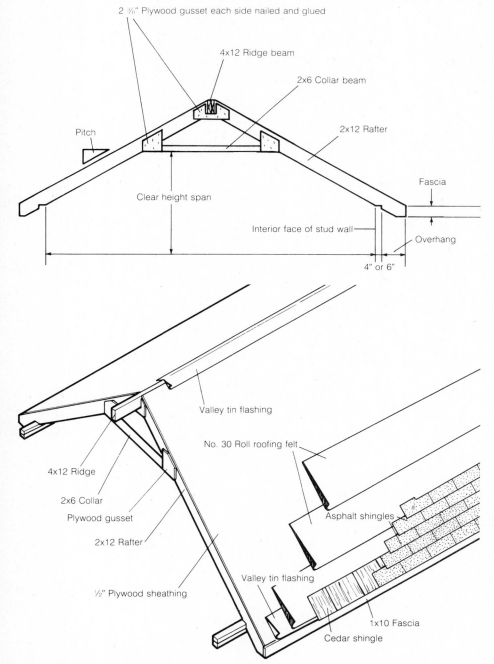

A 1x8 or 1x10 fascia finishes off the rafters. Install flashing at the eaves and the ridge line. Lay overlapping rows of 30 lb. roofing felt and then place shingles.

Project continued on next page

that sets into the rough opening with enough space around so you can level the window. Use shingles to level and brace the window in its opening. Many of these come with built-in flashing that acts as a nailer and is nailed to the exterior sheathing.

Patio doors must be installed as complete units. The doors often can be removed so the threshold can be anchored to the concrete or sill member below. The door frame inserts into the opening, with shims added until it is level and plumb.

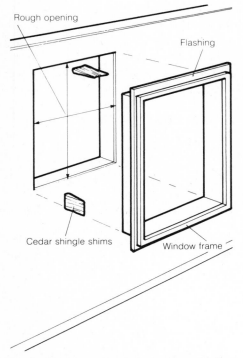

The flashing around a window acts as a nailer. Nail this to the sheathing. Use shingles as shims to level and plumb the window.

Step 14: Adding Exterior Siding

Once the window and doors are in place, the exterior siding can be installed. In this case, a narrow clapboard style siding will be installed to match the existing house siding. This material comes primed and is ready to install using box nails. The siding comes in 8 to 12 ft. lengths, up to 16 in. wide, depending on the manufacturer.

Before placing the hardboard siding, apply a 15 lb. felt over the sheathing. Make sure that the felt covers the entire wall surface and butts to the window and door openings. Keep it level, since the white stripes will aid siding

alignment. Staple or nail the felt with a heavy duty staple gun.

Remove the clapboard siding from the shipping container piece by piece. Lay the first panel so it extends beyond the bottom of the sheathing by about ¼ to ½ in. Face nail the panel with galvanized box nails. Usually, most manufacturers specify the number of nails required for each panel. Complete the entire side. Make sure that when butting two ends together they are flush and true. Some panels are designed to be overlapped with each other — a desirable feature if you are installing the sheathing yourself.

Build up the corners of finish 1x4s or 1x6s. The siding will look uneven if you try to miter the corner; it is better to butt up against a finish piece of material. Seal the connection with caulking. Once the wall has been completed, some finishing of edges may be required by installing 1x2 or 1x4 finish strips. Use only galvanized nails, or fully recess the nails and plug with a filler. If you don't, they could rust and spoil the siding.

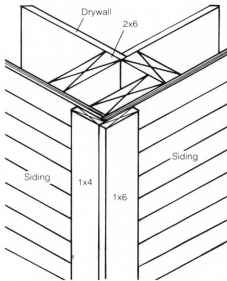

To create an even-looking joint, butt 1x4s or 1x6s against a finish piece of material. Use caulk to seal the connection.

Exterior Painting At this stage, almost all the exterior work has been completed except for the final coat of paint. If you selected a factory-painted siding, all that is needed is the finish trim. Be sure to prime all surfaces before painting.

Step 15: Finishing the Interior

Insulation All the interior walls and ceilings should now be insulated. Most insulation comes in the form of roll or batt. For the wall application, select an R-19 roll insulation for studs at 24 in. centers. Buy the type faced with Kraft paper. Another option is to have it foil-faced, which will eliminate the need for a vapor barrier. No matter which one you select, staple it securely to the studs and fill all crevices.

To cut the batts, use a bare hack saw blade. Always wear gloves, since the material flies all over the place. We also suggest wearing a face mask when installing fiberglass insulation.

The roof should be insulated before the ceiling is installed. These rolls come in 16 in. widths. Fill all crevices at eave and ridge lines. Do not worry about lapping several layers over each other in those zones, unless a vapor barrier is attached. In this case, slash the vapor barrier on all but the outermost (inner-facing) layer.

If you selected kraft-faced batts, you should install a separate vapor barrier. The vapor barrier prevents condensation from destroying the wall, keeping it away from the finish interior surface. The vapor barrier is generally a 4 mil or 6 mil polyethylene sheeting that comes in a roll. It is clumsy to maneuver, so get some help. Attach it with staples. Cover all wall and ceiling surfaces. This vapor barrier installation may be delayed somewhat, until the electrical work has been done.

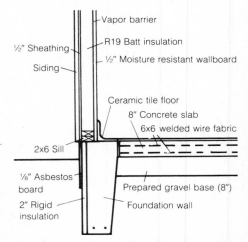

Pour the concrete slab floor after you position any additional floor drains. Welded wire reinforcing mesh strengthens the slab.

Installing the Concrete Floor Slab

By the time the enclosure is completed, the in-ground pool also should have been finished up to installation of the coping, liner and the deck support and deck forms.

Level the entire interior area and prepare it for installation of the concrete slab. Install any additional floor drains now. Check that the floor surface will pitch to the floor drain. Block out the areas that are to be poured. Where a large expanse of concrete slab is to be poured, contractors often will pour in a checkerboard pattern. This allows the concrete to be surface-finished, reduces the number of forms required, and controls the cracking of the slab.

Lay at least 6 in. of compacted gravel over the entire area. Tamp it well, using a mechanical or hand tamper; the more compact the better. Install all pool accessories, such as the diving board base and the slide.

Before pouring the concrete, clean the forms. Place a sheet of 6x6 #10/10 welded wire fabric. Pull the fabric up as the concrete is poured, so that the fabric ends up about 2 in. above the gravel base. Do not let it settle to the bottom. Where the concrete is to be used on the south side of the enclosure, pour an 8-in. concrete slab to act as a heat sink. In this case, use a double layer of wire fabric.

After each section has been poured, finish the surface by screeding, darbying, floating and troweling. This procedure is described in Chapter 3. After the troweling has been completed, you may want to install a hardener to reduce the absorptive qualities of the concrete. Cure the green concrete for at least three days; then strip the forms. Try not to step directly onto the concrete during the curing time; walk on boards placed over the slab for about a week.

Putting Up Interior Finish Materials

The surface you select should be as moisture-resistant and free of maintenance as possible. The ventilation system should be installed before placing interior surface.

Paneling If you have selected wood paneling or wood tongue and groove siding (T&G) as a finish material, it can be placed directly over the vapor barrier and nailed into the studs. The wood T&G siding should be placed horizontally across the studs, using casing nails. Try to conceal the nailheads as much as possible.

Paneling can be carried all the way up the wall into the ceiling. It is good looking and there are several types available, including knotty pine, cypress or cedar.

Joints between panels and between panels and openings must be finished. Use finish trim or moldings that are mitered. Recess all nails and fill in the holes. Paint is recommended for all exposed trim pieces. For both paneling and T&G boards, apply at least one coat of clear sealer.

Moisture-resistant wallboard Another option is to install gypsum wallboard that is specifically designed for high humidity situations such as a pool environment. This installs directly onto the studs, using corner beads where necessary. Once the board has been installed, the joints and nail indentations should be taped and plastered using a joint compound. Care should be taken to smooth all joints; you may have to sand all the connections after the first coat dries. Another coat should be applied to even out all the surface imperfections before painting or applying another finish material. This option is the least expensive one available.

Hooking up the utilities The plumbing connections, filtration system and waste lines should be tested and connected. Complete the filling of the pool and test all machinery. Test all lights.

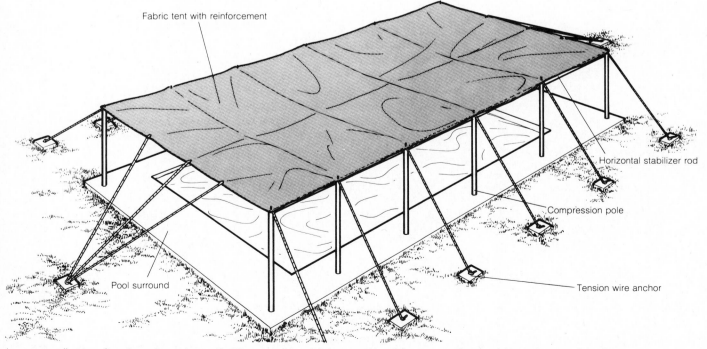

Fabric tent with reinforcement

Horizontal stabilizer rod

Compression pole

Pool surround

Tension wire anchor

In a warm climate, often the only enclosure that is needed is a fabric tent with reinforcement. Suspend the tent on tension wires.

6
HOME SPAS & HOT TUBS

The fastest-growing form of water recreation for the single- or multiple-family residence is a hot tub or spa. Neither one of the items is new. If fact, hot tubs and spas have been in use for centuries in many different cultures. In the United States, however, most sources agree that California is responsible for the resurgence of popularity of the hot tub and spa—and that popularity has spread. The California climate is particularly suitable for the hot tub. Although the original hot tubs were fashioned from old wine vats and water tanks, the modern version is a prefabricated wooden staved tub with metal hoops that hold the vertical staves in place and keep it watertight. To replace the earlier open flame to heat the water, the modern version has a built-in water heater with a circulating system.

Even if you don't have the space to provide a luxurious deck or landscape job for the hot tub, you can still create a private alcove or niche.

CHARACTERISTICS

Exactly what are these phenomena called the hot tub and spa? The hot tub and spa share one thing in common. They both are relatively small containers that can accommodate from l to 6 people in a warm to hot water environment. However, the tub and the spa differ in what they do and the type of installation required. Some people prefer the beauty and qualities of wood used in hot tubs versus the options of shapes, colors and sizes available in spas. Either one can be fitted with hydro-massage jets and both use recirculating hot water systems. One main design consideration is whether you prefer an outdoor or indoor location. Spas are more common indoors than are hot tubs. For the exterior location, similar considerations should be given to locating the tub or spa as for swimming pools. Whether you decide on as hot tub or a spa, they both are available in kit form. Most manufacturers provide a complete system ready for installation for a moderate price.

A Hot Tub Package

The hot tub is a modified barrel with straight sides and a wooden bottom. The size varies from 2.5 to 7 ft. wide with an

Spas can contribute to the most luxurious of bathtubs, with such additional features as built-in seating and temperature control.

average depth of 4 ft. Some tanks are oval in form. The barrel form is made of carefully tapered wood staves that are beveled on both sides with a dado cut at the base for the floor. The staves are often tongue-and-grooved to facilitate the assembly, but that is not necessary for the operation of the tub. The verticals are held together with steel hoops. Because of the round shape, the two or three round hoops compress the staves against each other to form a watertight container.

The tank recirculates water by means of a pump, filter and hot water heater. The water is usually introduced into the tub from several inlets. The tub normally sets on grade. The tub floor rests on heavy wood joists, which in turn are supported by the ground or a reinforced slab.

Materials The material most commonly used in the hot tub is vertical grained clear or all heart redwood, because it resists rotting and decay, provides excellent heat retention, and has excellent ''swell'' qualities.In other words, the staves swell when they are constantly soaked; the resulting compression is what keeps the tub watertight. If the tub is well maintained, the wood should last 12 to 16 years without needing replacement. Another popular wood is teak. Teak is a very expensive material, but exceptionally durable and free from the defects of less expensive wood. Teak swells enough to bind the vertical staves together and will last far beyond a redwood tub. Other wood materials, such as mahogany, cypress, cedar and oak are used. These are found less frequently than redwood or teak. All the material that is furnished in kit form will be kiln dried to insure dimensional stability.

Location The very nature of the wood suggests that if the kiln-dried wood is in direct contact with the ground, it could rot. Therefore, a specific requirement of a hot tub is that it be built on grade, not in the ground. The on-grade installation is a very economical solution, since the plumbing and electrical installation can be easily connected. The hot tub can be placed indoors or outdoors, but is most often seen in an outdoor setting.

Means of Access Since the tub is built on grade, you need a means of access. On the one hand, a simple ladder to a platform will suffice. However, the hot tub is often built in conjunction with a surrounding wood deck or as an integral part of a larger swimming pool area. The large deck offers an area in which to rest and relax.

Home Spas

The distinctive characteristic of the spa is its one-piece construction. The spa is similar in operation to the hot tub but is available in a variety of colors, materials and shapes—square, round, oval, rectangular and octagonal, to name but a few choices. It is manufactured in fiberglass, metal or concrete. Often, spas are easier to install and maintain than a hot tub. The prices for the two are comparable. The support facilities, such as pumps, filters and heaters, are similar.

Basically, a spa is an in-ground pool. It is designed to be placed on a bed of sand that cushions the mold and allows it to move when subjected to shifts in the soil.

When at all possible — and if it does not interfere with safe use — locate your hot tub to take advantage of any spectacular view.

Usually built of molded fiberglass, the spa is designed to be set into the ground or patio area, especially in conjunction with a swimming pool. The water capacity is equal to that of the hot tub. The water in a spa swirls in through jets located along the sides. It can become a whirlpool bath for those that might require or desire that option.

Fiberglass Spas The fiberglass shell has a smooth, hard finish that often includes built-in seats and steps. There are provisions for underwater lights. The spa ranges in size from 4 ft. to 9 ft. in diameter and up to 5 ft. in depth. The shapes range from round, square, octagonal, oval to freeform.

The fiberglass shell comes with two types of linings, acrylic and the gelcoat. The acrylic lining is a tougher finish than the gelcoat. The acrylic performs well

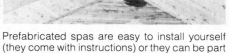

Prefabricated spas are easy to install yourself (they come with instructions) or they can be part of the contractor's landscaping.

Some outdoor spas are built into the landscaping to resemble ornamental garden pools, helping to focus and define backyard design.

A concrete spa often is trimmed inside (or even outside) with tile, with exterior faces stuccoed in any of a number of textures.

One of the simplest pool covers is this plastic one, which helps keep out airborne debris (and unexpected visitors).

For a clean-line look, the deck can be built so that the top of the spa or tub unit comes flush to the deck's walking surface.

In hot or windy regions, build a shelter to provide sun protection while still offering the necessary ventilation.

when subjected to chemical action and resists abrasion better. The main drawback is that it is much more expensive to repair if damaged. No matter which lining is selected, the fiberglass spa should be reinforced at all stair edges, seats and around all outlets and inlets. The fiberglass should be free of any rough edges and should have a uniform color throughout.

Concrete Spa The concrete spa is a swimming pool in transition. It originally started as an extension of a swimming pool, slowly changed into a self-contained smaller pool, and finally separated completely from the swimming pool area and became a standalone. The concrete spa has a long life compared to some other types and is easily maintained, depending upon the method of construction. Gunite, poured in place, masonry and hand-packed are the most accepted methods of construction. A gunite spa with a very hard cement finish is considered the equal of any other type of spa. A tile water table is placed at the water line to aid in the removal of algae.

Metal Spa The metal spa is available in many of the same shapes and sizes as a fiberglass or gunite pool. It is generally a customized pool. The interior liner is an enamelized coating that is applied and then baked. More esoteric models are shaped in a variety of flora and fauna forms. The sizes available are similar to those of the gunite and fiberglass spas.

NOTES ON BUDGET

The cost of a hot tub and spa are comparable, even when adding in the cost of patio and plantings. Both cost about as much as a small deluxe above-ground swimming pool.

When looking at the tubs or spas, base your selection on potential use as opposed to current demand. For example, selecting a two-person tub may be satisfactory for the immediate need in terms of economics and size. If you ever plan to have tub parties, a 4 or 5 ft. unit may be able to accommodate five people. Select something a little larger. The cost difference is not that much. All kits come complete and ready to operate.

SITE CONSIDERATIONS
Indoor vs. Outdoor

Hot tubs and spas require a minimal amount of space. This is one of the main reasons that they are particularly popular on sites of very limited size. When full, a hot tub can weigh as much as 6000 pounds. This alone is a good reason for outdoor installation. In some cases, people have been known to install a hot tub in the basement of their house so it could be used in greater privacy and more frequency.

Since this industry began in California, where the climate is temperate, it made sense to place the unit out of doors. The spa, on the other hand, lends itself well to

below grade installation because of the one-piece construction. When the spa is fitted with whirlpool jets, it can become like a larger-than-life bathtub. Privacy is an important consideration in the placement of the hot tub and spa, since most users prefer nude soaking in the warm water.

Exterior Installation Your best outdoor spot is a level part of the site, away from boulders, big trees, roots and underground utilities or overhead power lines. Always place the tub or spa out of drainage patterns if your weather becomes cold and wet. The location of a hot tub or spa on your property can determine the frequency of its use. Orientation, protection and security are among the many issues. The design of the area around the tub or spa is critical to successful operation. By placing the spa or tub near the main house, it will generate more back-and-forth traffic than one located farther away from the house. The amenities that are part of the tub or spa surround can also determine the amount of activity.

The spa or hot tub can be the social center of your house and yard. Depending on the size of your yard and your budget, you can create almost any hot tub or spa relaxation center, from the simple to the most ornate. What enhances the installation is the surrounding deck(s) and seating areas and the method by which you integrate the installation into your landscape. On a larger lot with a swimming pool, you may want to integrate the spa alongside or near the pool. The hot tub is most often located in a private area of the garden or deck.

A southern exposure is preferable, except in extremely hot climates. Select a spot where the prevailing winds will not bother the bathers. It will make soaking more enjoyable, as well as keep the water

Although hot tubs are usually placed outdoors, interior locations are feasible as long as there is adequate support beneath.

Differences in elevation can be handled with creative use of varying deck levels, turning a drawback into a design benefit.

Plan your surrounding area carefully, being sure to provide safe, convenient stair access covered in a water-resistant material.

warmer. Install wind breaks such as hedges, low plantings, screens and fences to control the air movement, while at the same time insuring privacy.

Indoor Installations Most interior installations are located in northern climates where the winters are most severe. In fact, in more severe climates the potential owner will be forced to install the tub or spa indoors. An indoor hot tub or spa can produce the same greenhouse effect as an enclosed swimming pool. If you plan to locate the tub or spa in an interior space, the room should be fitted with a good negative pressure air system that combines a fresh air intake with the potential for recirculation. The interior walls should have a vapor barrier installed. Moisture-loving plants can help control the humidity.

Many potential owners of the tub or spa think that they will be able to sit in the water for several hours. This is a misconception, since most relaxing soaks last a short period of time. It is then advisable to get out and rest. Since you will get in and out of the tub or spa continuously, select an area where you can do so with ease. Do not get stuck in an out of the way corner. The hot tub or spa, while able to fit into a large closet, should be enjoyed visually as well as spatially. Make sure that you have enough room.

Sloping Sites

There can be no doubt that placing the hot tub or spa on a flat piece of ground is desirable. It is costlier to install a hot tub on a sloping site. The excavation of the hillside must be carefully cut and the base well prepared. The grade must not be permitted to "lean" against the tub, since the tub was meant to withstand the outward pressure of the water, not the inward pressure of the earth. If the soil is not overly stable, the cut portion will have to be reinforced with a brick or block wall if it is open to view. If the cut portion is not visible, a concrete slurry will do.

Another option for a sloping site is to build a concrete well in which the tub is placed. A drainage system for the well, such as a sump pump, is required to keep the area dry. On a sloping site, the position of the surrounding deck may be somewhat limited due to the need for a recessed area in which the tub can sit. Construct the deck with removeable sections in order to get at the drainage and supply systems.

Building Code Requirements

When considering installing a hot tub or spa, you should determine if you will require a building permit. This varies from region to region. Each region may have different requirements which you must meet in order to receive a permit to build. Do not go ahead without one (if applicable). The building code office could fine you and make you remove all the work that has been done. Some communities require that temperature control thermostat cut-off controls be installed to reduce the possibility of high heat. Others may require a locked top on the hot tub or spa.

Planning the Surround

Hot Tub A wooden hot tub goes with a wood deck. The deck, whether large or small, can comprise a series of level changes, either as short steps or broad levels, to get people up to the tub seat. In some cases, a wood deck can link the house with the tub, thus bypassing a lower level, which could be strictly for entertainment. If you have a two-story house on a slope and the second story opens out onto a two-level deck, one way to integrate the tub and the deck is to have the upper edge of the tub be level with the upper level of the deck. When not in use, the tub could be covered over and the deck used for other purposes. This scheme takes advantage of the fact that the hot tub must sit on grade and not be recessed into the ground.

Spas A paved patio can receive a spa below grade. It is a good idea to install the spa and its plumbing before paving the area around the spa. The specific location of the spa on the patio should be carefully located with respect to doors, ladders,

Outdoor settings can be enclosed with a structure built around the tub or spa.

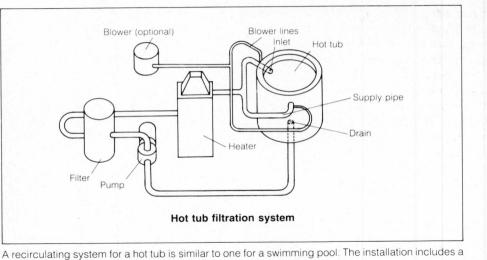

Hot tub filtration system

A recirculating system for a hot tub is similar to one for a swimming pool. The installation includes a filter, pump and heater. A blower for creating turbulence is optional.

fences and stairs. Always locate the spa at a reasonable distance from major obstacles. If your spa is integrated with a swimming pool, separate them with an extension of the pool surround, a bridge-like area or ceramic tile, provided you have the space. (If you combine the installation of the spa along with that of a pool, the overall cost of the spa will be far less than if you install it separately.) When installing a spa alongside a pool, use the same types of materials so that there is visual continuity between the swimming pool and the spa.

Overhead Protection For climates that are excessively hot or rainy, you might want to consider incorporating an overhead structure with the deck or patio to protect the tub or spa. A semi-enclosed structure such as a gazebo or lanai can filter the sun's rays, thus making the area in and around the pool appear cooler.

Electrical Requirements
The electrical requirements for a hot tub and spa are quite similar. Both types require electrical connections to power the pump, heater, blower unit and underwater lights in the spa. Most manufacturer's require that a 230 volt, 60 amp service be installed. This may require some addition to your present electrical service. It is recommended that you retain a qualified electrician to do the work. All electrical work must be properly grounded to conform to the National Electrical Code. All wiring should be installed in rigid conduit with waterproof fittings in and around the spa and tub. All outlets must be grounded and require Ground Fault Circuit Interrupters for safety.

In the case of a spa, the electrical wiring to the control panel must be installed underground. Provision should be made for this hookup and for low voltage underwater lights if applicable. The illumination level required to light the tub or spa area is determined by the type of use and activities planned. In many ways, the requirements are similar to swimming pools. Refer to those sections in the previous chapters. Either way, you should select the light fixture and type before installing the tub or spa. That way the two can be properly integrated into the landscape or enclosure.

Setting Up the Water System
No matter which type of hot tub or spa you select, you will need a filtration system that includes a heater, pump and motor, filter system and piping. This part of the system is similar to that of a swimming pool. The water chemistry requirements are similar as well, as are the water testing procedures. The filter must be sized according to the number of cycles and the gallonage of the tub or spa.

The pump is the water mover in the system and is rated from ¾ to 2 horsepower, depending upon the tub size. The water is sucked into the pump from the recessed drain. The pump assembly—brass, bronze or plastic—is composed of two parts: the motor and the impeller assembly. The housing for the impeller includes a lint trap or leaf basket. The water is drawn through the trap and pushed out by the impeller to the filter. The filter—either a sand, diatomaceous earth or cartridge—removes impurities from the water. For an interior operation, the filter can be a car-

tridge type, since there are fewer pollutants in the air.

Once the water has moved through the filter, it passes on to the water heater where the water reaches temperatures of up to about 100° F. There are many types of heaters available: tank, flash or convection. Each one offers specific features that a manufacturer may recommend as best for its type of operation. The heater selected depends upon the size of the spa or hot tub, the location—in or out of doors—and severity of the climate. Whether you select a gas fired or electric heater, you must make provisions for service.

Once the water has been heated, it is then injected under pressure into the tub or spa. Turbulence is acheived through the water inlet nozzle. The one most frequently used is a venturi jet, which decreases the water flow through a pipe while increasing the velocity. Air is mixed with the water to provide some bubbles. If continuous bubbles are desired, a blower that injects air into the water medium is placed between the heater and the water inlets. In some models you can dial the amount of turbulence you desire. Once the water has been injected into the tub or spa, the cycle then repeats itself. (The addition of hydro-massage jets or venturi jets, especially in spas, may require a higher capacity motor for the pump.)

In a whirlpool spa you may have up to two discharge pipes that feed two separate pump motors. This system supplies the pressure necessary to provide maximum venturi action of the inlets. The whirlpool can be added to a hot tub as a kit, if desired. A hot tub and spa have readily available controls that can turn the heat off or

This enclosure (The Environment) lets you control temperature, humidity and water flow — from a fine mist to a heavy rain.

Plants flourish around an enclosed pool because of the room's high humidity level.

An outdoor spa provides a bubble for weather protection, with a table for convenience.

Serenity and simplicity characterize the backyard setting of this spacious retreat.

Brick in a pool surround can be cut to fit as needed around a pool's curving perimeter.

A vinyl-liner pool with a concrete surround will often fool the eye, at first glance appearing to be an in-ground concrete pool.

Kidney-shaped pools seem particularly desirable in lots with lush greenery.

Tile rimming the pool edge can become part of the design, as in these built-in flanking planters.

This pool is the focal point for a luxurious backyard entertainment center. At one end, a tiled spa is separated from the rest of the pool, but easy access is still provided between the spa and pool.

A dark blue tile finish contrasts with the masonry and deepens the color of the water in this pool and spa combination.

This really is a pool, but it is built to blend in with its rocky New England surroundings.

An oasis in the desert sun, this pool dominates a southwest backyard because all the other space elements are designed around it.

Cleverly disguised as a woodland scene, this New England site uses plantings and rock gardens to subtly integrate pool and landscape.

Decor for an indoor pool area should match the scheme to that of the rest of the house.

If possible, orient pool enclosures with large expanses of glass so the glass faces south.

Heavy concrete walls and masonry floors retain heat that enters through a skylight roof.

A complete relaxation area is centered around this pool, which is an enclosure that is attached to the house.

The landscaping for this vinyl-liner pool emphasizes and dramatizes its free-form shape.

A fencing and pool surround, when built of wood, should use redwood or pretreated lumber.

Facilities for changing or eating can be as simple or elaborate as your budget permits.

Massive stone accents the geometric and unusual lines of the pool.

A changing room can be built to resemble a small, stylish house.

The rounded shape of the pool helps soften the formal effect of the plantings and layout in this yard.

RELATING A SWIMMING POOL TO LIVING AREAS

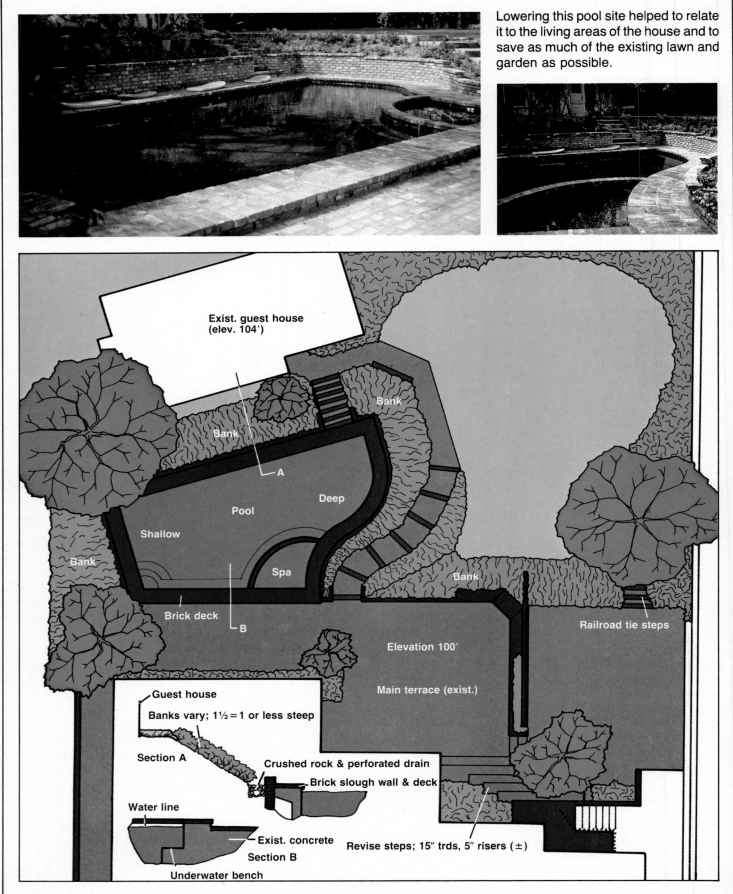

Lowering this pool site helped to relate it to the living areas of the house and to save as much of the existing lawn and garden as possible.

Exist. guest house (elev. 104')

Bank

Bank

A

Deep

Pool

Shallow

Bank

Spa

Brick deck

B

Bank

Railroad tie steps

Elevation 100'

Main terrace (exist.)

Guest house

Banks vary; 1½ = 1 or less steep

Section A

Crushed rock & perforated drain

Brick slough wall & deck

Water line

Exist. concrete

Revise steps; 15" trds, 5" risers (±)

Section B

Underwater bench

BUILDING A POOL ON A SMALL SITE

This house is set on a very small site, overlooking Los Angeles, Santa Monica and Beverly Hills (on a clear day, one can see Catalina Island). The major portion of the redwood deck already existed, so there was very limited remaining level area in which to place the pool. This, and the position of the pool, led to an extension of the deck, as shown.

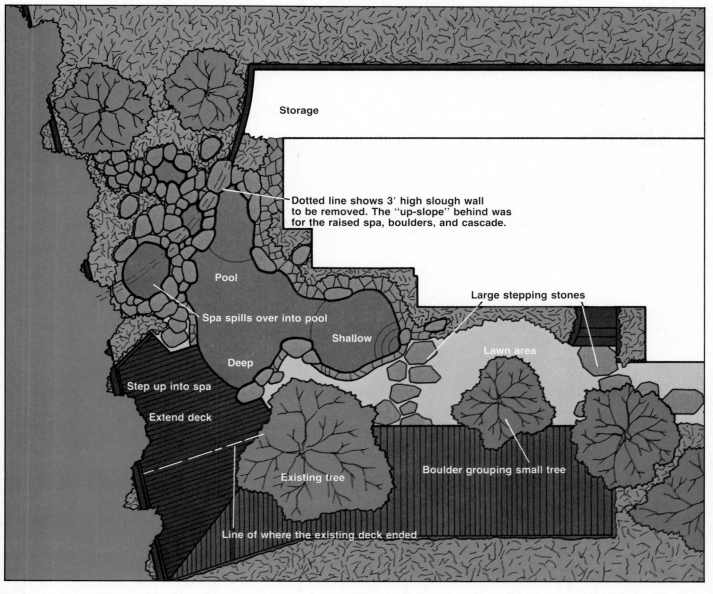

Storage

Dotted line shows 3' high slough wall to be removed. The "up-slope" behind was for the raised spa, boulders, and cascade.

Pool

Spa spills over into pool

Large stepping stones

Shallow

Lawn area

Deep

Step up into spa

Extend deck

Boulder grouping small tree

Existing tree

Line of where the existing deck ended

LANDSCAPING CONSIDERATIONS

Sliding glass doors lead from the living room to a patio with a gas-fired barbecue. The patio adjoins the pool, with its spa and a sunning area. To supplement the pool as an entertainment center on this large site, a ping pong area was added not too far from the pool. In addition, a firepit was built as part of an out-of-the-way picnic location in groves of trees that were laid out to resemble a natural camping retreat.

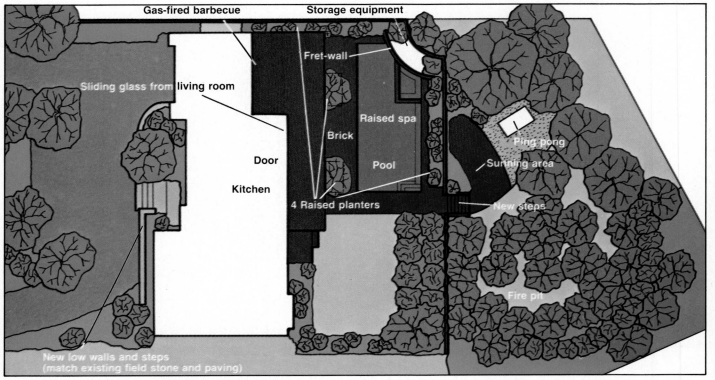

LANDSCAPING CONSIDERATIONS

The owner of this backyard desired a minimum of paving around the swimming pool. In addition to the paving, boulders were placed to enhance the natural appearance of the design. Bamboo was transplanted to the surrounding area; since only about 50% were expected to survive, the bamboo plants were crowded into the bed.

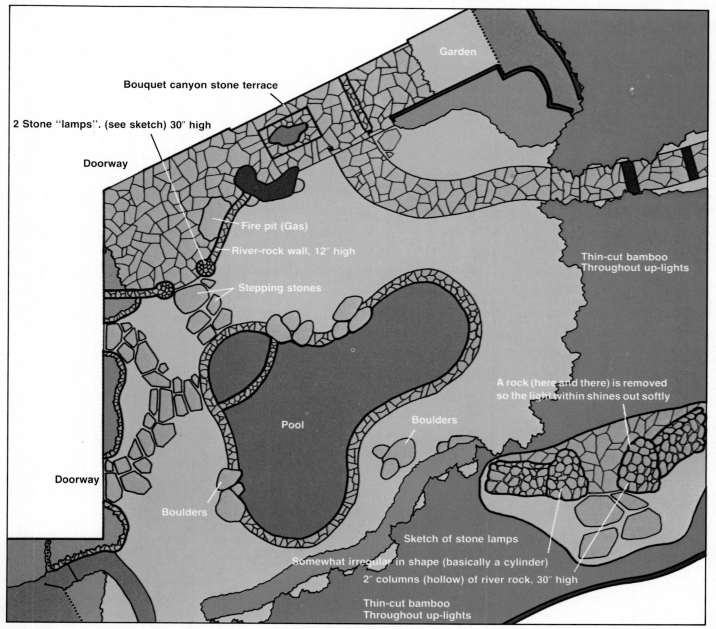

Bouquet canyon stone terrace

2 Stone "lamps". (see sketch) 30″ high

Doorway

Garden

Fire pit (Gas)

River-rock wall, 12″ high

Stepping stones

Thin-cut bamboo Throughout up-lights

A rock (here and there) is removed so the light within shines out softly

Pool

Boulders

Doorway

Boulders

Sketch of stone lamps

Somewhat irregular in shape (basically a cylinder)

2″ columns (hollow) of river rock, 30″ high

Thin-cut bamboo Throughout up-lights

BUILDING A POOL ON A SLOPE

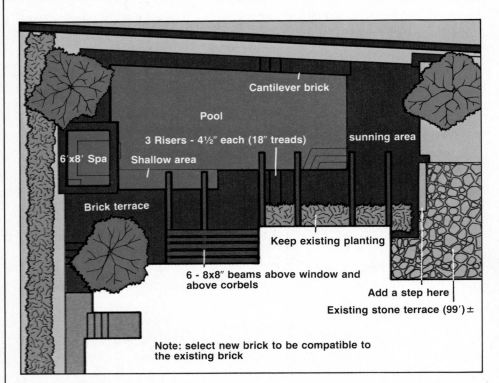

Cantilever brick

Pool

3 Risers - 4½″ each (18″ treads)

sunning area

6′x8′ Spa

Shallow area

Brick terrace

Keep existing planting

6 - 8x8″ beams above window and above corbels

Add a step here

Existing stone terrace (99′) ±

Note: select new brick to be compatible to the existing brick

The varying elevations made this design a challenge. All new construction was forced onto the area southwest of the existing stone terrace. A pool, spa, and sunning area were created within this area. Due to the limited space, one of the questions that arose was whether or not the pool equipment center also could be used as a passageway.

BUILDING A POOL IN LIMITED SPACE

This backyard offered very little level outdoor space. The graduation of the land required careful planning for and setup of drainage.

At first, a wooden deck was proposed to the west of the pool, but this idea ultimately was rejected. The needs of two small, active children prompted the decision for play space north of the pool.

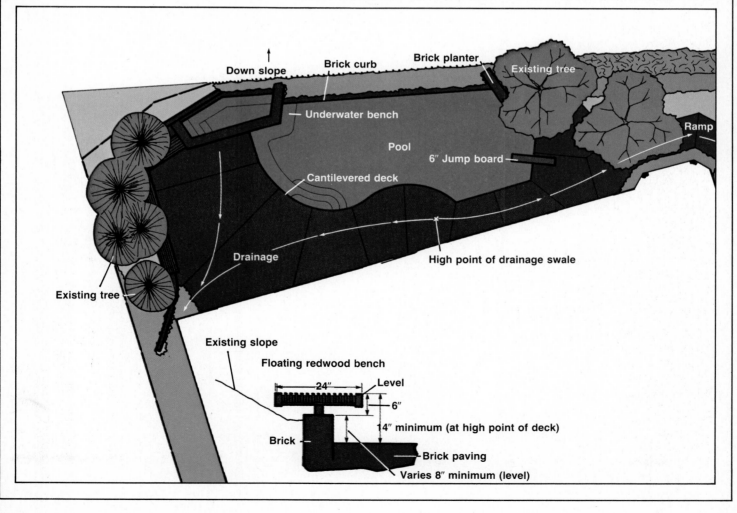

Down slope

Brick curb

Brick planter

Existing tree

Underwater bench

Pool

Ramp

6" Jump board

Cantilevered deck

High point of drainage swale

Drainage

Existing tree

Existing slope

Floating redwood bench

Level

24"

6"

14" minimum (at high point of deck)

Brick

Brick paving

Varies 8" minimum (level)

A pool, spa and wading pond serve this area. They all use the same water source, with differing temperatures.

Steps circle this hot tub for easy entry. The protective cover should always be on the tub when the tub is not in use.

This deck comes right up to the coping for safety and contrast in color and texture.

With careful attention to seating and tables, an interior hot tub or spa can become an indoor entertainment center.

Hot tubs can be considered an "attractive nuisance" to neighborhood children and pets. You should always place a cover on one when it is not in use.

Spas built are often placed next to pools, with plumbing run from the pool to the spa in order to cut piping costs.

shut the entire operation down. In addition, the whirlpool installation can have a set of controls that modify the amount of water action.

Water Supply The water supply for a hot tub or spa can be obtained from a garden hose. There is no permanent water hookup required. Just add additional water as needed to compensate for any lost due to evaporation or splashing.

SAFETY GUIDELINES

Hot tubs and spas located outdoors pose many of the same safety problems as swimming pools. The units are attractive, fun and interesting to use. People, especially children, want to take a look without proper supervision. It is easy to fall in a spa or tub without the proper safety measures.

Tub or Spa Covers

A cover that keeps unwanted intruders out is a must. The cover must be rigid enough to prevent a small child from falling in as well as secure enough so that it cannot be simply pushed off. There are several types of covers available for the tub and the spa that meet these requirements. Wood covers roll into a tight package and are insulated to maintain the water temperature. Another type resembles the pool blankets used on swimming pools. It attaches through a set of rails that keep the cover from collapsing inward.

Fencing

Another safety measure is proper fencing, similar to swimming pool fencing. A fence that also serves as a privacy screen is often your best choice.

Health Considerations

Benefits Warm water and swimming pools have been used for years to help people relax and keep physically fit. A spa or hot tub introduces the massaging action of whirlpool jets. The hot water relaxes the muscles; the jets stimulate the movement of the blood in the body. In the case of the whirlpool bath, hydrotherapy jets are placed all around the tub or spa sides. Once the water is in motion, the pump(s) keep the water active. The hydrotherapy effect, or whirlpooling, is achieved only if the jets are all angled in the same direction. A blower can add bubbles that have little or no therapeutic value, but which many owners find pleasurable.

Design for Safety

For most, a deck or patio is an integral part of the living area. As a result, the placement of a tub or spa in the deck or patio area can present hazards. If you do not design proper level differentiation, guests might fall or slip into the spa or tub. To prevent this occurrence, plan for a wooden or masonry level change between the patio and the spa or tub.

The Jacuzzi (a commercial name quite often heard) is one type of whirlpool that does produce therapeutic massaging action in the water. The original model was developed to provide relief from rhumatoid arthritis. There is no doubt that some hot water soaks and whirlpool baths do help certain afflictions. The degree of assistance can be measured only on an individual basis. Be sure to check with your physical therapist or physician about using a spa or hot tub to verify if it will help your health.

Potential Health Hazards Some cases have already been discovered in which a tub or spa is a decided detriment to health. Some of the problems include: dizziness, heart attacks, heart-related problems, bacteria-related problems and high blood pressure, to name but a few. Pregnant women, especially in the first four to five months, are advised not to use a hot tub or spa.

Danger: Do Not Fall Asleep One of the most serious dangers comes from falling asleep in the tub. There have been a number of instances where bathers have fallen asleep and died. In other cases, the bathers have not controlled the temperature properly, causing serious burns to the body. The use of alcoholic beverages while bathing can strain the heart, affect one's heat-regulating mechanism and cause drowsiness. Electrocution can be a reality if a plugged in TV or radio falls into the water. This problem may be eliminated by installing a GFI circuit to all outlets within reach of the tub or spa. In fact, the National Electrical Code requires this device out of doors.

Exposure or overuse can be a problem as well. Water temperatures should never go above 104° F. and preferably never exceed 100° F. Hot tubs and spas can be relaxing and beneficial to ones health, provided they are installed and used correctly., Be certain to check with your physician before you financially obligate yourself. They are not for everyone.

INSTALLING AN INTERIOR SPA

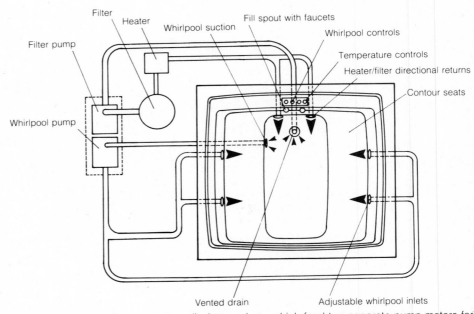

A whirlpool spa may have up to two discharge pipes, which feed two separate pump motors for maximum water movement.

The interior spa installation is a relatively simple procedure. The most serious problem is often whether or not the spa will fit through the doors. Another major consideration is that, once the spa is in place, the appropriately sized electrical service must be supplied (check the manufacturer notes).

If the spa is in a basement, there is no need for any structural support. A spa on an upper floor, on the other hand, does require structural support. The spa is a self-contained unit; it requires no drain opening or plumbing connections to other house lines. It is filled with an ordinary hose. There are PVC plumbing lines that connect the jets in the spa to the housing containing the pump, filter and heater. These connections can take up to eight hours to complete; many homeowners prefer to have the unit installed by the supplier.

Spas are filled with a garden hose or from a water supply in the house. Before using the spa, make sure that the surfaces are clean and the bottom is free of debris. Once the spa has been filled to the correct level, it should be run for at least three hours daily for the first seven days with chemically treated water. The base drain is connected to the pump, which will empty the spa through the switching of a bypass valve.

To keep the spa at the desired level, replace water lost through evaporation every one or two weeks.

Interior location not on grade

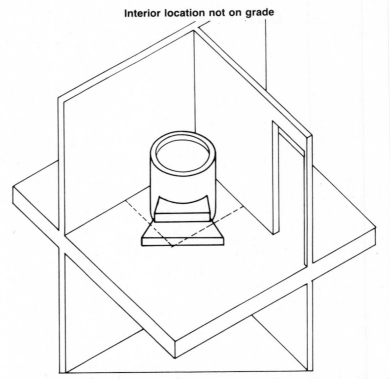

When installing an interior spa anywhere other than on grade, position it along a load-bearing wall. Consult a structural engineer before installation.

CONSTRUCTING A REDWOOD HOT TUB

Research the available tub kits careful-ly. Compare what is offered in each kit price. Determine what the installation price would be as a separate item; some dealers include the installation cost as a part of the price. Make sure that the dealer has been in business for some time and is able to provide you with a number of installation refer-ences. Call the references and ask not only about reliability, but also about any history of delivery of faulty parts, or advice and repair supplied by the dealer.

As you settle on a kit, plan not only the location and the tub size, but the total landscape package. Decide now whether you will have a wood deck as part of the area design.

MATERIALS AND COMPONENTS
Most hot tub kits come equipped with a standard range of materials and con-nectors. Before beginning the assem-bly, lay out the pieces so othey can be checked against the manufacturer's parts list. It is frustrating to begin work on the kit only to realize that something is missing. The list of pieces supplied includes but is not limited to the follow-ing items:

(1) solid redwood, cedar or mahog-any tub, 5 ft. in diameter, 4 ft. high: including two seats, floor support joists, 3 steel hoops and necessary fittings and hardware;

(2) one-horsepower pump and mo-tor assembly;

(3) high efficiency cartridge filter;

(4) 24-hour automatic tub time clock including built-in override with remote air switch;

(5) electric hot water heater (12kw-220v) with built-in bypass and pressure relief valve;

(6) four jet hydromassage system that is fully controllable within the tub;

(7) 45 ft. of hose;

(8) suction grate, recessed drain, necessary plumbing, hardware and miscellaneous accessories;

(9) illustrated manual.

Also included may be some of these options: tub bubbler; a stair kit and platform; a winterizing kit; a water test and treatment kit.

The remaining materials required will be those for the preparation of the supporting concrete slab, if you do not already have a suitable area.

Tools Needed
In the kit, the factory has milled all the pieces so that each piece will fit snugly together. Do not try to exert tremen-dous force as the kit was designed to be erected with the simplest of tools: a carpenter's square, a rubber hammer, wrenches, hand plane, screwdriver and a drill.

CONSTRUCTION PROCEDURES
Most hot tubs have been successfully located on an on-grade, reinforced concrete slab that ranges from 4 to 6 in. in depth. When you consider that an average tub will hold as much as 6000 lbs. of water for a five ft. tub, it is very important that the base be able to with-stand the load.

If you plan to install the tub or spa on a wood frame floor, make sure that the floor is capable of supporting the load. You may have to install additional sup-ports or stiffen the floor. Check with your local inspector or structural engi-neer to verify the structural safety of what you have in mind.

Step 1: Excavating the Area
Once you have selected the area in which you will place the tub, you will have to strip the topsoil from a 6½x6½ ft. area. If you want the slab even with the ground, excavate to a depth of 8 in. If the slab is to project 4 in. above the ground level, you may decrease the excavation to a depth of 4 in. Once the area has been excavated, level and tamp the exposed soil until it is smooth and compact. Check the level from side to side and diagonally,using a car-penter's level.

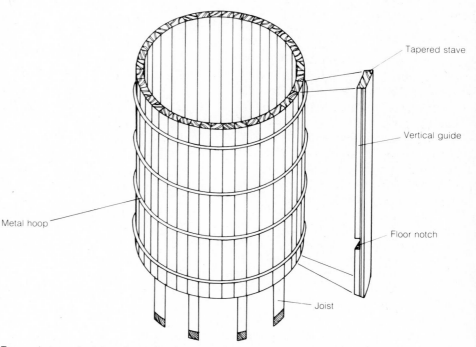

Tapered staves lock together tub unit components and anchor the tub.

Project continued on next page

Step 2: Placing the Fill

Place 2 to 3 in. of sand into the excavation and again level carefully. You can use a rake for this purpose.

Placing the Forms Install a 2x6 wood frame inside the perimeter of the excavated area. For our example, the dimensions of the form are 6 ft. on each side. Once the exterior form boards have been installed, level them. Then select one corner on the high side of the excavation, if possible. Raise the forms so that this corner will be about ¾ in. higher than the low side to allow for proper drainage. Then stake the forms securely to prevent any movement during the pouring. Oil the forms with motor oil.

Step 3: Adding Reinforcing

Having staked the form boards in place, check the forms for square. Place ½ in. deformed steel bars that are 5 ft. 9 in. long, running in two directions so that they form a grid. In this example, 5 bars will be evenly spaced in each direction. To raise the bars off the sand bed, place bricks under the bars. Tie the bars together with wire obtained from the reinforcing bar supplier.

Step 4: Pouring and Finishing the Concrete

If at all possible, arrange with you local concrete supplier for a truck delivery. If not, you may want to rent a concrete mixer, or simply buy premixed bags. Place the concrete as described in Chapter 3. Once the concrete is in place, it should be finished (as in Chapter 3) and cured.

Step 5: Assembling the Tub

If you have help from a couple of assistants, your tub could be assembled within three hours. Move the kit to the site and unpack the pieces. Make sure all the pieces are there and in the proper order. Decide how the piping is to be connected and where the filter system will be located.

The joists are laid down first on the slab. Make sure that all pieces are the correct distance from each other and that they are level. Shim each with a wood cedar shingle until the level has

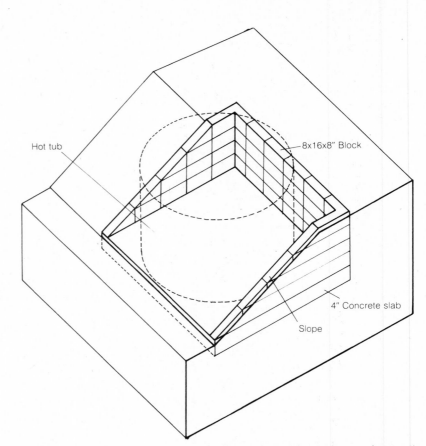

1   On a sloping site that does not have stable soil, you must reinforce the area of cut earth with a wall of brick or block.

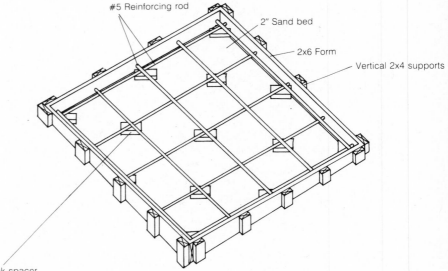

2   When placing the fill under the tub, install 2x6 pieces inside the perimeter of the excavated area and under the reinforcing.

been achieved. (The kit will offer the option of installing a wood pier block under the joist locations when the concrete slab was poured. If you had installed the pier block, the floor joists could be toe nailed into the pier blocks at this time.)

Placing the Floor Boards Once the joists are placed, trued and leveled, place the floor boards. Lay them bev-

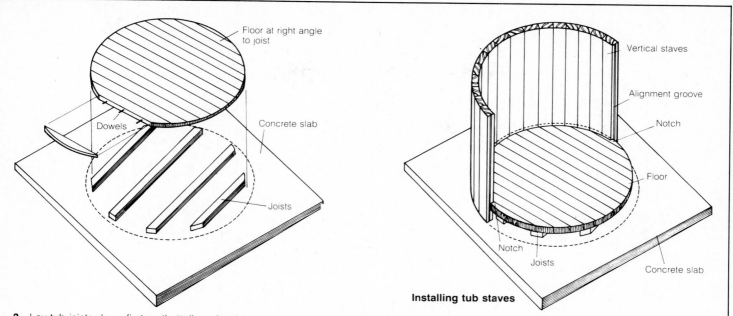

Installing tub staves

3 Lay tub joists down first so that all are level and at the correct distances from each other. Then place the floor boards.

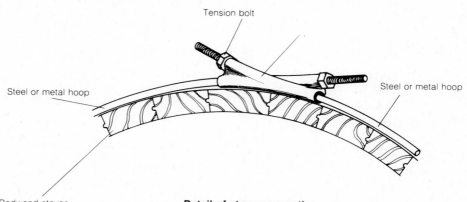

Detail of stave connection

eled side down, over the joists. Place the center board first. This should lie at a 90° angle perpendicular to the floor joists. The boards are either doweled to each other or tongue and grooved. They should fit snugly. Once the floor boards are in place and all the edges line up to form the circular shape, the vertical staves can be installed.

Step 6: Installing the Staves
The staves are put in place and must be perpendicular to and resting on the floor boards. If in doubt, use a carpenter's square to check the 90° angle. Each stave has a notch or a croze. This is a routed section that fits over the end of the floor board. The method may differ by manufacturer. Place each stave notch over the floor board by gently tapping with a rubber hammer. Later the metal hoops will draw the staves in tightly, so do not worry that the edges are not completely seated. Some of the staves may have to be trimmed with a plane if they do not fit properly.

Step 7: Installing the Hoops
Put the lower steel hoop in place first. Most manufacturers provide a specific height above the floor boards. In one model, the location is directly over or slightly above the notch. To keep the hoop level, drive small nails into the exterior of the stave to hold the hoop in

place. Once you tighten the hoop, remove the nails. Center the first hoop lug over a stave joint with the remaining lugs centered over successive stave joints. Slightly tighten the lower hoop to stabilize the staves. Install the remaining hoops at the locations indicated by the manufacturer. Nail as required to keep the hoops in place. Make sure the lugs are centered over the stave joints. Stagger the lugs so that they are not centered over the same joint.

Tightening the Hoops Work from the bottom up, tightening the hoops until they are snug against the staves. Repeat the sequence six to eight times until the staves are fully butted, true and round. Have someone inside the tub begin to hammer the lower part of the stave while the person on the outside tightens the lugs. This ensures

that the edges of the adjacent staves end up flush to each other. Since the watertightness of the tub is dependent on this phase of the operation, do not rush it.

Step 8: Installing the Plumbing
Most tub kits come equipped with staves predrilled for the plumbing connections. Trenches should be dug if the plumbing pipes are to be placed underground. At this point you may bring in the electrician to install the 220 volt power line needed for the heater and the pump. The installation of each component will be outlined by the manufacturer's illustrations.

You will have to install the hydromassage jets in the predrilled holes. These are installed with a wrench. Make sure the gasket is evenly pressured. Do not tighten too far; otherwise

Project continued on next page

you may strip the connection. Install the recessed drain in a similar manner. If the manufacturer has not drilled the holes, you will have to perform this operation using a drill bit with a diameter sufficient to accommodate the plumbing connections.

Step 9: Final Touches
If you ordered a blower with the kit, now is the time to install it in line. Make sure the piping connections are fully seated. Once the plumbing and electrical connections are made, place the tub seats in place and anchor as directed by the manufacturer. The step to the rim should be installed prior to filling the tub.

You are now ready to fill the tub for the first time. Be prepared to take the time to fill and drain the tub a number of times. The wooden staves must be given the opportunity to swell. As the redwood swells, it gives off a coloring called tanin. To rid the water of the tanin, it is necessary to drain and refill the tub several times daily for a period of two to three days until the coloring is imperceptible.

Once the tub is full, start the system to see if any leaks develop. If you find some small leaks, the hoops might not be tight enough. Check the plumbing connections before throwing your hands up in the air. If there are major leaks on one side, the verticals may be out of plumb and you will have to start again.

Once you begin regular operation, the water should be drained at least three times a year to as much as once a month. This depends on the frequency of use and by the number of people using it. Food, drink, suntan lotion or soaps should not be permitted into the water. They tend to clog the filter and reduce the longevity of the mechanical system. Normally, hot tubs are drained into a garden or into a floor drain.

DESIGNER SPA JOB
The client's first concern was to maintain the esthetics of the existing house. The new addition was to have the appearance of having "always been there". This was accomplished by designing a hip roof into the plan, employ-

The intent was to construct an addition that would house a Jacuzzi pool that could be easily enjoyed by the homeowner and his family and friends.

The Jacuzzi tank on a 12-in. base of ¾ in. crushed stone, under 4 in. of concrete. Tank construction is of 2x6 jointed heart or clear cut redwood; plumbing is of P.V.C. plastic.

Below-deck material is wolmanized, treated against rot. Vertical beams are heart-cut redwood 4x4s, resistant to twisting due to moisture. Rafters and roof boards are "D" select pine, chosen for its lack of large knots and its acceptance of stain and sealer.

ing the identical roofing material and keeping exterior colors the same as existing ones. All vertical and horizontal lines would take on the massive and heavy appearance of the existing building.

The next concern was to build a low maintenance structure. This was accomplished by using top-quality products throughout all of the construction details.

Ease of operation was the final concern. This meant that preparing and entering the pool — and leaving and locking up — should be simple operations.

This was accomplished by the use of conveniently located storage compartments for the safety cover of the pool, which easily disassembles into four lightweight pieces for storage. All controls are below seat level and are easily operated by lifting hinged hatches.

Surfaces not scheduled for stain and sealer were first painted with alkyd primer and then covered with 2 coats of dark brown paint.

7
CREATING ORNAMENTAL GARDEN POOLS

Addition of a garden or ornamental pool to a yard or enclosed patio space enhances the area and affects the atmospheric qualities. The sight or sound of water can have a calming and soothing feeling, lending an aura of well being.

BUILDING CODE REQUIREMENTS

In most areas one does not need a building permit to construct an ornamental pool. In new construction, the permit would include the pool if it were a part of the original contract. In other cases, it is usually up to the local agency whether or not a permit is required. This will depend on such points as size of the pool, or if it comes under the jurisdiction of the plumbing or electrical codes. Check with your local inspector. For some locales, setback requirements may apply.

ORNAMENTAL POOL CHOICES
Prefabricated Pools

The ornamental pools available commercially are varied and are designed to perform a variety of tasks. Perhaps the most popular, accessible and reasonably priced are the preformed pools, which come in laminated fiberglass or injected molded plastics. The typical size is 4x6 ft. and the pool is intended to be set into the ground. A preformed pool will survive most weather conditions. In many cases, it does not come equipped with a drain and, therefore, must be cleaned on a regular basis.

Fiberglass Pool The fiberglass pools have one major advantage over all the other varities: they are more rigid and durable than their counterparts. As a re-

An ornamental garden pool can add beauty and grace to a backyard setting. Goldfish or waterlilies add an extra touch.

The pool should be planned as part of the overall setting. Instructions for the gazebo project are in Ch. 10.

sult, this type of ornamental pool tends to be expensive. It is available in styles that resemble natural stone, shale, an outcropping or even a simulated waterfall.

Concrete Pools

The in-ground concrete pool, either precast or free formed, is probably the most widely used type of pool because it offers the greatest variety and flexibility of design. The more popular geometric forms can be integrated inside the house as well as in a garden outside. The pool generally has a wall thickness of 4 in. and is reinforced with a welded wire fabric. The construction of an in-ground concrete pool entails the same procedures as those outlined for an in-ground swimming pool, except that the sizes, depths and thicknesses of the materials are scaled down to meet the dimensions of the ornamental pool. The structural requirements mean that this usually is the most expensive type of pool.

Vinyl Liner Pool

For a natural look that is less geometric and fits effectively into the topography, a vinyl liner ornamental pool is recommended. It is simply a 20mm (or thinner) liner that is spread over a natural or manmade depression. Surrounded by local stone or other suitable edging, the pool becomes a part of the natural landscape.

In-ground and Above-ground Masonry Pools

Many garden pools are often thought of as ornamental even though they might perform a much more important task for the house and especially the garden: all water lines could originate from it. An above- or in-ground masonry pool can provide water to the landscape while blending into the garden scheme.

For an above-ground masonry pool that is less than 16 square feet, the base should

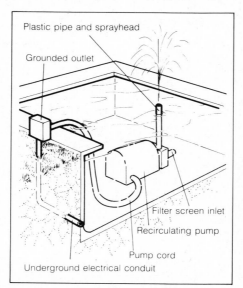

If you desire, your pool can hold a fountain. The installation requires a power outlet, which is protected by a GFIC.

be at least a 4-in. concrete slab. If the pool has dimensions of 4x5 ft. install a 6 in. base slab. Masonry pools should have a concrete base that are reinforced with welded wire fabric or reinforcing rods.

In most masonry pools, the masonry — brick, stone or tile — is used only as a veneer over a concrete base and walls, and the masonry thus is nonstructural. The freedom of selection of pattern and structural bonds, as well as the type and coloration of the brick and mortar, make the in-ground and above-ground masonry pool a popular choice for many gardens.

Fountains

The ornamental pool is often enhanced with the addition of a fountain. A fountain requires pumping facilities and must be maintained on a regular basis. It adds acoustical and visual beauty to the garden.

HOW THE ORNAMENTAL POOL WORKS
Pools Without Pumps and Drainage

Several types of ornamental pools do not require recirculating water and do not have a fountain. These pools generally are required simply to contain a body of water. However, if the pool is not properly maintained, the water can become stagnant and odorous. A shallow saucer pool set into the ground is probably the simplest.

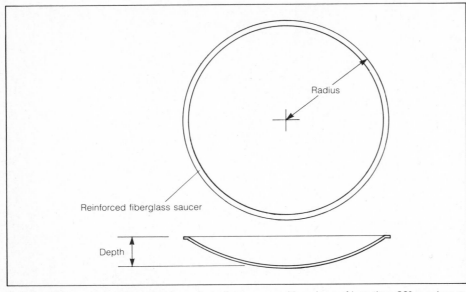

A pool can come in prefabricated form. A shallow saucer with a slope of less than 30° requires no recirculating pump. The rigid, durable form has a long life.

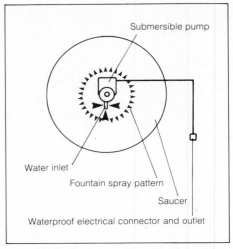

A submersible pump draws water into its center and moves the water out at the edges. The pump size depends upon the pool size.

Shallow Saucer Pool The shallow saucer pool is particularly suited to northern climates, since wall damage is prevented by the slope of the sides. The slope is 30° or less, which essentially eliminates the horizontal force exerted on a wall by ice formation. You can install this type of pool without a recirculating pump because the water is so shallow.

The operation of the saucer pool is very straightforward. Once in place, it is filled with a garden hose. Because the water is not aerated, the pool must be emptied often and cleaned on a regular basis to keep excessive bacteria and algae from forming. If you contemplate a natural setting with fish or aquatic plants, you may want to add an overflow channel with a wier to drain excessive water from the pool.

Pools With Drainage

Not quite as simple, but still easy to manage, is a pool that includes a floor or base drain, which is installed when the pool is installed. The drain, usually made of PVC, is set in the base with cement and then run to a low spot in the site or to a sewer line. If the pool is to have some form of recirculating water system, the floor drain can be connected to the inlet part of the pump. This allows the pool to be drained above ground.

Pools With Recirculating Systems

If you want a pool in which water is to be sprayed, dropped or moved, you need a recirculating system. Most larger pools will include a recirculating system. The aeration of the water provided by the sys-

tem reduces the need to clean the pool or even to replace the water. There are two types of recirculating systems: the submersible and the conventional. Both pumps require a pool water inlet. Once the water has been pulled in through the pump, it is then pushed out through a series of outlets (dependent on the size and design) to repeat the cycle. The inlet side is fitted with a filter to remove any debris that might be floating on the surface of the water.

Whether you select a conventional or submersible pump, its assembly must be checked on a regular basis. The conventional pump is usually self-priming to speed up the startup of the pool. The submersible draws the water in and through; an impeller assembly attached to the pump housing forces the water towards the outlet. The pump itself never comes in con-

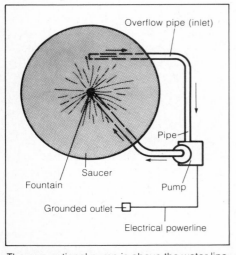

The conventional pump is above the water line. The water moves through a pipe to the pump. It is then sent out the fountain.

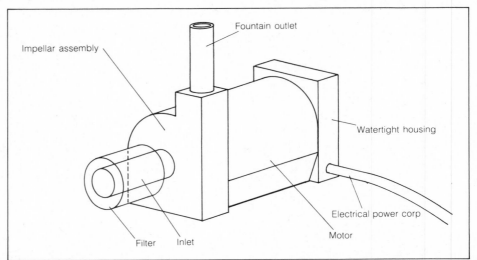

The aeration supplied by a submersible pump helps keep the water clean so that it is capable of sustaining small plants. The pump motor itself is completely enclosed.

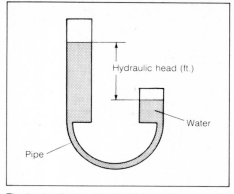

The hydraulic head is the distance between the pump inlet and outlet. The farther the distance, the harder the pump works.

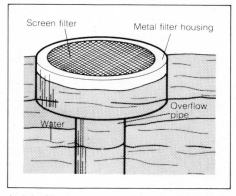

An inlet filter trap removes large particles of dirt from the water, thus reducing the possibility of pump damage.

tact with the water. It is usually made with case iron or heavy plastic enclosing the motor. Submersibles are available in a variety of sizes that can handle from 75 to 3,000 gallons per hour.

Position The submersible is not built in; the conventional recirculating system is. The submersible is made to sit on the bottom of the pool.

Hydraulic Head Another factor in the selection of the pump is the hydraulic head. This is the distance from the inlet of the water to the outlet. If the water outlet is much higher than the inlet, the pump must perform extra work to push the water up that additional height. Select a pump that will work effectively for the volume of the pool as well as for the head.

Wiring Details Since the conventional and submersible pumps are in contact with the water, most come equipped with a diaphram-operated switch and enclosed-pump housing. In addition, most pumps will be equipped with a thermal overload protection device. The submersible comes with a power cord having a three-pronged plug that connects to a grounded outlet.

Fountains Many of the pumps can be

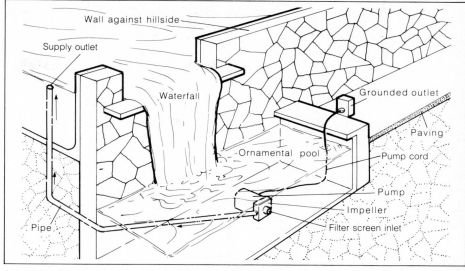

A waterfall takes advantage of the acoustical appeal of running water. The recirculating pump cycles water from the lower pool area to above the falls to begin the cycle again.

connected to a variety of fountains to achieve a wide range of effects. Waterfalls, water chutes and the like all rely on a pump and gravity to achieve the desired effect.

Filters If the pool will be subjected to a lot of debris, a inlet filter trap is strongly recommended. This type of filter is located just below the top surface of the water. The inlet itself is an additional way of maintaining the water level of the pool.

Water Supply

For most installations, the house water supply system is adequate to meet the needs of an ornamental pool. The pools are usually filled with a garden hose, although in some cases the pool is connected

directly to a pipe having a water supply valve similar to that in a water closet tank. In this case, a ½-in. water line can deliver an adequate supply.

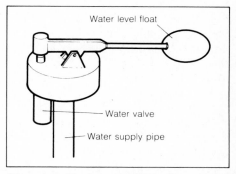

Although most pools are filled with a garden hose, some have a water supply system that works like a water closet system.

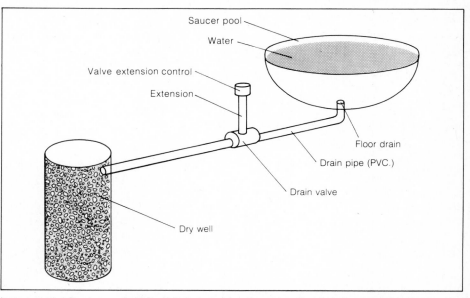

Larger pools often have a built-in drain for emptying the water. The drain leads to a low spot or to a dry well. The system is controlled by a valve.

Drainage

Larger pools require some form of drainage in order to empty the pool for cleaning or repair. One option is the gravity floor drain that is connected to drain tiles emptying into a low spot on the site or a dry well (if permitted). Another alternative, more frequently used, is to employ the pump and drain to void the pool. This eliminates a lot of unnecessary piping.

Filtration Systems

Most ornamental pools do not require any form of filtration. For a large reflecting pool, you may want to install a small filter system to enhance clarity of the water. Filters used on submersible pumps are a trap type that connect to the inlet side of the pump. The water is pulled in through the filter on its way to the pump. The capacity of this type of filter/pump arrangement varies from 100 to 1000 gallons of water circulated per hour.

Some systems are available where the filter has a reusable foam sleeve that filters the water and recirculates it through the pump. Keep in mind that the pools still need to be cleaned on a regular basis. Although the installation of a filter reduces the cleaning frequency, it does not eliminate it completely.

Enclosures

If you select a conventional type of pool pump and filtration system, locate the apparatus within several feet of the pool. In most cases, the equipment is recessed in an in-ground storage chamber that is waterproof and well ventilated. If you do not want to invest in an in-ground chamber, the pump assembly may be placed behind a wall or under a bench and enclosed with a material compatible with the surroundings. The submersible pump does not require any enclosure.

FITTING THE POOL INTO YOUR LANDSCAPE

Whether your ornamental pool is to be formal, rustic or natural, you must plan for its intended placement and size. The specific location on your site has a lot to do with how you can utilize the pool.

Space Requirements

The majority of ornamental pools available commercially range from 36-in. saucers to 18 ft. long reflecting pools. Most of the pools come with depths ranging

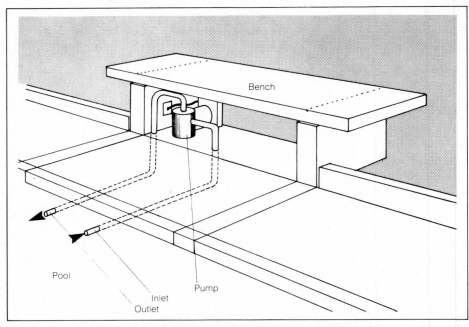

Oftentimes a conventional pump assembly can be disguised by a bench or other structure near the edge of the pool.

from 5 in. to a maximum depth of 18 in. Hence, most sites can accommodate an ornamental pool.

Weather Conditions

When deciding whether to add an ornamental pool to your site, you must take climate into account. For colder climates subject to freezing and thawing, you must exercise more care to select a pool type that will withstand the dimensional changes brought on by the cold. If you select a concrete pool, it should be placed firmly and deeply enough so that frost heave will not shift its position. In addition, the pool should be reinforced with a welded wire fabric so that it will not crack or break up because of the cold. Other pool types, such as shallow saucer shapes, fiberglass pools or the newer vinyl liner pools, do well in most climates. In warm regions, placing a reflecting pool beneath a tree can lower the temperature in the surrounding area by 10 to 15 degrees.

Level and Slope

Overall, a level spot for the pool is preferable because installation is easier. Make sure the area selected is free of tree roots and large rocks and even underground utilities. Some of the pools can be set above or below the ground, on platforms or recessed in a shallow excavation. Always make sure that the drainage is away from the pool; a heavy rain can fill the pool with topsoil.

Slope The design depends on the effect that you wish to achieve with the pool. Slope can provide the gravity feet that keeps pool water moving. With a recirculation system, it could keep going for quite some time. However desirable a flat level piece of ground is, the use of a slope for a decorative pool can enhance its effect.

Seasonal Care of Materials

On a seasonal basis, the pool should be drained and scrubbed out with soap and water. If there are cracks or chips in the material, they should be repaired. In some concrete pools, the surface may need to be repainted with an appropriate waterproof paint.

Winterizing the Pool During winter, in cold climates, drain the pool by half. If you have a fountain, disconnect the housing and remove the spray jets. Once this is done, place a large wood log in the middle of the pool. When the water freezes, the log prevents a huge block of ice from forming, thus reducing the potential for damage. A pool cover is recommended even if it is just a sheet of plywood placed over the opening in the severe winter months. If you have selected a saucer pool with less than a 30 degree slope, concern yourself only with the suggested maintenance schedule of the pool manufacturer.

BUILDING A SQUARE, TIMBER-EDGED ORNAMENTAL POOL

The prefabricated pools offer a wide range of options, but the in-ground concrete pool offers you the chance to design and build to your specific requirements. For the purposes of demonstration here, we will give instructions for an in-ground square pool. The steps covered in this example also apply to a variety of free forms and other geometric shapes. The edging material presented here will be a rough sawn timber.

This design was developed to complement a garden gazebo. The pool, measuring 8x8 ft. overall, was framed into a brick masonry patio area. The pool included a conventional pump arrangement connected to a center-mounted water jet.

Materials List

The quantity and list of materials will vary according to the size and specific design. If you are in doubt, take the plan to the local concrete supplier to determine the amount of concrete and reinforcing you need. To complete this pool, you will need these items: concrete; reinforcing; wooden 2x2 in. stakes, 24 in. long; 6x6 #10/10 welded wire fabric; 30 bricks or evenly matched stones; 3x10 rough sawn cypress or outdoor wood; plumbing pipe ¾ PVC; 2x6 edge forms; 2 gallons black silicone paint.

Tools

No matter how proficient you may be in building, one of the most important tools you can have is another helping hand. Select help based on the skills that may be brought to the project. Basic tools you may require will be: shovels; wheelbarrow; carpenter level (48 in.); hammers; pliers; rented reinforcing bar cutter; 1-in. o.d.(outside diameter)x36-in. galvanized pipe; skill saw; nails; hand tamper; trowels; darby; screeds.

Construction Procedures

Step 1: Preparing the Site Pick a site that is flat and free of large stones and tree roots. One way to make sure that the site is satisfactory is to dig several test pits slightly deeper than the actual pool. This will also tell you how

A square, timber-edged pool and fountain can add to your leisure-time enjoyment. The pool can be formed of concrete, as here, or prefabricated.

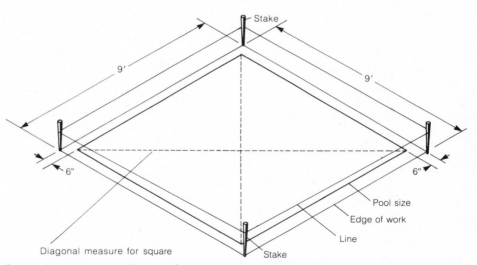

Select a flat and level site. Stake out the pool; then erect a stake-and-string outline 6 in. farther out on all sides to allow for the concrete walls of the pool.

the soil will behave when you pour the concrete. Once you have determined that the site is satisfactory, start the pool layout.

Step 2: Staking the Excavation The walls of the pool are to be made of 4 in. of concrete. You must allow for this thickness, and also give yourself some working room, when you excavate. Therefore, for an 8x8 ft. pool, excavate a 9x9 ft. hole. Pound stakes to mark each corner of the excavation. Run string lines around to all four stakes. Make sure that the outline is square to your plantings, pathways

or patio. If not, adjust the string lines until you have achieved the correct position. The next task is to square the stakes. (Refer to Chapter 3 for details on how to square the stakes,using the 3-4-5 triangle approach.) Drive the stakes far enough into the ground so that they will not shift during the excavation. Batter boards (discussed in Chapter 3) also are helpful in establishing reference marks. For very small pools, however, they are not required.

Level the four stakes with a carpenter's level or line level. Find the highest corner of the site and pound the stake

Project continued on next page

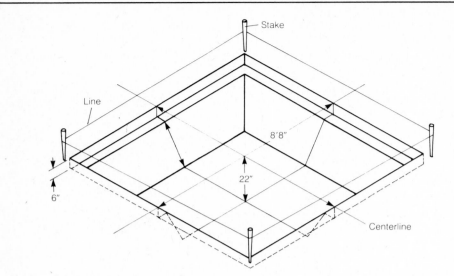

The pool itself will be 18 in. deep. The excavation must be 22 in. deep to allow for the concrete bottom. Note the shelf that defines the edge of the pool.

so it is 6 in. above grade at that point. Then align the other three stakes to that height.

Step 3: Excavating for the Pool In

this design, the edge of the pool will slope downward at a 45° angle until the bottom of the pool is reached. The soil must be removed to conform to this

shape. The depth of the pool will be 18 in. Keep in mind that the thickness of the concrete must be accounted for, which will be 4 in. Therefore, the excavated depth will be 22 in. from grade. The slope will extend 18 in. toward the center, producing a diagonal measurement of 25.2 in. Refer to the diagram for the layout of the sloping sides. Lay at least 4 in. of gravel fill before placing any of the reinforcing steel.

As the soil is removed from the excavation, place it to the side so it can be removed easily. Shape the excavation in layers rather than attempting to go to the full depth at once. This will help level the entire opening. If an area is too low, do not try to fill it in; level everything to the low spot. Be careful to adjust for the increase in overall depth. Keep the soil moist so that the excavated slopes and base will maintain their shape.

Once the excavation has been completed, mechanically tamp the area so

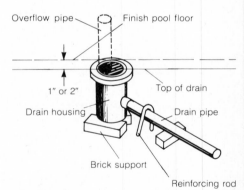

Support the drain and pipe with bricks. A bent reinforcing rod holds the pipe in position during the concrete pour.

that the soil is smooth and properly consolidated. If a depression now develops, let it alone. Let the concrete fill it in.

Step 4: Installing Pool Supply and Drain The pool in this example has a floor drain that is a combination of 1½ in. PVC overflow painted black, a 1½ in. coupling that is unthreaded, and the 1½ in. drain. The arrangement is illustrated in the drawing. To place the drain piping, dig a small trench. Lay the piping to the dry well or other drain point and then backfill. Place the drain and the attached coupling in position, with the top of the coupling 1 in. below

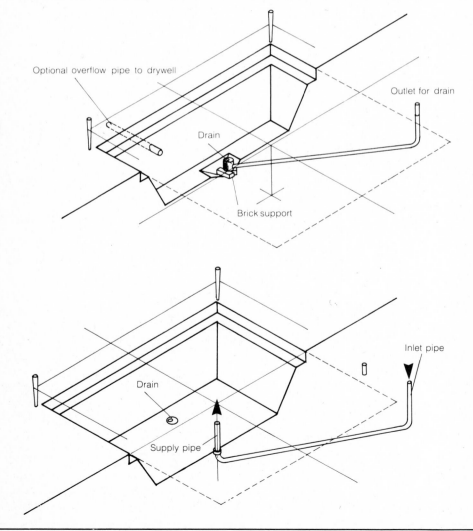

the finish level of the bottom of the pool. Stuff the end of the opening coupling with a rag or cap so that the concrete cannot enter. Once the assembly is in position, stabilize by placing a brick underneath it and a bent reinforcing rod over it. Drive the ends of the rod into the ground. After the line has been stabilized, check the level and the vertical dimension by measuring between the drain and the top of the pool to insure accurate placement of the drain.

The supply line is a ½ in. PVC pipe that will enter the pool in the exact center. Lay this pipe and stabilize it in a similar fashion as you have the drain coupling.

Step 5: Installing Reinforcing
Once the drain is in place, you are ready to install the reinforcing.

Corner and intermediate bars Cut ⅜ in. reinforcing rods into 18-in. segments. Use a bar cutter rented from the reinforcing supplier or rental store. Drive one bar in each corner of the excavation, centered in the thickness of the 4-in. wall. Place them 8 ft. 4 in. apart, with the top of each bar 2 in. below the tops of the corner stakes. Continue to drive additional 18-in. rods into the ground, 4 in. from the string line. Each side needs 6 intermediate rods driven to the same elevation as the corner rods.

Edge bars After all the rods are in place and the level is checked, bend them to form 90° angles. All that is needed is one continuous bar tied so it aligns with the tops of the vertical rods. Repeat this until you have outlined the perimeter. Tie the bent rods to the vertical rods using short pieces of tie wire. Overlap the ends of the horizontal bars at least 6 in. and tie the ends together. If any of the bars are short, place a short piece in between the two longer ones. Overlap the ends of longer bars with the shorter piece by at least 6-in.

Welded wire fabric Once the edge rod is in place and firmly tied to the vertical rods, you should be ready to place the 10 gauge welded wire fabric in place. This will require several bricks. Set the single bricks along the bottom and sides of the excavation. The bricks will support the fabric and

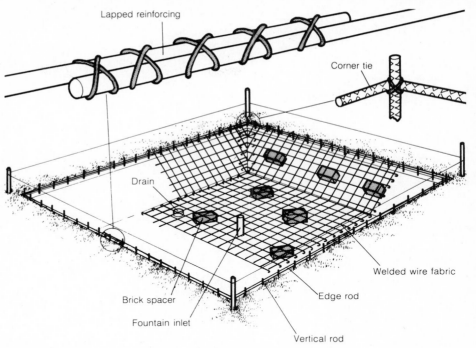

Reinforcing mesh is held up by bricks placed along the pool bottom.

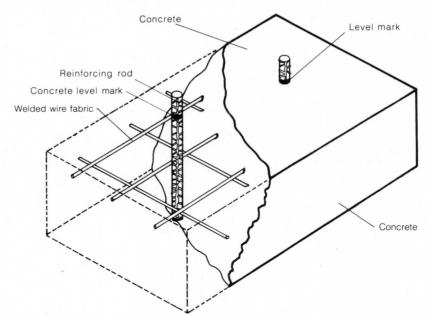

These rods in the pool bottom have been marked to indicate the depth of the slab.

keep it from touching the bottom and sides of the excavation.

It will be important that the concrete, when poured, encircle the fabric as much as possible. Bend the sheets of fabric to the shape of the bottom of the pool. Extend the sheets up the sides and slightly over the top of the horizontal bar you recently installed. Overlap the sheets several inches and tie them together with the short metal ties. After all the fabric is in place and tied together,

er, secure the fabric to the horizontal edge bar. Then cut off the excess with wire shears.

Depth gauges You will need to place several rods in the base on the pool floor. Drive these in so that they extend 6 in. above the floor and walls of the pool. Measure down 2 in. on each rod and paint a white stripe around each. The marks will help you make sure that the concrete will be a uniform 4 in. deep. Drive a rod in each

Project continued on next page

corner at the base of the slope and one in the middle. You may also drive several along the length of the wall.

Step 6: Installing the Edge Form Place the edge forms for the top of the concrete base, on undisturbed earth around the perimeter of the excavation. Using 2x6 lumber and duplex-headed nails, nail together an edge form and place it 3 in. outside the reinforcing. The top of the form should be 6 in. above level grade. The top should be level with the corner stakes and fit to the inside of the corner stakes. Once the form is nailed together, it should be established with 2x4 stakes inserted on 24-in. centers around the entire perimeter. Oil the inside faces of the boards with a generous coat of motor oil.

Step 7: Pouring the Concrete Now it is time to pour the concrete. For ease of installation, you may want to span the excavation with several 2x12s so that you can work the center of the pool without having to stand in the excavation.

The concrete should not be dropped into the form, but gently placed as much as possible. Otherwise, the concrete will separate. Use a shovel to work the concrete into the forms. Keep the concrete flowing until the concrete is level with the marks on the rods that were driven in the bottom and sides of the pool. Use a ⅜-in. rod to consolidate the concrete around the mesh. This will remove any air bubbles. Level all depressions and keep the concrete flush with the tops of the rods.

Step 8: Finishing the Concrete To smooth the concrete, use a float. In this case the standard float (24 in. wide) is satisfactory. (For a free-form pool, the float would have to be custom-made so that a smaller blade would form to the curvature.) Smooth the concrete until the surface is level and free of rises or depressions.

At this point, drive down the rods, which are at or just below the surface, so they are farther into the ground. Then smooth and shape the walls and floor of the pool. Leave a slight depression around the drain coupling. Once the overflow pipe is removed, the depression assures that the pool will

drain properly. Trowel until the surface is very smooth and well shaped.

After the steel troweling, spray the inside surface with a garden hose. Gently wet the inside of the concrete just enough to moisten it. Take a stiff broom and draw it across the surface of the concrete until the entire surface is gently roughed with the broom finish.

Step 9: The Final Touches After the concrete has cured for at least three days (refer to Chapter 3 on in-ground concrete pools), remove the edge forms. Check the edges of the concrete for cracks or spalling. If you notice cracks or holes, fill them in with patch cement.

Piping Unplug the drain coupling and install the overflow pipe and supply pipes in place. Cut the overflow pipe to the desired pool water level, 1 in. below the top of the concrete edge. The supply will be cut off at this elevation if no additional nozzle or jet is to be used.

Painting Paint the inside of the pool with two coats of black silicone or

similar paint. If you are planning to have fish in the pond or aquatic plants, purchase a powdered or liquid neutralizing agent that seals out the harmful alkalis of the fresh concrete. This process allows the fish to survive. Follow the directions on the package as to the duration of the treatment.

Step 10: Installing the Wood Surround After the pool has cured for at least a week, you can install the heavy wood 3x10 cypress or exterior wood edging board. To do this, you will require a drill and ½ in. masonry bit. In addition, you need twelve ½-in. lead expansion shields and hex head bolts with washers. Drill a ½-in. hole 4 in. from each end of the 8 ft. concrete side wall, and drill another hole in the center. Install the expansion shield with the bolt in place. To simplify the task, drill holes in the wood at the same time that you drill the concrete. After placing the lumber on the edge, bolt the lumber snugly in place and toenail the corners to each other.

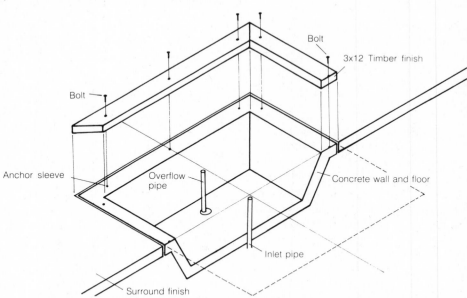

After the concrete cures for three days, remove the edge forms, unplug the drain coupling and install the overflow and supply pipe lines. Then install the timber beams.

BUILDING AN OCTAGONAL TILED POOL

An attractive way to finish a garden pool is to cover it with ceramic tile. Select a tile that is specifically designed for outdoor use. You also must choose an adhesive and grout based on latex-portland cement. These are specifically designed for outdoor applications.

Design your pool so that the length and the width of the walls are even multiples of the tile you have chosen. This will avoid small awkwardly cut tiles. Be sure to allow for grout lines as you plan.

CREATING THE POOL
Step 1: Excavating the Area
Set out a stake-and-string outline of the pool. Then set batter boards and excavate to the depth required by local codes. If possible, lay the plumbing lines below the footing. If not, these still should be set before the footing is poured. Lay a 2-inch base of gravel in the part of the excavation that lies beneath the pool bottom. Set in ½ in. plastic pipe between the position for the submersible pump and the spray head. Set in 1 in. plastic drain piping between the center drain and the drain site. A coupling and second pipe lead to the overflow drain location. Hold the pipe in place with small rocks. Then add 2 more in. of gravel base over the pipes. Pour the footings.

Step 2: Setting the Forms
After the footings cure, build a form of 2x6 lumber. To create the octagonal shape, cut the ends of the formboards at a 45° angle. Butt tightly and brace with 2x4 stakes. Install 2x4 spreaders in the tops of the forms. After pouring the fountain, tamp to avoid honeycombing.

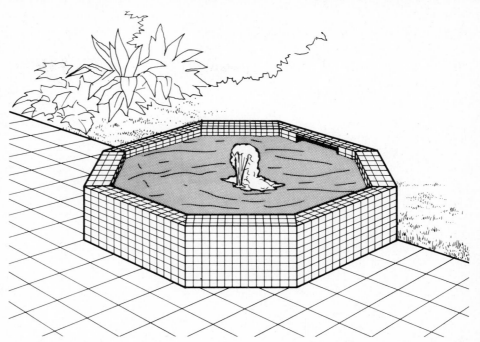

This octagonal ornamental pool is of poured concrete, over which tile has been laid on both the exterior and interior wall faces.

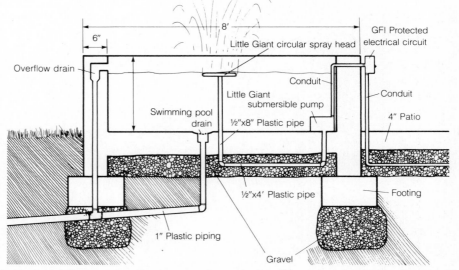

The pool design utilizes a submersible pump and a fountain. The overflow drain is formed into the pool walls. Slope the concrete down to the floor drain in the pool bottom.

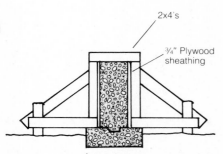

The walls of the pool must be constructed of ¾ in. plywood securely braced with 2x4 braces. Oil the forms for easy removal.

Step 3: Pouring the Floor
Screed the top of the concrete level; float finish. After seven days of curing, remove the forms. Install the drain and fountain head. Pour and float the floor to slope gently to the drain.

Step 4: Preparing the Concrete for Tile
The concrete surface must be level to ⅛ in. to hold the tile. Use a cold chisel and hammer to knock away any protrusions that are left from the seams of the form boards. To repair any holes left by air bubbles that were not tamped out before the pour, first flush the area with water. Then make up a mix of 1 part mortar cement and 4 parts sand. Add enough water to create a fairly slushy mixture. Trowel the mixture in place, level and allow to cure. Use the mortar where needed to provide a level tiling surface. Once this has cured, apply at least three coats of basement waterproofing mixture to seal the fountain.

Project continued on next page

TILING PROCEDURES

Step 1: Tiling the Tops of the Walls

Once the waterproofing has dried, apply a prime coat of the portland-latex adhesive of the same type that you will later use to adhere the tiles. Use the flat side of the adhesive trowel for this job. Once this coat has dried, you are ready to begin tiling.

Dry lay a set of tiles along one of the sides of the pool. Remember to allow space for the grout lines. If possible, arrange the tiles so that all cut tiles will fall at the corners. Remove the tiles and apply a coat of adhesive with the saw-toothed edge of the trowel. Press firmly so that the notches in the trowel leave trails of adhesive that show up as separate, distinct rows. Use a wriggling motion to set the tiles in the adhesive. Lay all the full-size tiles on each wall first.

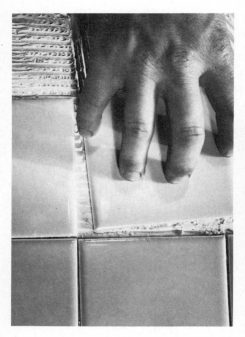

As you work, frequently check the vertical and horizontal grout lines for level. This is especially important later, when you work on the sides of the pool walls.

To seat the tiles firmly and prevent air pockets, use a beating block. This is a carpet-covered wood block equal in size to at least two tiles. Slide it across the tile surface, tapping the block gently with a hammer as you go.

Cutting Tiles Once the full-size tiles are in place, you must determine cut tiles to fit as needed. This job is easier if you rent a tile cutter from the tile dealer. If you have planned correctly, you will need a small triangular piece at both ends of each row to fill in the corner area.

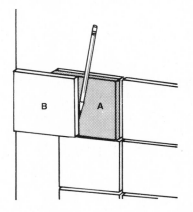

Place a loose tile, Tile A, on top of the last full size tile at one end. Slide the loose tile over, adjusting it so that it fills the empty space. Now place a second loose tile, Tile B, exactly aligned over the last full tile, sandwiching Tile A in between. With a felt-tipped pen or a sharp object like an ice pick, mark along Tile A as shown.

Now put the tile, glazed side up, into the tile cutter. Place the blade so that you allow for the thickness of the grout line. Score a line across the tile. Remove the tile from the cutter. Set the tile on top of a wire such as a coat hanger, aligning the scored line and the wire. Place one hand on either side of the tile and press down. The tile should snap in two (wear safety goggles for this task to protect yourself from bits of clay and glaze.)

Step 2: Tiling: the Outside and Inside

Plan the tile layout for the outside so that cut tiles will fall at the base of the pool. Apply adhesive as above. Lay any cut tiles last. You can tile the entire inside of the pool, or you can tile to below the waterline, as desired.

Step 3: Applying the Grout

Allow the tiles to set up for at least 24 hours. Then mix up a batch of portland-latex grout according to the manufacturer's directions. This is applied with

a soft rubber squeegee. Work the squeegee at an angle to the grout lines to completely fill the joints and prevent any air pockets. As soon as the grout becomes firm, use a wet sponge to remove all the excess from the faces of the tiles. To shape the grout lines, run the handle of an old toothbrush along the joints. Then clean the tiles and smooth the joints with a damp sponge. Allow the surface to dry; polish with a soft cloth. Cure the grout according to the manufacturer's instructions.

8
ABOVE-GROUND POOLS

An above-ground swimming pool is a worthwhile alternative for those who want backyard swimming time but cannot afford the expense of an in-ground pool. The in-ground pool may be three to ten times as expensive as an above-ground pool. An above-ground pool normally comes in kit form, designed and packaged to fit into a station wagon and be driven home for assembly.

The above-ground pool is a very noticeable structure. All too often, the pool is simply placed in the middle of the property without any consideration for the view of the land. While the above-ground pool does not have the same overall aesthetic as an in-ground pool, it can enjoy the same integration into the overall landscaping scheme. On the other hand, the above-ground pool can be moved if the original location is not acceptable. (Since an above-ground pool can be moved, it is generally not taxed in the same way an in-ground pool would be.)

The above-ground pool comes as a kit that includes: 4-ft. high galvanized steel or aluminum perimeter walls, vertical supports and a vinyl liner. Generally, the filtration equipment is included in the basic kit. Pool accessories are often considered optional, although a pool ladder might be included.

WORK SEQUENCE
The assembly usually takes one to three days, once the basic site preparation has been completed. The typical above-ground pool assembly consists of the following procedures:
    (1) preparing the ground by removing the topsoil;
    (2) leveling the base soil and compacting it;

Vinyl liner above-ground pools can be integrated into a second-story deck in order to achieve a pleasing, unified backyard design.

During the installation of an above-ground pool, pull back the sand edge from the edge guide to aid insertion of the pool wall.

(3) laying down the bottom form rail;

(4) unrolling the pool wall and placing it on the bottom rail;

(5) joining the wall sections;

(6) putting the vertical supports in place; installing the top finish panel;

(7) placing the preformed cover;

(8) laying the vinyl liner;

(9) adding water;

(10) installing the filtration system and pool ladder;

(11) installing decking, railings, stairs and landscaping after the pool is finished.

COMPARISONS WITH AN IN-GROUND POOL

An above-ground swimming pool operates similarly to an in-ground one in that it recirculates water in the same fashion, uses chemicals for bacteria control, has a filtration system (and sometimes a heating system) and requires maintenance. The above-ground pool differs from the in-ground pool in that it always must be winterized, which means that the pool must be drained during the winter season. The liner need not be removed, but all the pool equipment and accessories should be stored. The liner of the above-ground pool must be changed a number of times over the life span of the pool. This is because of the seasonal changes that the pool undergoes. An in-ground vinyl liner pool need not be emptied or filled at such a frequent rate. The average life span of an above-ground pool is 15 years or less.

Building Code Requirements

In most areas, the building codes are not as specific for the above-ground pool as they are for the in-ground one. For pool security, the 4-ft. height of the pool wall is considered adequate, so a fenced-in yard is usually not required. However, codes do vary from location to location; verify those for your area before purchasing the above-ground pool. You will probably need a building permit, which can be obtained upon written request and payment of a nominal fee.

SITE CONSIDERATIONS
Available Land

An above-ground pool requires a relatively small area. Most pools come in sizes ranging from 15 to 28 ft. diameter circles or from 12x24 to 21x41 ft. ovals. The pool is a self-contained structure that does not rely on a wide area around the pool for support. The access requirements of an above-ground pool are quite different than those of an in-ground pool. In most cases, the above-ground pool is entered by means of a ladder to a deck. In the case of a sloping site, the deck might extend to the high side of the pool, making access much easier but still requiring less ground space than an in-ground installation.

The most important consideration is the flatness of the site. Once the area has been selected, the remaining area can be left alone or integrated into a recreational area adjacent to the pool. In addition, plan for fence heights, and pool water drainage. Locate the pool in an area where there are no underground utilities. If you have a tile field for your sewage, keep the pool well away from that area, even if it is relatively flat.

Privacy Concerns

Privacy in an above-ground pool is difficult to obtain without extensive site development. Because the pool sits 4 ft. above grade, the swimming activity can be seen from quite some distance. Even a very high fence would not necessarily provide all the visual privacy you may desire. Nonetheless, the most readily available privacy is gained from enclosing the yard with a fence. The pool also may be placed so that your house or garage helps hide it from the neighborhood and forms a sheltered enclosure for the noise and activity. Another alternative might be dense shrubs around the pool. Security from unwanted guests should be considered; if you have a deck, an access-ladder drawbridge arrangement may be adequate. If you do not add a deck, a fence around the pool is suggested.

Relationship to the House

This is generally based on the available land. Remember, however, that the farther the pool is from the house, the more difficult it will be to supervise the activity.

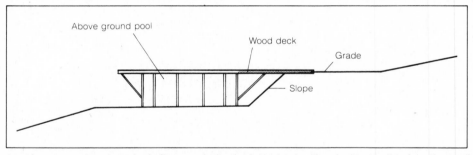

An above-ground pool can be built up against a rise in the land, with a deck extending from the pool onto the higher ground.

A raised deck with pool can become a family entertainment center. Note the unusual use of indoor/outdoor carpeting.

If at any time a swimmer is in trouble, proximity to the house might save him or her from disaster. On a smaller lot, the location may be predetermined and all that can be done is to decide on what landscaping features may be necessary to make it more or less a part of the house.

Location also may be determined by the availability of level ground. An above-ground swimming pool can be effective if it is built up against a rise in the land. It is not recommended, however, to try to negotiate building on land that has a gradient over 6%. If possible, use the house to shelter the pool. In some cases, a leanto roof structure can be extended from the house over the pool to increase its year-round usage. A second-story deck attached to the house and leading down to the pool can also prove a very effective design.

Soil Conditions and Types

Generally most sites are suitable for an above-ground pool. The major exception is thin, sandy soil or excessively pebbly soil. Most other soil types, even dense clay, form a good support base for the pool. To determine the suitability of your soil, the simplest method is to observe your site. Check to make sure that there is

an adequate drainage pattern away from the house and away from the proposed pool site. Is there any standing water? It may indicate a high water table or poor draining soil that may not be adequate to support the pool. If in doubt, consult your local building inspector or a qualified excavation contractor. They will be able to tell you if the soil is satisfactory for installation.

The typical 16-ft.-diameter round pool will contain enough water to exert 250 lbs. per sq. ft. pressure on the soil underneath the pool. If the soil is not compacted or consolidated enough to support this weight, the soil will give. The ground settlement could cause the liner to rupture or the walls to buckle. It is, therefore, important that the ground under the pool be well prepared and level. A professional excavator should be hired to remove the sod or topsoil. Once the lowest elevation of the pool site has been determined, all digging and leveling should be to that point. A contractor, using proper equipment, can clear and grub the site, level it and provide the proper level of compaction far better, more quickly and possibly more cheaply than if you had done it yourself.

Dealing with a Pebbly Soil Where a 'pebbly soil' condition exists, concrete

block should be placed under the vertical support locations around the perimeter of the pool wall. Washed mason's sand should be laid and compacted over the base soil in the area that will support the vinyl liner.

POOL TYPES AND DESIGNS

The main design options available with an above-ground pool are more limited than for in-ground pools. The most common type of above-ground pool is round because it is less expensive and because a circle contains the maximum volume with the least surface area. Because of the strength of the circle to withstand outward pressures, the round pool does not require diagonal bracing at the vertical panel supports. If the pool is oval, the flatter side of the pool requires additional bracing by diagonal legs that support the side of the pool wall. There are other forms advertised, but they are more complex in their installation requirements. When deciding on a pool, look for kits that are well built, and instructions that are clear and excellent, with illustrations of the assembly procedures. If you are not building the pool yourself, select a manufacturer and installer with a reputation for quality work.

Prefabricated Kits

As previously mentioned, nearly all above-ground pool manufacturers make their pools available in a prefabricated kit form. The type of material and construction method varies from manufacturer to manufacturer.

Kit Materials A typical above-ground vinyl liner pool kit consists of: ground rail of steel or aluminum; pool wall in steel or aluminum; jointer connector piece for the wall panels; vertical supports; finish top seat connector; vinyl liner, 20mm average thickness; ladder; nuts and bolts and appropriate tools.

In addition to the above, the following can be made part of the kit: filtration system; skimmer; vacuum system; chemical supplies; pH test kits; accessories.

Some above-ground pool kits offer an angled bottom, which allows a gradual slope down to a deep end. These require a more comprehensive soil base preparation and more extensive excavation. The extra depth does add tremendously to the swimming pleasure when compared to the more typical flat bottom.

An above-ground pool built on a slope can be partially recessed in order to help create a "deep-end" and to avoid breaking up landscape design.

Materials and Components Most above-ground prefabricated pools are constructed of an aluminum or hot-dipped galvanized steel frame with a baked-on vinyl finish. The walls of the pool usually are fabricated from corrugated or ribbed 4-ft. high sections. The sections are aluminum or galvanized steel sheets with a baked-on vinyl finish. All accessories are of similar material and finish.

Recent developments in the technology of reinforced fiberglass have produced a prefabricated pool structure composed of 1¼ to 2 in. thick preformed plastic/fiberglass panels that connect to the vertical supports in a similar fashion as the steel or aluminum. These come in a round or oval form and provide insulation between the outside air and the water. Their cost is somewhat higher than the standard steel or aluminum panel unit.

Vinyl Liner The vinyl liner is the major component in the entire assembly, since it is the element that contains the water. The vinyl liner should be at least 20mm thick, with maximum tensile strength, and have surface embossing to prevent skidding. The liner also should resist tears, chemicals, and ultraviolet light. The manufacturers provide expandable liners for either a pool of continuous depth or a graduated slope to a deep swimming area. The liner expands to fit the graduated bottom contours, thus avoiding the need to preform the ground precisely to fit exact dimensions. This allows an excavated pool with a deeper and possibly wider swimming area than is possible with alternative, strap systems.

Safety Issues

An above-ground pool does make it more difficult to simply wander into the water since people must climb a ladder to get into the pool. If you have an extended deck, however, you must take the same safety measures as the code requires as for an in-ground pool.

To enhance the appearance of the pool or if attaching a deck to the pool, the minimum requirement would be for indirect lighting coupled with selected task lighting aimed at the ladder and the swimmers in the pool. All lighting must conform to those standards established by the National Electrical Code.

EQUIPMENT AND FUNCTIONAL SYSTEMS
Mechanical and Electrical Requirements

The plumbing, mechanical and electrical requirements for an above-ground pool are minimal. Depending on the climate, a swimming pool water heater may be required. In this event, you must provide a gas line or oil line to the heater. Aside from the needs of the filtration system pump motor, little electrical power is required. This can normally be acquired by the installation of a waterproof outlet within 3 ft. of the pump motor. The circuit should be used solely for the pump to eliminate any interference with the house operations. The circuit should be a mini-

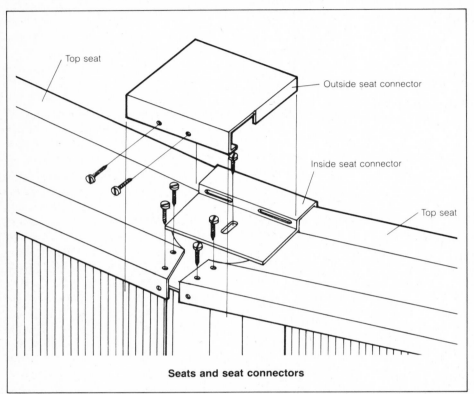

Seats and seat connectors

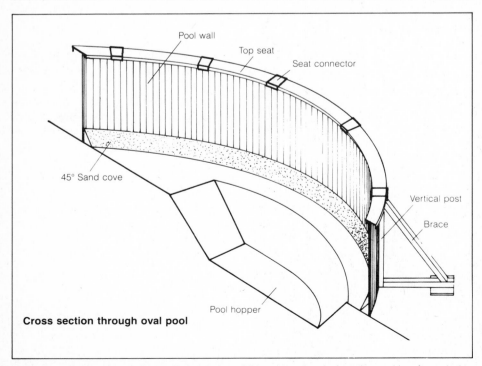

Cross section through oval pool

This cross-section through the pool shows the additional bracing (using diagonal legs) needed to support an oval pool.

Shown are the main housing and the face piece for a skimmer assembly. A gasket goes between the outside face piece and the liner.

The filter basket fits into the skimmer housing base. It can (and should) be removed from the top for daily cleanings.

mum 30 amp, preferably with no. 10 wire. Consult an experienced electrician for local requirements; do not attempt to do the wiring yourself. Most codes require that the filtration system be located at least 3 ft. from the pool proper. No additional power requirements need to be provided unless you are planning to power the deck or patio area around the pool.

Water Supply and Drainage

Most of the water supply and drainage requirements for an above-ground pool resemble those for an in-ground one. Probably the most noticeable difference is that the above-ground does not require a main floor drain, which reduces the amount of piping required. In addition, most models provide for the inlet to enter the pool above the coping instead of below the coping as in the in-ground pool. Other minor differences are noted below.

Drainage An above-ground pool is drained only when repairing or replacing the lining and during the winterizing. If the pool is to be moved to a new site, it is drained. When drainage is necessary, use the filter as a pump. As the water is evacuated, make sure that it drains away from the house and the pool. Try not to undermine the pool by allowing the water to enter into the gravel base.

Filtration System The filtration system operates similarly to that of an in-ground pool. The major difference is in the size of the filter and pump necessary to drive the system. Sand, diatomaceous earth or cartridge filters may be used for an above-ground pool.

To connect the filtration system, remove the knockout plate or hole in the pool wall. Cut the liner to correspond to the opening. The skimmer fits into the opening and extends down below the top of the pool wall. Flexible pipe connects the skimmer. Remove this and the filter and place it in storage in order to prevent damage. The filter size is determined in a similar fashion to that of an in-ground filter system. An 8- to 10-hour filtration cycle is often recommended. Always select the filter and pump based on your pool size; do not oversize.

Enclosures Above-ground pools do not usually have enclosures for the mechanical equipment. If there is a deck, the filtration system is placed underneath to conceal it partially. Any filter system needs to be easily accessible and cannot be tightly enclosed, since the filter must be no further than 3 ft. away from the pool. Generally the filter is left to stand alone.

The skimmer door must be free to move. The water level (indicated by horizontal marks) will be about 2 inches below the top of the face piece.

An inlet hose connects at the midpoint of the filter, with the outlet at the top. The opening at the base is for filter backwashing.

BUILDING AN ABOVE-GROUND POOL

Always assemble the structure exactly as the manufacturer's instructions indicate. There is little room for any deviation from the instructions, since otherwise the panels will not fit or connect properly. Read and completely understand the assembly sequence. If you are in doubt about the instructions, consult your kit supplier. If you decide to build an above-ground pool yourself, get some help; you may need one or two additional hands.

This discussion concentrates on site preparation and assembly of a circular 18-ft. diameter pool with a deep end. The methods also apply to other pool sizes, both circular and oval.

DESIGN
Make sure you see as many different models in at least three showrooms or sites. Compare assembly instructions and the features provided for the price. Also compare dealers, since you will probably be depending on them for information and for future supplies.

TOOLS AND MATERIALS
In additon to the pool kit, you will need the following items: nails (2½ in. long); 12x12 patio blocks (if necessary); ball of heavy string; bag of 3 in. clothespins; 2x2x4s; duct tape; 3 wood stakes (2x2x2x18 in.); mason's sand.

You will also need these tools: 48-in. carpenter level; hammer; flat end shovel; 12-in. tape measure; garden rake; mechanical or hand tamper; garden roller; carpenter's saw; 2⅞-in. wrenches; sifting screen to remove pebbles; sharp knife.

Once you have gathered all the tools and materials, lay out the pool kit to make sure all the pieces are there.

Step 1: Site Preparation
Pick a day to work that is not windy or overcast. The sun helps dry out the ground, and the lack of wind helps when installing the pool wall. Keep in mind the size of the inside diameter of the pool (in this case, 18 ft.) and the clearance radius, which adds an additional foot to each side. The diameter then equals 20 ft.

Drive a stake in the exact center of the pool. With a shovel and a depth-level tool, remove the topsoil or sod in the entire clearance radius area. Fasten the depth-leveling tool to the center stake and rotate it around the area until you achieve level. Check this by placing the carpenter's level on the leveling tool. Do not attempt to fill in low spots. Use those as the base elevation and then lower the high spots to the low ones. Make sure that the area is free of pebbles, gravel, sticks, stones and roots; these could puncture the liner.

Redwood pool surrounds offer moisture-resistant properties as well as good looks.

A-Brace for an above-ground pool resembles the in-ground one; the base gives stability.

External water pressure in an oval pool could cause side wall cave-ins. Flat metal plates added in front of the guide rails are filled with concrete to reduce liner side thrust.

Step 2: Deep Pool Excavation

This pool will include a deep swimming area, which is 36 in. deeper than at the perimeter area.

POOL EXCAVATION DEPTHS

Fig.	Pool Diameter					
	15′	16′	18′	21′	24′	28′
A	8′6″	9′	10″	11′6″	13′	15′
B	7′6″	8′	9′	10′6″	12′	14′
C	6′	7′3″	8′3″	9′9″	11′3″	13′3″
D	3′6″	4′	4′6″	5′6″	7″	9′
E	4′	4′	4′	4′	6′	6′
F	1′	1′	2′	3′	3′	3′
G	2′6″	3′	2′6″	2′6″	4′	6′
H	3′3″	3′3″	3′9″	4′3″	4′3″	4′3″
J	2′	2′6″	3′	3′	3′	3′

From the inside of the clearance radius circle, measure 30 in. toward the center. This will form the outside edge of the deep pool area. Using the dimensions given in the chart, with the center as a reference, stake out the deep pool area. The maximum depth of the deep area will be 36 in. below the excavated floor of the pool. Keep in mind that you are shaping the deep pool area to the desired form. Remove the dirt slowly until the desired shape is achieved. Once again, do not try to fill in low spots. They will simply wind up as soft areas and produce a deformed shape under the pool.

When the bottom is shaped, smooth and consolidate the entire area with a mechanical tamper. Check the level again and smooth out all rough spots.

Step 3: Installation of Bottom Rail

Using as a reference the stake that should still be in place in the center of the excavated area, mark out the inside pool radius with string. Assemble the bottom framework (the vertical end cap and the bottom rail). Form the circle by sliding the bottom rail into the vertical end cap piece. Complete the circle and adjust until the dimension is equal all the way around.

Sand is placed up to side forms and smoothed, but not over the guide rails.

To smooth sand, begin at side ledges, move into deep end and then do the shallow end.

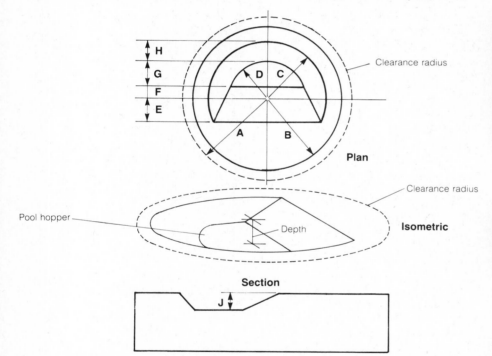

When staking out and excavating the deep pool area, the maximum depth will be 36 inches below the excavated floor of the pool.

Unroll the pool wall panel; place in the rail; metal clips hold the ends together.

For a bottom rail and post support in unstable soil, the base lies on a concrete block.

Project continued on next page

If the soil is not very stable, place one patio block under each vertical end cap; center each block. Make sure that the rail and entire bottom assembly are level.

Step 4: Installation of Wall Panels

Position the wall panel so that the directional arrow printed on the panel points upward. Begin by installing the end of the wall at the center of a vertical end cap. Uncoil about 6 ft. of the wall panel at a time and insert it into the groove in the bottom rail. Try not to dislodge the bottom rail during the process. Complete the entire perimeter. If the ends do not meet, adjust the bottom rails until the ends just touch.

Keep the two end pieces together while you slide on the joint piece over the formed ends of the panel wall sections. Once in place, the joint piece should be even with the top of the formed hooks on the wall. If the joint piece does not slide on easily, adjust the bottom rails. When the joint is in place, measure the inside radius.

Oval Pool Variation In this case, brace post before placing the wall.

Step 5: Installation of Vertical Supports

At each vertical end cap, install the vertical support. Properly seat the vertical over the end cap and use the screws provided to fasten the lower piece. Complete this procedure for the rest of the pool. Check the radius alignment to keep the wall plumb and level.

At this point, the skimmer and water

Pour a sand edge along the wall and floor after the side wall panel and coping are in place. Rake to a 45° angle between floor and wall; pour cement over the shaped end, moistening lightly. When hard, this will protect the liner.

Place end caps around pool radius

Position bottom end caps, which will hold the support posts, around the pool perimeter.

Bottom rail installation

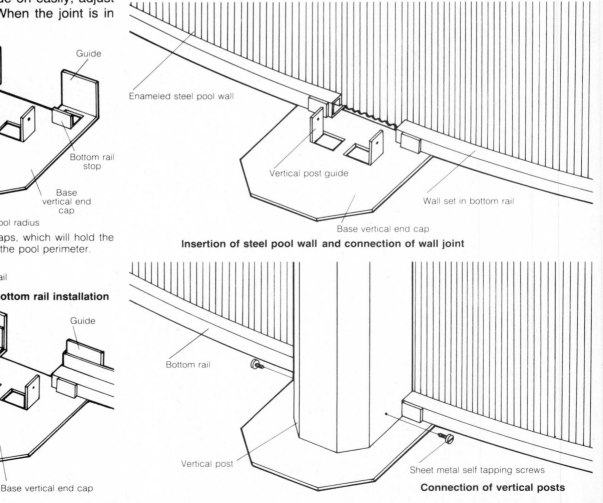

Insertion of steel pool wall and connection of wall joint

Connection of vertical posts

inlet cutouts should be taped closed if you are using over-the-edge devices. If not, tape the edges of the openings using the duct tape. Make sure that the openings are free of burrs.

Step 6: Installation of Upper Vertical End Caps

The upper vertical end caps must be properly seated. The notched end should face toward the center of the pool.

Step 7: Installation of the Seat

You will notice that each vertical end cap has a number of holes in it. Select the correct holes for the 18 ft. pool; otherwise the seats will not fit properly. Using four No. 10x⅜ screws, attach the seats to the vertical end caps. If your particular model does not include the embossed numbers or letters, use a felt tip marker to mark the hole locations.

Attach all the top seats around the entire perimeter of the pool. Then attach the top seat connectors. Attach the inside connector before you slide the exterior connector over the interior. Repeat this procedure until all the top seats are in place. Align all the pieces so they appear to be uniform.

Step 8: Installation of Base Cove

The base cove is a vertical structural element. It prevents the water pressure from forcing the pool liner out from under the bottom rail. In most cases, the manufacturer will not assume any responsibility for the integrity of the pool and the liner if the base cove is omitted.

There are two methods for installing the base cove. The first is to use screened damp earth to produce an edge 6 in. high by 9 in. wide. The second and the more reliable method is to use a preformed cover base from the manufacturer. Purchase the prefabricated preformed base with the kit. It will help greatly in the assembly of the pool and insure successful pool operation.

Step 9: Installation of the Vinyl Liner

Place a level layer of mason's sand over the base of the pool. Tamp the sand well over the entire area. Remove the center stake. Smooth the area again; you might do this with a trowel or similar tool.

Once the entire surface is smooth, place the vinyl liner on top of the seat. The liner should be loose and overhang the outside of the pool by about a foot. Hold that end and unroll down the middle of the pool as you would unroll a carpet.

Begin to work in both directions from where the liner overhangs the edge. Unfold the liner and drape it over the seat and down the outside of the pool about 24 in. The center of the liner should just touch the pool floor in the center only. All other parts of the liner should not yet touch the floor. The bottom edge seam of the liner at this point should be no more than 12 in. from the top seat.

While the liner is uniformly draped

Unfold the vinyl liner and adjust until it just touches the pool bottom. Pull taut and slip the liner under the rope restraint.

over the entire perimeter seat, hold the liner in place with 2 clothspins on the underside of the seat. Clip the liner carefully around the entire seat. Gently place a garden hose in the pool and begin to fill. The liner will stretch as the water begins to cover the bottom. Check the sidewall to make sure that no section is overly taut. Any area that feels tight should be released by unclamping the clothespins in a little and allowing the liner to feed into the pool. Reclamp the clothespins and repeat the procedure around the perimeter. Perform this task slowly, because you are fitting the liner to the shape of the pool and the deep bottom.

As the pool continues to fill, make sure that the liner does not fall into the pool and thus allow the water to escape. Water between the liner and the pool wall can cause pool failure. When the pool has 24 in. of water in it, stop filling.

Retain the liner's upper edge with the rope while filling the pool. When the liner is partially filled, place it under the coping.

As shown, the vinyl liner for an oval pool requires more bracing than for a square or circular one because of greater water pressure.

Project continued on next page

With the help of two to three people, raise and hold up the liner from three seat sections. Remove the attaching hardware at the seat connectors, three seats and three vertical end caps. Make a return hem in the edge of the liner as illustrated. Smooth the liner against the side of the pool wall and secure to the top of the wall by pressing the provided plastic coping piece down over the vinyl liner, which was folded over the top of the wall. Once this is done, place the stabilizer rails over the plastic coping piece. The stabilizer rails come in two pieces, the smaller fitting into the larger. Make sure that the pieces telescope into each other by at least 6 in. Pull all the parts back in position.

Repeat this same procedure for another three sections, making sure that the liner is properly folded and is smooth between each successive section.

Step 10: Completing the Assembly

Once the pool is assembled, with the liner and all the seat sections in place and fully connected, install the skimmer and inlets.

The skimmer assembly comes with a faceplate that is put in front of the liner and through-connected to the skimmer assembly on the outside of the pool. Insert the faceplate and gaskets until firmly seated. Cut out the liner for the opening. Use the inside of the faceplate as the template. This same procedure may be used for the water inlet if it is a through-the-wall type.

Now finish filling the pool up to the level indicated on the faceplate of the skimmer. Finally, connect the filter system and start it according to the manufacturer's instructions.

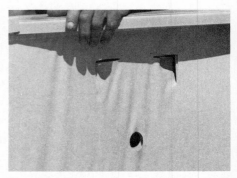

Placing the restraining lip of the vertical post, which restrains and supports the wall and liner, over the top of the wall panel.

Tape the skimmer assembly housing to its opening on the wall panel. Cut the vinyl at the corners and the vacuum opening.

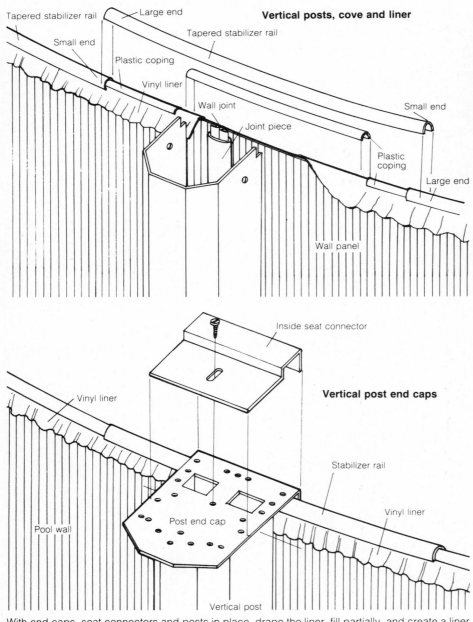

Vertical posts, cove and liner

With end caps, seat connectors and posts in place, drape the liner, fill partially, and create a liner hem with plastic coping. Then add the stabilizer rail.

Screw in the exterior face piece; use brass screws to prevent corrosion. Remove remainder of the liner covering skimmer opening.

9
MANMADE NATURAL PONDS

A Natural Pond

A pond can be either a natural pond, which is a "bulge" in a very large drainage system, or a self-contained pond, which is a body of water that is completely divorced from the hydrology of the area, such as a vinyl liner installation. The self-contained pond can be built anywhere, as long as there is some type of water supply or source and landform and soil material can accommodate a large body of water.

The pond as discussed here refers to a small, enclosed body of water that is smaller than a lake but larger than a pool. We are assuming that it will be used primarily for water recreation and aquaculture. Both the natural and the self-contained pond can be manmade; each has similar requirements for water quality and filtration. This chapter is only applicable

to a very select number of sites. Not everyone has a site of unlimited acreage, nor the time and economic resources to invest in the creation of a pond.

REQUIREMENTS FOR A POND
The Natural Pond

The natural pond utilizes certain topographic features of the landscape, such as a depression, a small river or a stream basin, in which a dam or retaining berm is introduced to contain the water and raise its level to a minimum depth of 6 to 8 ft. If the pond uses a natural water supply, a weir (an obstruction built with a controlling aperature) is used on the outlet side of the pond to allow for overflow. Once the pond begins to fill, the sides of the pond can be faced in a variety of materials, including a sandy beach.

A Self-contained Pond

The self-contained pond does not have the luxury of a natural water supply. However, it still must reflect the topographical features of the landscape. The primary differences between the natural and the self-contained pond is that the self-contained pond is lined with fiber or vinyl sheeting in order to contain the water. The sides of the pond are then finished in a variety of facing materials. The water supply could be from a well or a commercial supplier. This source is supplemented with rainfall and/or a garden hose.

Water Sources

Most natural ponds derive their water from such sources as a slow moving stream or rainfall. A natural spring located in or alongside the pond is also a source.

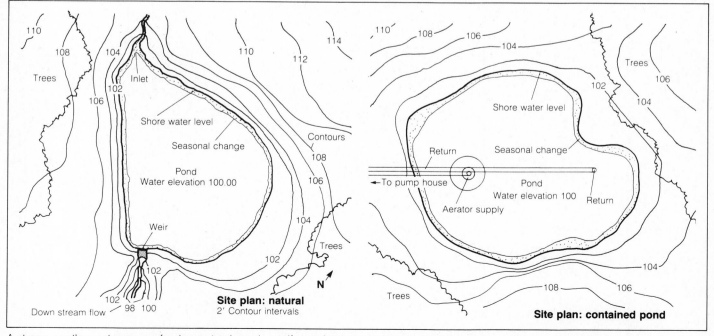

Site plan: natural
2' Contour intervals

Site plan: contained pond

A stream or other water source feeds a natural pond; a self-contained pond needs a circulating system. The shape reflects topography.

The manmade pond also requires a water source in order to avoid stagnation. The usual source is an artesian well, the water table itself, a stream or drainage runoff.

Water Table

If the depression lies below the water table, the hydraulic pressure exerted by the water table will maintain the water level in the pond. In this case, the water may appear to be stagnant or just sitting there but in reality it is a part of a much larger sheet that is moving slowly toward a river or stream. The pond formed as part of the water table will rise and fall seasonally as the water table rises and falls.

A Mechanically Fed Pond This is very expensive. Try to use the natural sources available on the site before resorting to any mechanical solutions. If this is the only choice, an aerator can increase the oxygen content of the water, which can then support a larger amount of aquatic life. The rainwater that leaches into the pond will provide certain chemicals that are necessary to support life in the pond. Preferably, the water should not be chlorinated. No drainage requirements are necessary if the pond is self-contained.

Consistency If the water source dries up during the summer months, the level of the pond will diminish accordingly. If the water level falls to the point that the overall temperature of the pond increases, the pond life may die. Therefore, try to choose a source that is consistent. If a prolonged dry spell is in the offing, there is little that can be done other than to periodically refresh the water from another source.

Controlling Water Level The water level of the pond should be kept fairly constant. This can be achieved by raising and lowering a weir. This device is placed on top of a dam to control the amount of water passing over the dam. In the spring, when water is more abundant, raising the level of the pond can help compensate for summer evaporation and possible dry spells.

To integrate the pond with the site and to strengthen the pond's sides, you can edge the container with large, natural boulders.

When you plan the position of a pond, be sure to investigate the runoff and drainage patterns to avoid potential pollution problems.

Runoff and Drainage

Most manmade ponds are located in areas that tend to collect water. Therefore, the drainage patterns of the site channel rainwater or effluent into the pond. This may be a blessing or a fatal error. The water that is being discussed is not absolutely clean, but the pond can tolerate a certain amount of impurities. However, if the runoff is full of pesticides and the like, the effects are obviously negative ones.

Pollution Problems Because of drainage and runoff patterns, you must take a large area into consideration when you plan. You cannot simply look at the area that is right around the site. A broad view will help you know if a stream-fed pond will overflow after a heavy rainfall or if the pond will be polluted because someone upstream is leaching undesirable material into the water supply. To determine the quality of the water, send samples to the state for evaluation.

If the site is to be situated near livestock, the effluent from the area could leach into the pond and increase the algae content to the point that the pond could no longer survive. If this situation is unavoid-

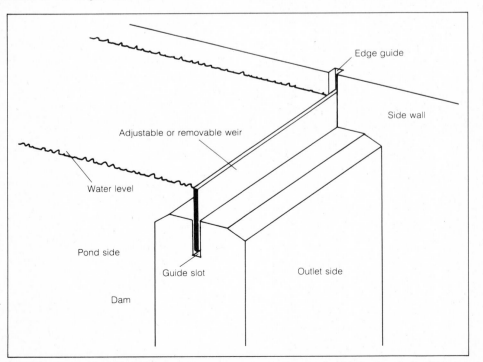

To maintain a fairly constant water level in a natural pond, utilize a weir. This design can be slid open or closed to control the amount of water going over the dam.

able, you may have to increase the size of the pond so that algae controlling elements are able to maintain a "balanced" condition.

Cycling

Cycling is the life process in the pond water itself. The cycling process relies on the energy of the sun. With this energy, living material is built up from inorganic constituents. The matter decomposes into its original components, which are then available for the start of another life cycle. This continuous chain of events is ultimately what supports other life forms in the pond water environment.

Temperature

The temperature level of the water must be moderate enough to support a temperature gradient from the water surface to the bottom of the pond. This temperature stratification allows different organisms to exist at various levels. If the pond is too shallow, the stratification tends to disappear because of a reduced temperature gradient. The temperature rises and destroys the plant and aquatic life.

Problems Due to Climate

Whether a "self-contained" or "bulge" pond is selected, the climate has a lot to do with its longevity. In areas that are very arrid, the evaporation rate may be such that a pond will dry out or become saline in a very short period of time. In such a setting, you should not construct a pond.

If a pond is located in a very cold climate, evaporation is not a concern, but you may have to increase the depth in order for the pond to support aquatic life. A shading tree may be desirable for the enjoyment of the pond, but if the pond is located in a region where acid rain is a problem, the leaching of the rain into the pond could make the pond environmentally dead.

Soil and Container

The structure of soil ranges from organic material to solid bedrock. Within these extremes lie the soil types that are most often encountered: gravel, sands, silts and clays. Normally, each site has a profile of a mixture with some of each one. There is no one best soil type for a pond. A combination of factors maintain the water level

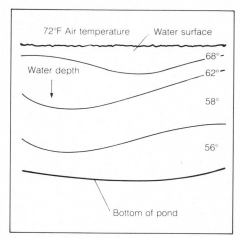

To operate successfully, the pond must be deep enough to allow for temperature gradients. Each level supports different organisms.

in a pond, not simply the soil. However, the pond must have a liner. It is the impervious quality of the lining of the pond that maintains the integrity of the container.

A Natural Liner Most natural ponds have many layers of sediment that over the years have formed to create an impervious lining. The newly constructed pond requires some help since it does not have this liner nor does it have the benefit of time to make it watertight. The lining most frequently used is clay. Clay is unique in that it can hold a tremendous amount of liquid without allowing the fluid to move from or sink into the pond. After the water is in place, the liner is added by sprinkling the clay over the water. When a clay liner is introduced into a newly formed pool, the pool water generally becomes stabilized.

Vinyl Liner For ponds that are self contained or excavated in areas in which the bottom of the pool will not sustain any form of clay liner, you may have to use a manmade vinyl or rubberized liner to retain the water in the cavity. This is an expensive alternative to the more natural manmade liner.

Information Sources There are several sources available that will aid you in determining the adaptability of the soil for a pond. Probably the most used is the soils engineer. This person can be retained privately or contacted through your state's Department of Natural Resources. This office will also provide soils and hydrology maps that will give you useful information about possible locations and requirements of your site. Another source for soil information is a soil or water well-drilling firm. These people generally have a high level of expertise in identifying the soil type and the level of the water table.

Topographical Issues

The shape and the size of the land determine the feasibility of locating a pond on a site. To determine the suitability of your site you need some perspective on the physical shaping of the land. The first, and probably the most expensive, way to determine this is to perform a site survey to locate all physical features. The survey records the elevational differences of the site. The second method, which is by far less expensive and time consuming, is to obtain a United States Geological Survey map of your particular quadrant. This shows similar information to that in a site

The container of a pond prevents the water from seeping away. The best type of container is a natural clay fill. This is sprinkled over the water after the pond is constructed.

survey, but is not as detailed. The survey maps may be more than adequate for your particular purpose.

The topography of the site is the vertical and horizontal shaping of the land. The device that is most often used to measure the rise and fall of the land is the contour. This is simply a line that traces a given height over a site. On the USGS map, each contour will be 5 to 10 ft. apart vertically. As can be seen here, the contours can be shaped in a variety of ways. The closer the contours, the sharper or steeper the drop or rise in elevation. Look for what appear to be depressions in the landform, a stream bed or pool area, a part of the property that is lower than the rest of the surrounding area or a particular feature that could contain water.

The USGS map or the survey map will indicate if there is a high water table and its location. This information can also be obtained by referring to hydrology maps of your quadrant. If the area does have a high water table, the location of the pond may be predetermined for you, since a dip or excavation that extends below the water table will assure you of a workable pond.

ENVIRONMENTAL PROTECTION CODES AND ASSISTANCE

The ponds that are described in this chapter rely on the natural landform for their existence. In doing so, they change, or have the potential for changing, the balance of the landscape. If a water stream or small river is blocked or its path changed, the environmental protection laws of each state come into play. Always verify what laws are applicable before you proceed with any plans.

Some of the regulations can offer you valuable assistance. As you are comtemplating the placement of the pond and its size and shape, the state Department of Natural Resources or its equivalent would like to assist you in your endeavor. Most states have incorporated into law wetlands preservation acts or similar legislation. These laws protect water resources in any natural form. They are to protect the public interest, but also to assist the property owner in preserving and enhancing those natural features.

NATURAL FEATURES

Each site can be said to have a unique "signature," certain identifiable, intangible features that contribute to a site's overall qualities. A stand of trees shaped a particular way is seldom replicated on any other site. The shape of the land relative to a stream or rock outcrop is a permanent "signature" and thus should be incorporated into the overall design.

Look to the site for the clues. By observing and carefully recording the natural features, textures and scale of the land, the placement of the pond will certainly become another natural feature once it has been fully integrated.

The shape of a hill or land surrounding the pool can be further developed by shaping protective fencing, plantings or even earth berms. Privacy or protection from the wind can be achieved by planting deciduous trees on axis to the wind direction. The location of out buildings can also be used to achieve a high level of visual privacy.

PONDSIDE CONCERNS
Pond Uses and their Requirements

An adequately sized pond will support almost all water activity that a swimming pool will. As long as the pond has a continuous water source and there is some associated water movement, the natural filtration system should work effectively.

Safety

The safety features associated with a pond are similar to those of a swimming pool. The most effective way to prevent water-related accidents is an effective water safety program. If specific instructions are necessary for the use of the pond, or certain areas are off limits to swimmers, make sure that the rules are clearly posted, that the areas are cordoned off and that all swimming activity is supervised. It is better to be safe than sorry.

Pond-related Structures

If adequate depths are provided, the pond should be able to accommodate all but the deepest of diving board requirements, as well as a slide and other water-related accessories.

One of the unique features afforded by a pond is the potential for a float. The float is an island unto itself and has always been the center of activity of any pond. Often incorporated into the float is a stair and a diving board. The float is usually anchored. It can be homemade or purchased and provides the more proficient swimmer with a haven from the shore.

BUDGET

The overall cost of a pond, when based on a per square foot basis, is quite inexpensive. However, since a pond is significantly larger than a swimming pool it will cost more on a lump sum basis. On the other hand, you will be getting far more in terms of water volume and usage. The main expenditure is the excavation of the pond itself. This may require several large earth movers to perform the work. An experienced excavator will use the proper equipment; however, the machinery is expensive to rent.

If any concrete work must be done, such as for a ramp, retaining wall or pond facing walls, include those costs in the overall figure. If the site requires a clay liner, you will need several dozen sacks of dry clay.

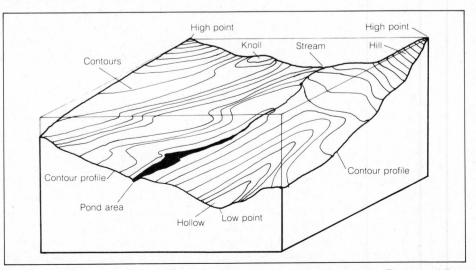

To select the best spot for a pond, you will need a contour map of your area. The curved lines indicate high and low locations as well as water supply and drainage patterns.

CONSTRUCTING A SMALL NATURAL POND

To demonstrate the particular requirements of the design and construction of a small pond, a 5-acre piece of land with a year-round stream was selected. The pond will function as a swimming pond and storage area for irrigation purposes.

Step 1: The Site Survey
The first step is to determine what part of the site is suitable for the pond. Begin by contacting a local licensed surveyor who will "shoot" your site. The result of the survey will be a drawing at a scale of from 1 in. equals 20 ft. up to 1 in. equals 250 ft. The drawing will show all the contours, physical site features and water source locations (if any). The site plan, as it is known, will be based on a certain elevation above mean sea level. The surveyor will leave a bench mark on the property so that when actual excavation is performed, all contour elevations will be based on the same benchmark or reference point.

Step 2: Information Gathering
Once the site plan has been completed, you should contact the state for hydrology information as well as soil information. At the same time check to make sure that the applicable state or local codes are adhered to.

In the event that hydrology maps and/or soil identification maps are not available for your region, you may have to retain the services of a driller to determine the level of the water table below the ground elevation and the type of soil material underlying the surface. The drillers will drill at least one hole and measure the water level. Make sure that a reading of the water table is taken after 24 hours. That will provide a more accurate reading.

Step 3: Developing the Design
Once the survey is complete and you have decided on a location, you are ready to develop the design. In this example, a 22,500 sq. ft. area has been selected on the lower portion of the site. As can be seen from the illustration, the lower area is fed by a brook that delivers enough water to service the pond on a year-round basis. The

lower end of the site will have to be built up with a barrier in order to retain the water to the indicated elevation. The pond design should allow for a natural rise and fall of the water table by at least two feet either way. This will account for any seasonal changes in the volume of the water.

To further encapsulate the feeling of the site, which is small scale with very little primary growth, a small island will be placed on the north side of the

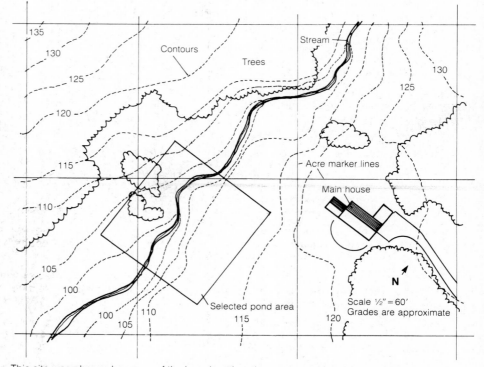

This site was chosen because of the low elevation, the presence of a stream to feed the pond, and the relationship to the house. The size will allow for water recreation.

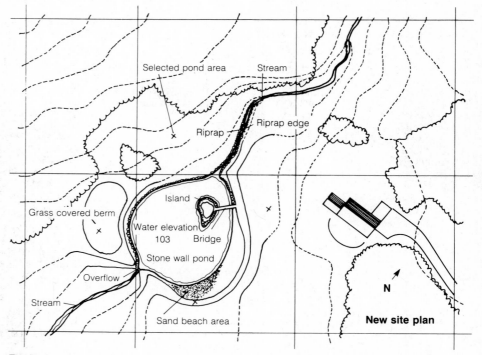

The final design, including an island, will look like this. The riprap edging, a foundation wall of loosely laid broken rock, will support the stream and pond walls.

Project continued on next page

pond. The owner desires to install a bridge over the water to the island and have the island large enough to accommodate a small gazebo with several deciduous trees.

Preparing a Rough Sketch Once the scope of the project has been determined, make a copy or tracing of the site plan and prepare the rough sketches that outline the actual water level desired, the shape of the island and any other development such as a beach area or locations where the sides of the pond are to be reinforced with a stone wall.

Final Drawings Once these drawings have been completed and you have finished the sketches to the point that they include all the details, retain a draftsman or engineer to complete the drawings that you must submit for a permit. The state or local authorities will require a stamped drawing by a licensed engineer or architect in order to approve the work.

Designating Materials The final drawings should also indicate the choice of paving or surfacing materials to be used. The illustration shows a cross-section through the pond indicating the type of materials required to complete the design. Notice that the overflow pipe is a circular cast concrete pipe standing vertically just below the surface of the highest point desired. If the water level is to be raised above that point, a collar can be installed on the end.

Step 4: Acquiring a Construction Permit

After the drawings are completed and stamped, submit them to the proper authority at the state and/or local level. Part of the submission will be a requirement to fill out an Environmental Impact Statement. This may vary from state to state. The EIS simply requires you to describe the scope of the project, what it is to do, what it may effect and how you are planning to accomplish it. Once the permits are issued, you may begin the project. The permit process can take a long time.

Step 5: Excavating

After you receive the permit, the excavation may begin. It is strongly recommended that you retain an experienced excavator, as he will know the proper type of machinery to use. In cases in which the ground water is excessive, the excavation may be performed with a drag line. Here, the brook will be diverted slightly until the proper depth of the pond is achieved. The material removed from the excavation will be placed in the low end opening as a dam. This material will be further compacted so that it will not fail when the water reaches the design height.

Step 6: Compacting the Excavation

Once all the rough excavation has been completed and the rocks have been removed and placed under the island, the finish excavation can be undertaken. This part of the process requires the careful compaction and shaping of all the underwater surfaces in order to reduce seepage when the pool is filled. For those surfaces below water, this is not feasible. If your design includes a sand beach, now is the time to place it in the appropriate area.

Step 7: Finishing

Once the finish excavation has been completed, the finishing materials and overflow pipe can be installed. If a stone wall was selected to finish the edge of the pond, now is the time to install it. The stone, which can be field stone, should be placed into a wood form of the desired height. This is normally 8 to 12 in. above the mean water level. The stones are packed tightly into the wood forms and then a stiff concrete is placed around the stones. This produces an excellent surface edge at a reasonable cost. If severe freezing and thawing are possible, the placement of two or three No. 6 reinforcing bars in the stone layers will tie the wall together more effectively. The bars do not guarantee that the wall will not crack.

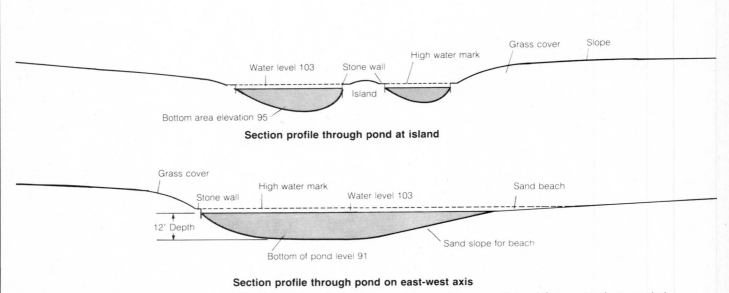

Section profile through pond at island

Section profile through pond on east-west axis

The sketches and drawings you prepare should anticipate both high and low water conditions, as well as reinforcement where needed.

The island can now be built up. Place gravel into the cavities around the stones forming the base of the island. Follow this with 2 to 3 ft. of topsoil. Tamp the topsoil well to reduce settlement of the earth around the stones.

Also install the overflow at this time. The outfall from the pond should follow the line of the original brook. To do this, you must pour a concrete box with the outfall pipe located out of one side and the overflow pipe emerging from the top.

Step 8: Filling the Pond

Once the finishing materials are in place, allow the brook to fill the pond. Once the pond begins to fill (the process may take several weeks) you may have to further increase the watertightness of the pond in order to reduce the seepage. Keep in mind that no matter how well the base was compacted, it is still quite porous. To fill the pores of the bottom, sprinkle granular or powdered clay over the filled portion of the pond. You may do this in layers. Once the clay has been sprinkled over the water it may take several weeks for it to subside enough to see the results.

Step 9: Final Clay Seeding

After the water has reached the level of the outfall (this may take a full season) you may have to apply a final seeding of the pond with clay if the fill rate is not fast enough. In the interim, swimming and other activities are permitted.

Final Note

While the description has referred to a specific design, the procedures described are similar to many other types of pond designs and should give you full seasonal use of the pond on a year-round basis.

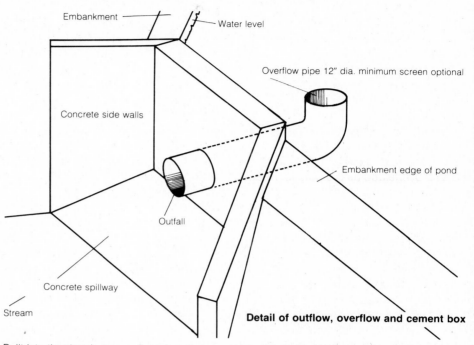

Detail of outflow, overflow and cement box

Built into the dam is an overflow pipe. Its top ensures the desired high water level, which can be raised by a collar extension.

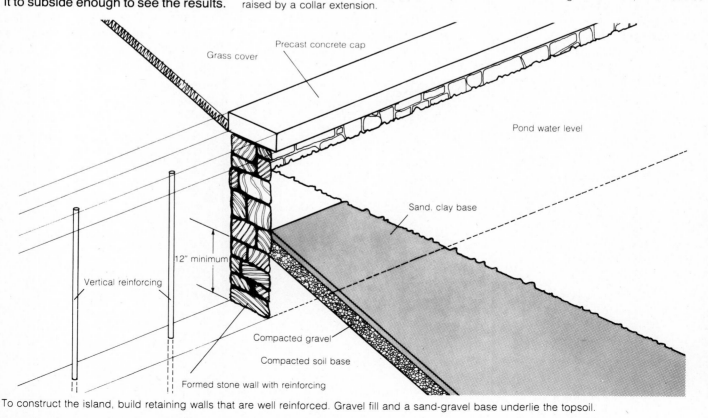

To construct the island, build retaining walls that are well reinforced. Gravel fill and a sand-gravel base underlie the topsoil.

10
POOLSIDE STRUCTURES: CABANA, LANAI, GAZEBOS, FENCING

The deck or patio around a pool can be further enhanced by an area for lounging, eating, sunbathing, entertaining or changing. Poolside structures, such as a lanai, gazebo or cabaña, will help create a water recreation center in your own backyard.

TYPES OF POOLSIDE STRUCTURES

There are many different types of poolside structures. Some of the more interesting ones are free standing and can be adapted to a variety of yard dimensions and shapes. These structures are normally of wood, which means they can be easily built by the home craftsperson. In some cases, the structures can be expanded as space requirements increase.

The Gazebo

The traditional gazebo is an enclosed, lightweight, free standing wood structure that has always stood off by itself somewhere in a garden as a place to which people go to contemplate or simply to enjoy the sun and breeze. A gazebo added to a poolside environment becomes more than just an observation space. It provides tremendous entertainment potential.

The gazebo is generally no larger than 12x12 ft. and can be as small as 5x5 ft. The shapes may vary considerably. The most common shape has a raised central monitor flanked by pitched roofs or a cupola sitting atop a gable roof. Some are circular, but these are more difficult to construct. A gazebo requires very little in the way of a foundation, and its design is flexible enough to fit any motif. Most often, it is one story in height, with the possibility of an attic space or viewing platform.

The Cabaña

Cabañas almost always sit directly next to the swimming pool area. They are free-standing, single-story structures most often constructed of wood or masonry. The cabaña can be a very simple structure or as elaborate as needed, designed to fit a variety of motifs. It can be fully enclosed or a simple outdoor privacy shelter.

The purpose is primarily to house changing space and shower rooms. It also can hold the swimming pool mechanical equipment and storage for pool accessories or lawn equipment. A cabaña is ideal if there are lots of people using the swimming pool on a regular basis, or if the pool is some distance from the main house.

The cabaña varies in size from a 4x5 ft. up to a 9x12 ft. shed. It can have doors, solid or translucent walls, and a roof. It

This gazebo made of redwood is designed to provide both ventilation and shade.

A fence can serve a number of useful functions — from providing security to simple decoration. Here lattice panels fill in the open space between stringers to provide both.

needs a minimal foundation and can be placed on a concrete slab. If you install a shower and/or toilet combination, you must provide for water supply and sewage. Some owners have expanded the definition of a cabaña by installing an outdoor fireplace, refrigerator and even a small kitchen.

The Lanai

The lanai originated in Hawaii as an outdoor room that was pleasant to be in no matter what the weather, had a beautiful view, and provided shelter from the prevailing winds and the harsh sun. The more modern versions attempt to incorporate all those features in what is an open patio space that is semi-enclosed with a sunscreened rook and wall system. The modern version of the lanai has evolved to accommodate a variety of climates.

The lanai is most often constructed of wood posts and rafters with a lattice or lathe open roof. If your climate is mild, a lanai may offer just a filter for the sun and protection from the prevailing breezes. In a wetter climate, the lattice can be replaced with a translucent corrugated plastic or fiberglass panel to channel away the rain. In a northern climate with fewer warm days, a glass roof panel, instead of the lattice, can focus the sun's energy to warm the space below. In southern climates, where the insect problem is severe, the addition of screens in place of or in addition to the wood walls transforms the lanai into a ''Florida room.'' Where the sunlight is very intense, the addition of canvas coverings or solid thatching provides welcome relief during the hotter parts of the day.

The lanai has no specific size, but is generally rectangular in form with a roof that is pitched similar to a leanto. It is a free-standing structure that can be attached to the house or act as a transition between the house and the swimming pool. It is a marvelous space in which to entertain, and it is affordable since the degree of enclosure is entirely up to the designer. The lanai is almost always 7 to 8 ft. in height and constructed of outdoor wood such as cypress, redwood, treated pine or cedar. Inset side wall panels can be constructed from a variety of materials — canvas, paper, screen, glass or plexiglass.

Fences and Screens

A fence or screen is one of the most economical and frequently used poolside structures. A fence consists of vertical members; a screen has openings in the framing that are set so as to allow air and light to penetrate. Most often a wood construction that is 3 ft. to 7 ft. high, a fence is an excellent solution to a lot hemmed in on both sides with other houses. A pool owner needs security and privacy; a fence or screen helps achieve that end. There are fences of wood, chain link, and masonry, as well as those that look like walls. Screens usually are of wood. Each will do a satisfactory job. Select a fence design and material in terms of the total landscaping. The best design offers both attractiveness and privacy.

The foundation for a fence consists of little more than a series of holes, 24 to 36 in. deep, in which the vertical posts are set. Once the posts are in place, the remaining part of the fence is mounted. Integrate the fence with a gazebo, cabaña or lanai to tie all the elements together and achieve greater unity of design.

CLIMATIC DESIGN ISSUES

When selecting a poolside structure, consider what kind of seasonal changes are going to occur and how you will use the structure.

Placement and Structure

A gazebo or cabaña should be placed according to the orientation of the swimming pool to the sun. If the pool is on an east-west axis, there will be maximum sun exposure to the south along that axis. Because any structure to the south of the pool would shade the pool, it would not be advisable to place a cabaña or gazebo there unless there were extenuating circumstances, such as privacy or access requirements. The coolest part of the site is to the north. If the swimming pool is located on the north side of the house, there will be places that do not receive direct sunlight. Because the north face is normally quite sheltered, it may not require an overhead structure except as protection from the elements.

The overhead structure may be placed so that it extends the amount of time it can be used in a season. For example, if the swimming pool is located to the south face of the site or house, a cabaña could be placed to the east and connected by a lanai with the main house. This would provide not only additional space, but an alternative to the constant southern sun. Extending a deck or patio in combination with a lanai can offer the owner the alternative between types of sunlight during the daylight hours. In this way, the placement of the poolside structure takes advantage of climatic differences to the benefit of the user.

The colder the climate, the more desirable sun access will be. The hotter the climate, the more protection is required. A very windy orientation becomes a perfect location for a cabaña, and possibly a fence, to act as a windbreak. The gazebo, when placed adjacent to a pool, may provide some protection from the sun for the swimmer.

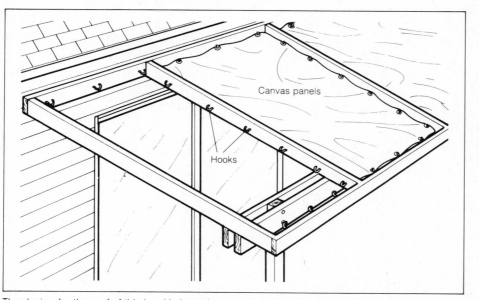

Canvas panels

Hooks

The design for the roof of this lanai is based upon open window frames. For protection from winds and rain, canvas panels can be lashed into place. The walls are of plywood.

Types of Climates

Here are some general guidelines according to the type of region you live in.

Northern Climates Your primary requirement is to extend swimming days and block prevailing winds. We suggest that you use masonry walls and pool enclosures that are heated, in combination with a patio or deck.

Arrid Climates Your major concern is shelter from the sun. Areas should be open to catch the breeze. We suggest a lightweight lanai to encircle the pool, and open masonry walls or canvas shades.

Temperate Climates You can use a variety of shelters. Gazebos are one excellent choice in this climate.

Southern Climates Plan structures that will offer protection from insects and from rain. We suggest using screen enclosures along a lanai motif. Gazebos also work very well.

SITE CONSIDERATIONS

In previous chapters, we stressed the importance of locating the swimming pool in areas that were not subjected to unusual climatic variations. A southern orientation and plenty of open sun access into the site were considered desirable. The poolside structure, whether a lanai, gazebo or cabaña, should enhance the previous design decisions. For more information on the placement, orientation and organization of a swimming pool area, refer to Chapters 1 and 2.

Soil Conditions and Types

Your local pool dealer, excavator or contractor should be consulted as to the best foundation for your particular type of soil. Most of the poolside structures are lightweight enough so that the foundation requirements are relatively simple. Any area of the site that has been determined as satisfactory for the installation of a swimming pool should be more than satisfactory to support a poolside structure.

Relationship with Existing Structures

Of all the structures that are involved in the design of a swimming pool environment, the lanai is the one structure that will come in contact with the house or garage. The gazebo or cabaña are normally free standing units. Probably the most visually important aspect of attaching a lanai to an existing structure is the compatability of materials. The use of similar or complementary materials, such as brick and wood, or similar types of wood together, reduces potential problems that might occur in the future. The lanai roof should pitch away from the structure to which it is connected to reduce leakage in the main structure. The slope also keeps a solid lanai roof free of debris.

Building Permits

Prior to the construction of any of the projects, ask your local building inspector if a building permit or certificate is required. You will probably need to submit a drawing or verbal description indicating the location, size and materials to be used. In some localities, each phase of the work must be inspected once it has been completed.

Always make sure that the project to be built is away from any underground utility and well inside the property setbacks. If you are installing a fence in addition to the above project, make sure that your community does not regulate the height of the fences. A visit to the building inspector's office will answer a lot of your questions.

COST COMPARISONS

After the initial investment in a swimming pool and the necessary pool accessories, it is sometimes difficult to increase that cost by a building poolside structure. However, compared to the primary investment in the swimming pool, the additional amount is not great and will represent a small percentage of the total figure.

If it is outfitted with showers and toilet room, a cabaña can be the costliest structure. A beach house or cabaña can even include a kitchen, lighting, television room, changing rooms and even a sauna. Cabañas also have been known to include laundry rooms. In some installations, the owner felt that the cabaña should be expanded to act as a small guest house for overnight visitors. Such an investment certainly increases the total and future worth of the property.

Then lanai is probably the least expensive poolside structure. Its requirements for materials are minimal, yet it does the most to shade and protect the open spaces below it. The gazebo can be elaborate or simple; the most elaborate gazebo kit can cost as much as a new car. The simplest can be very inexpensive as long as it is not outfitted as a small house. For those who include a spa or a hot tub in the gazebo, the overall price will rise.

THE FINAL TOUCHES

There are less significant but still important finishing touches that should be made to your gazebo, cabaña or lanai. For ex-

An open-sided lanai attached to the side of the house provides shelter and shade. The open-beamed overhang extends the design lines above the steps and shades the edge of the pool.

ample, include lighting to permit after-dark use. For a cabaña, changing-room lights for swimmers are always desirable. While the yard is torn apart during construction, have a licensed electrician install the electrical conduit to the location of the new structure, even though it may be some time before the hookup is completed. The after-the-fact addition of overhead lines is an unsightly solution.

Some aspects of the finer details of design might deal with the selection of appropriate hardware. For example, in a cabaña, select towel bars, door knobs and latches, hinges and vent fans to reflect a particular design motif. Mixing styles and types of hardware lowers the quality and clarity of the overall design. The addition of a decorative weathervane on the top of the cabaña or gazebo is an elegant touch and completes the design. If you desire handrails, the selection and design of the rail should be in keeping with the overall motif. Take care in choosing paint colors. Match the new structure with the main house through a wise selection of color of motifs. Or, use color to differentiate one area of activity from another.

CONSTRUCTION OPTIONS

Poolside structures, by their very nature, are unique and highly customized structures. With an assistant, you can build any of the projects offered here in a couple of weekends. The expense will be minimal. Most of the structures require a foundation and little vertical or supporting structure. The structural skeletons call for standard fasteners available at your local hardware store or lumber yard. Connections are simple butt joints that can be through-bolted or nailed. Once the skeletal structures is up, the rest is simple finish work.

TOOLS AND MATERIALS

In addition to the wood frame members and pieces, the tools necessary to build the above structures include,

A cabaña beside a pool can be a simple changing area or an elaborate living space complete with kitchen. Lighting facilities will extend the cabaña's use into evening hours.

Hammers, finish and framing;
Table saw or skill saw;
Carpenter's level, preferably 48 in.
Hand saw, rough and finish;
Mitre box;
Drill and assorted bits wood, and concrete;
Shovels, rakes;
Wheel barrow;
Sledge hammer;
Screw drivers, pliers, crescent wrench;
Line;
Carpenter's chalk;
Measuring tape, rulers;
Sawhorses;
Transit or line level.

If modifications are made to the structures, such as the addition of special scroll work for the gazebo, additional tools may be required. Nails and nail sizes will be indicated where necessary. It is preferable to purchase the minimum number of nail types to avoid any possible confusion. Exterior nails should all be galvanized, if at all possible. All finish nails should be countersunk and holes filled to avoid staining of the wood.

BUILDING A CONCRETE BASE FOR YOUR PROJECT

Whether you plan to build a cabaña, gazebo or lanai, your project will require a concrete slab on which to sit. The shape will vary according to the construction you are erecting, but the process itself can be generalized.

CONSTRUCTION PROCEDURES

The construction procedures for the base can be applied to all the following projects (except the fence). Once the foundation has been completed, you should be prepared to begin erecting the superstructure, which is where differences show up. From that point on, each project will vary.

Step 1: Preparing the Site

In all cases, the site should be stripped of all topsoil prior to beginning any construction. Building on topsoil will result in settlement and deterioration of the structure, no matter how well it is built. Generally, topsoil is found within the first 6 to 12 in. Remove all of it from the area in which the project is to be constructed. Leave sufficient room so that heavy trucks can get to the site if concrete is being delivered. This may require removing a fence or even a hedge; plan ahead.

Step 2: Laying out the Concrete Base

The concrete slab that is to be dis-

cussed is known as a turned-down slab. It combines the qualities of a concrete slab with a reinforced edge seam that rings the perimeter of the slab. The edge produces a very rigid and stable surface. However, this type of slab is not satisfactory for use in very cold climates where the 16-in. depth of the edge remains above the frost line. As an alternative, you may choose a continuous footing to the correct depth

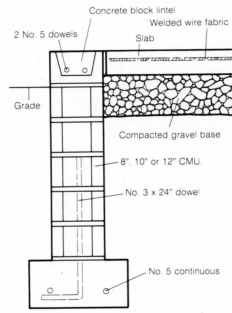

In areas subject to freezing, you need a continuous footing topped with a foundation of concrete blocks. The slab falls between the walls.

topped by concrete block walls finished with a concrete slab.

Using the plans given for your projects, stake out the corners of the slab. In the case of the gazebo, create the square outline first and then stake the intermediate corners. The process of staking out the base and the squaring of it has been discussed in Chapter 3. The steps are the same.

Step 3: Setting Up Batter Boards

Once you square the stakes and string the overall form, you build the batter boards as references for the forming and leveling of the slab. Since the slab will be exposed to the elements, it should be pitched slightly to assist in drainage. The batter boards, however, must be perfectly level.

Take four 2x4 stakes that are 24 in. long and drive them into the ground. Place them outside the previously set corner stakes, in the pattern shown. Once the stakes are firmly in the ground, nail 1x4 or 1x6 boards, approximately 5 to 6 ft. long, to the stakes so that the top of the board is 12 in. above ground level.

Next, level the boards. Use a transit or line level. Make sure that each corner is the same elevation (about 12 in.). Drive the stakes further in the ground to adjust the level. When the boards are level with each other, check them with a carpenter's level to make sure they are true as well as level.

String lines from board to board, making sure that the lines cross over the initial corner stakes that you drove in Step 2. Drive a nail in the top of each board and connect the line to it. Check dimensions again. Once verified, you can remove the initial corner stakes and their line. The site is now ready for the form boards.

Step 4: Installing the Forms

Take 8-ft. sections of 2x10s and place them under the string. Align the inner face of each board with the string. Stake each section with four 2x4s, making sure that the joint will have an additional stake on either side with a backup, as shown. Complete the entire perimeter until all the form boards are in place, nailed and staked.

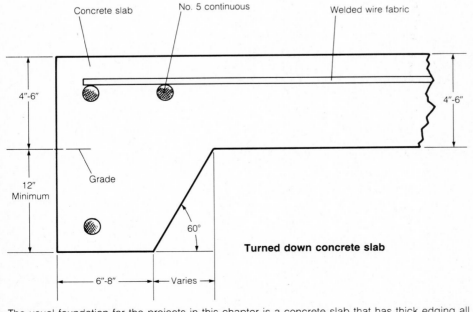

The usual foundation for the projects in this chapter is a concrete slab that has thick edging all around. Run reinforcing rods and mesh through the slab for stability.

Pitching the Slab At this point, create the pitch in the slab. The standard pitch should be ¼ in. per ft. For a 12 ft. pitch, the total drop would be 3 in. It is better to pitch in the short direction, if possible. However, for the gazebo, the perimeter should be the same elevation. The center will be raised so that the pitch is outward (the slab is "crowned.")

Step 5: Bracing the Forms

The form boards must be braced to prevent them from moving during the pour. Drive another 2x4 stake 12 in. behind each stake that is supporting the form. A ⅜ in. CD (Grade C on one side, D on the other) plywood triangle nailed to both stakes will be sufficient to brace the forms. You may substitute 1x2s at top and bottom.

Where joints occur between the form boards, nail a ⅜ in. CD plywood piece over the joint and stake the joint similarly to the others. Then check all dimensions and levels again. It will be too late to check if all things are square and level after the concrete has been poured.

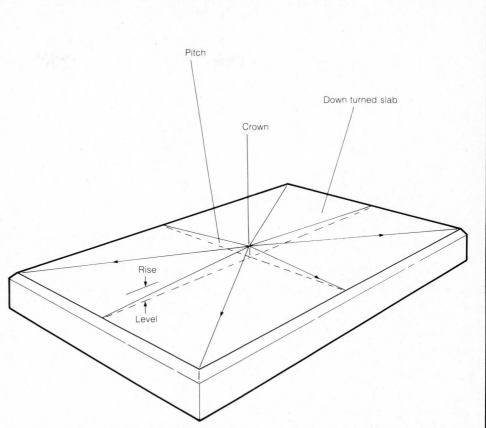

To ensure runoff, the slab must be pitched slightly. Finish the concrete so that the center is ½ in. per ft. higher than the edges. This is called a "crowned" slab.

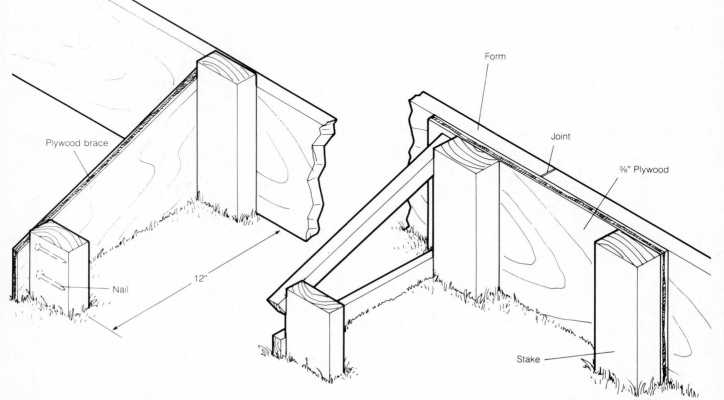

Place formboards. Brace the boards securely with 2x4 braces or triangles of ⅜ in. CD plywood. These keep the forms stable during the pour.

Project continued on next page

Step 6: Excavating the Trenches

Having completed the forms, dig a trench to form the extra thickness of the edge. This trench is 12 in. wide and 16 in. deep. Use the inside face of the form as a guide. Once the trench has been dug to the desired depth, taper the sides by shaving an additional 6 in. away from the top of the trench. Angle this cut down, so that the bottom of the trench remains 12 in. wide.

Reinforcing the Edge Once the trenches have been dug, drive a pair of ⅝ in. deformed reinforcing rods 6 in. apart, every 24 to 48 in. on center. The rods should be 3 in. below the top of the form board.

Step 7: Inserting Horizontal Reinforcing

To place the horizontal reinforcing bars in the trenches, buy 2⅝ in. bars that are 6 in. shorter than the length of the form (the form extends 3 in. on either end). The bars should be placed to the outside of the vertical rods and tied to the verticals using a tying wire. Set the rods at least 3 in. above the bottom of the trench. Repeat this procedure for each of the trenches. Overlap at the corners and wire together.

Repeat this same procedure for the top part of the vertical rods by installing another pair of rods around the perimeter. These should be 3 in. below the top of the form. Tie to the verticals and overlap and tie the ends. All horizontal steel should be in place and well tied. The reinforcing should not move.

Step 8: Adding Gravel Fill

After the rods are in place, place a 4 in. layer of clean gravel with no aggregate larger than 1 in., over the flat portion of the excavation. Make sure that no gravel falls to the bottom of the trenches. Place a 6 mil polyethelene sheet or vapor barrier over the leveled gravel and top with a 6x6 WWF #10/10 welded wire fabric. Tie the fabric to the horizontal rods using the tie wire.

Step 9: Pouring the Concrete

The pouring, placing, finishing and curing of concrete has been covered extensively in previous chapters. For detailed information, refer to Chapter 3.

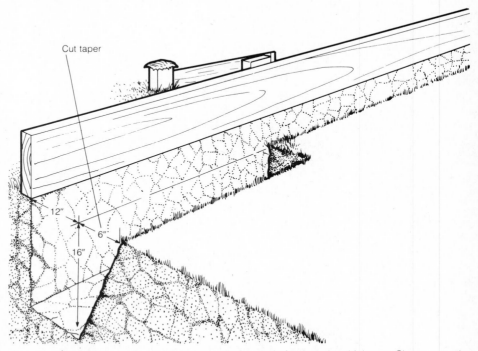

Once the form boards are in place, you can cut the angle for the edge thickness. Shave away the earth so that the top is 6 in. wider than the bottom for a strong edge.

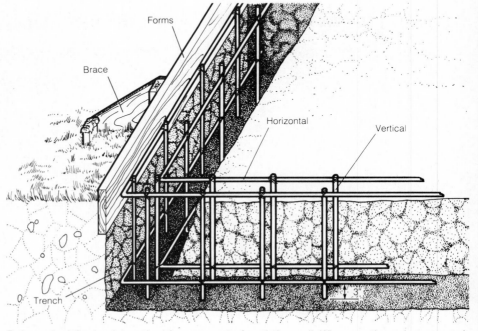

Deformed reinforcing is required for a concrete foundation wall. Whenever the rods cross each other, they must be tied together with wire for firm support.

BUILDING AN 8-SIDED GAZEBO

The gazebo offered here is made of wood. The structure is octagonal and requires a simple foundation. The superstructure is composed of 8 rafters connected at the leg and ridge pole. The roof and side covering are lightweight wood lattice inset panels. The 8 corner posts are directly connected to the concrete base. The gazebo measures approximately 12 ft. by 12 ft. to a side and measures 8 ft. to the top of the support beams.

Step 1: Laying the Foundation

The slab for the gazebo should be octagonal, slightly raised above grade. The center should be higher than the edges so that the slab tapers from the middle to the edges by a total of 1.5 in.

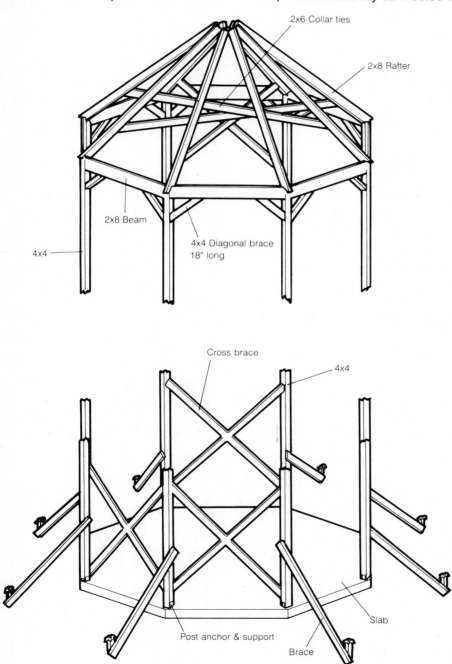

Materials List

8	Anchor (post)
8	½" Lag bolts
8	¾ Expansion shields
8	8' 4x4 Pressure treated posts
	Miscellaneous bracing
8	Post caps
	Assorted 10d galvanized nails
8	2x8 6' long beams
4	2x6 Collar ties 12' long
16	4x4 24" long diagonal ties
8	4x4 Ridge spacers
8	1x4 Fascia 6'
8	1x4 Soffit 6'
16	1x4 Joint caps
1	Finial (optional)
32	2x4x8' (clear studs) to be cut into lattice ⅜x1½
21	2x3 Top and bottom and side rail 6' long
7	1x6 Top piece 6'
14	1x2 Finish trim 6'

During construction of the framing for an eight-sided gazebo, all beams and other members must be securely braced to ensure stability. Collar ties support the roof rafters.

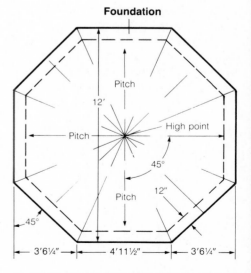

Foundation

As always, the concrete slab must be pitched for drainage, as shown.

Project continued on next page

Step 2: Installing the Post Anchor Bolts

To begin the procedure, locate the actual centerline of each post. Use carpenter's chalk to first mark the exact center of the floor slab. Once the center has been located, string a line between opposing corners in order to locate the specific centerline of each post position. Once the post center point has been determined, install the anchor bolt. This procedure will be repeated 8 times, once for each post. Two in. inward from the edge of the slab, install a ¾ in. lead expansion shield by drilling ¾ in. into the cured concrete to the necessary depth. The shield is installed by placing the bolt into the shield or using a setting tool and hammering it in place. Once in place, the shield should not move. Repeat for each post.

Step 3: Placing the Posts

After the anchor bolts have been installed, set the 4x4 post anchors. These post anchors should be installed with an offset washer to allow later adjustment if necessary. Install the post support inside each post anchor.

When all the post anchors and supports are in position, install the posts. Place a post cap on each post using 10d nails or nails provided. Once the cap is on, lower the post into the post anchor and nail the flanges of the post anchor to the bottom part of the post. To stabilize the post, provide a diagonal brace in two directions until all the posts are installed and interconnected. Use the galvanized nails provided with the connector or 10d galvanized.

Once the posts are in place, each post should be plumbed and braced properly so that the diagonal measurements made from opposite sides of the post are equal. After the posts are

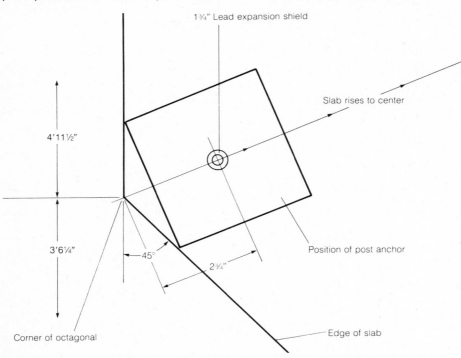

The corners of the octagonal slab meet at a 45° angle. When the concrete is cured, drill a hole in each corner for a 1¾ in. lead expansion shield to hold the anchor bolt.

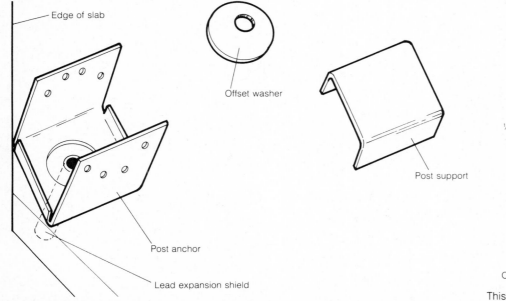

Once the shield is installed, secure the post anchor with an offset washer. This allows for later adjustments. Place the support in the anchor, set the post and nail securely.

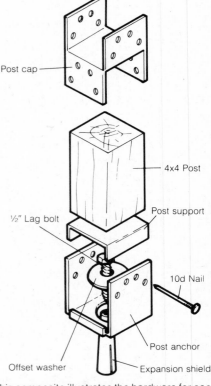

This composite illustrates the hardware for each corner beam. It sits on a post anchor and is topped with a post cap.

plumbed and leveled, go back and tighten the anchor bolts in the anchor posts.

Step 4: Installing the Beams

Bevel cut each beam on each side so that the end of the beam fits into one half of the post cap. This requires accurate measurements and cutting. Cut the bevel on one beam at a time. Make sure the bevel cuts are accurate by placing the beam into the post cap. Once the beam is in place, it should be nailed with 10d galvanized nails driven through the vertical flange. Repeat this procedure until all eight sides are in place and nailed. Check the diagonal dimensions again and adjust accordingly. The next step in the procedure is to install the rafters and the finial.

Step 5: Supporting the Rafters

Each corner of the octagon will receive one end of a rafter. Each rafter will be connected at the other end to a finial which will form the high point of the roof assembly. The end of the rafter that is to set on the beam must be notched and bevel cut so that it is supported by the beam yet provides sufficient overhang for an eave. The overhang should be 12 inches.

The ridge or finial end of the rafter must be cut short so that all eight rafters can come together forming an octagon. To keep the rafters together, bevel cut spacers are installed between the rafter ends and toe-nailed together. The entire rafter assembly should be rigid.

The finial can now be installed. The finial can be any shape or size desired since it can be a very personalized 'top' piece. It is placed in the center of the octagon formed by the rafter ends and spacers and connected using 10d galvanized nails.

The rafters are tied together by collar ties, which are 2x6 studs connected from the beam end of one rafter to an opposite corner one. The collar ties hold the rafters together so the entire assembly behaves as one piece.

Step 6: Bracing the Post and Beam

To set the diagonal bracing of the post and beam, use 4x4 wood sections that are bevel cut at the ends so that a 45° diagonal brace 18 in. long will be formed on each side of the post. Make connections with 16d galvanized nails. Try not to split or bruise the wood. The nails should be flush with the wood. Once the diagonal braces are in place, the external bracing can be removed.

Step 7: Building the Roof

The gazebo roof is a lattice one composed of diagonally nailed strips of ⅜x1½ in. wood pieces. Wood lattice can be obtained from most local lumberyards. Since it is quite expensive, considering the amount of waste that can be generated, another alternative is to use a table saw to cut Clear Construction Grade No. 1 2x4s into the ⅜ in. strips. Once you have enough of a supply, you are ready to start the lattice.

Before installing the lattice on the roof, attach a fascia piece composed of a 1x6 with a nailing strip to the top of the lower ends of the rafters. Then start nailing the lattice on a 45° angle. Use the width of the lattice, or 1½ in., as the space between pieces. If you desire more light, increase the spacing distance.

After nailing the lattice for the roof, the lattice joints over the rafters must be finished. This is done with a 1x4 that

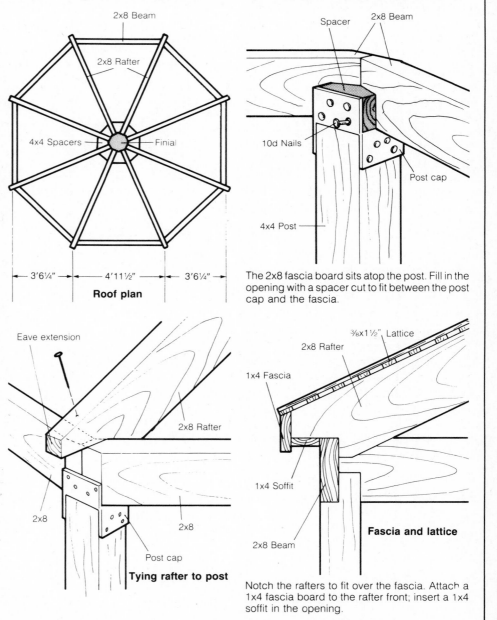

Roof plan

The 2x8 fascia board sits atop the post. Fill in the opening with a spacer cut to fit between the post cap and the fascia.

Tying rafter to post

Fascia and lattice

Notch the rafters to fit over the fascia. Attach a 1x4 fascia board to the rafter front; insert a 1x4 soffit in the opening.

Project continued on next page

caps the joint. Since the ends of the lattice joint do not lay flat, a 1x4 piece must be placed on each side of the joint. Make sure the sides adjoining are beveled so that they will create a flush joint. The finial or cap piece can now be installed. It can be a simple weathervane or a homemade design.

Step 8: The Railing and Entry
Locate the railing at a uniform height on each side except the entry side. Install top rail and bottom rail of 2x3s at the desired height. Normally, this is 36 inches. A vertical 2x3 nailing piece should be placed alongside each vertical post face. The lattice can then be installed on a diagonal, repeating the same spacing as on the roof.

With all the lattice in place, face-nail a 1x2 finish piece to the lattice to provide a finish trim. Then fasten a 1x6 top piece over the 2x3 top rail. The 1x6 will now become the finished top of the railing. Repeat this procedure for all the sides with latticework.

Step 9: Finishing the Gazebo
This completes the actual construction sequence of the gazebo. The builder can now add additional detail to the structure as desired. It is recommended that the structure be painted with a clear sealer. Addition of a bench, perimeter seating, and even a table will make the structure a more habitable and enjoyable space.

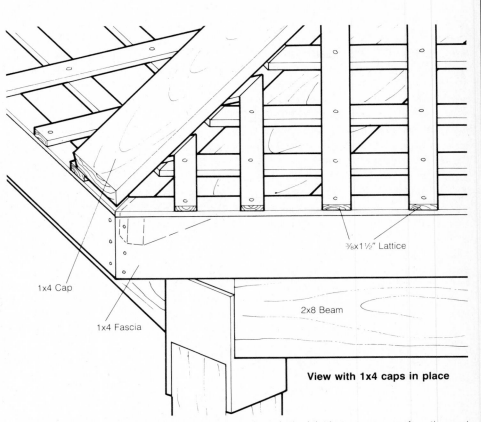

View with 1x4 caps in place

Install the roof using the width of the lattices as a spacer. At the joint between one roof section and another, install a 1x4 roof cap to create a neat, finished edge.

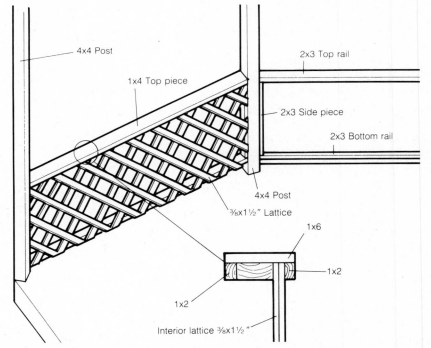

The sides of the gazebo repeat the latticework found in the roof. Use 2x3s for the top and bottom rails. Install the lattice and finish off with a 1x4 top railing.

BUILDING A 4-SIDED GAZEBO

Obviously, a 4 sided structure is less complicated to build than an 8-sided one. However, the basic sequence and nature of the steps are the same. Here are illustration details and a materials list for the less-complicated project. Be sure to carefully read through the preceding project before trying this one. Any procedural differences between the two are noted.

Materials List

10	2x8x14' Pressure treated lumber
30	2x4x10' Pressure treated lumber
8	2x10x10 Rough cedar
8	4x4x10 Cedar
16	1x6x10 Cedar
8	2x6x12 Cedar
4	2x4x8 Cedar, ripped to 2x2
2	2x4x10 Pine
32'	¾ Pine crown molding
6'	¾ Pine Quarterround
480'	¼x2" Pine lattice
4	1x6 12 Rough cedar for facing 4x4 posts

STEP 1: LAYING THE FOUNDATION

The foundation system for this design uses poured-in-place concrete corner posts that are 12 in. in diameter and 8 ft. 4 in. apart. To shape the postholes, use round 12 in. Sona Tubes or similar prefabricated forms. Place each tube about 36 in. deep.

To prepare the site, pinpoint the locations of the 4 posts; erect batter boards as described earlier. Check for square by verifying that the diagonal dimensions are equal.

Dig the holes. Place the tubes in the holes and brace the tubes to mimimize any movement during the pour. The tops of the tubes indicate the finished height of the concrete post—usually 6 to 8 in. above grade . Drive two #5 reinforcing bars in the bottom of each tube, with the tops of the rods about 3 in. below the tops of the tubes.

Pour the concrete. Then use a spare rod to consolidate the concrete by rodding it several times. Check the top level of the concrete. Install a post cleat in the exact center of each post while the concrete is still wet. Check the alignment of the post cleats, since

A four-sided gazebo offers an alternative to the more complex octagonal structure.

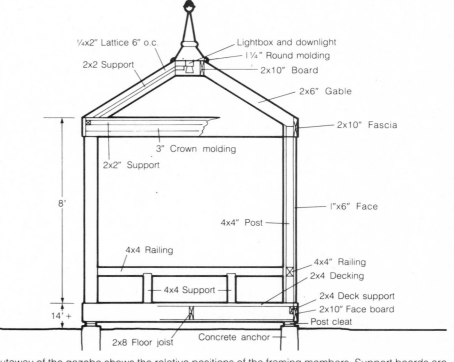

A cutaway of the gazebo shows the relative positions of the framing members. Support boards are necessary at the flooring and roofing levels. The railing is 36 in. high.

Project continued on next page

they will support the corner posts of the gazebo.

STEP 2: INSTALLING THE POSTS

Let the concrete cure. Place the 4x4 vertical posts. Each post must be leveled, aligned, and plumbed in both directions. Then install and tighten the anchor bolts that connect the post cleats to the posts.

STEP 3: LAYING THE DECK FRAMING

The deck framing for the four-sided gazebo consists of 2 sets of doubled 2x8 joists laid diagonally between corner posts. The ends of each board in the doubled set are beveled at a 45° angle to fit against the posts.

Set the first pair across the diagonal and nail the ends securely to the posts. Cut the second set in half, so that each half fits between its corner post and the center doubled set, which runs through the decking area. Fasten the center edge of each half joist to the posts.

Now install a set of braces that run between adjacent diagonals; this forms a triangle parallel to the sides of the gazebo. These braces fall half-way between the corner posts and the center cross. Bevel the ends of the braces at a 45° angle to form a secure joint. Nail securely.

Nail 2x10 face boards along the outside faces of the four posts. The top of the face board should be 1½ in. above the level of the diagonal 2x8s to allow for the thickness of the deck floor.

Along the inside faces of the faceboards, nail a 2x4 deck support. The tops of these supports fall 1½ in. below the top edge of the faceboards, on the same level as the diagonal supports.

Now cut and nail the 2x4 decking. In this design, the interior ends of the decking are cut at a 45° angles, and

the boards create a perpendicular design to the faceboards, as shown. Place the 2x4s about ⅛ in. apart so that air and water can pass through. Use galvanized box nails, even if the material is pressure-treated wood.

STEP 4: INSTALLING THE ROOF ASSEMBLY

Install the 2x10 fascia boards at the tops of the corner posts. The top edge of each board should be 5 in. higher than the tops of the posts. Temporarily

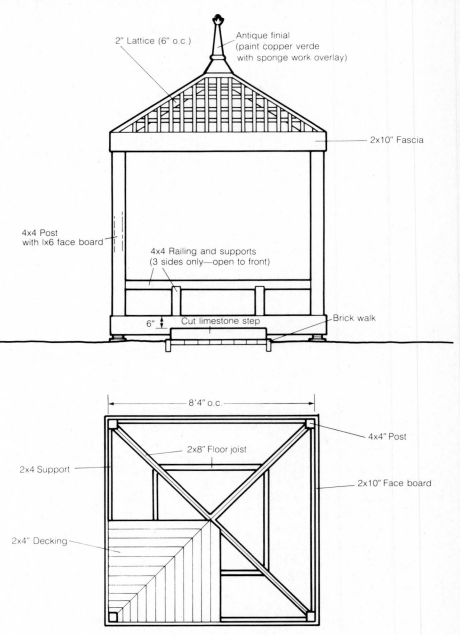

nail the boards in position. Then, using a wood bit, drill a ⅞ in. hole in each end of each fascia board and secure with ¾x8 in. bolts.

Build a center light box of 2x10s. This forms the roof peak to which the gable rafters connect. Create rafters from doubled 2x6s and bevel-cut at the upper and lower ends. Bolt the double rafters together with ½ in. bolts every 24 in. on center; stagger these bolts along the length of the rafter. Notch the rafters into the seat formed by the post and the fascia piece. Joints must be snug and well nailed. You need to support the rafters while you nail them into position.

STEP 5: INSTALLING THE FINIAL
The design of the finial is a personal one—try to have it reflect the spirit as well as the materials of the gazebo. Use the lightbox as the finial support base.

STEP 6: INSTALLING THE LATTICE
After the rafters and finial are in place, install the ¼x2 in. roof lattice. Custom cut each piece and install one at a time, rather than trying to fabricate the entire side at once. The work may take longer but you will be much more satisfied with the final product.

A 2x2 supports the lattice. Nail the support all the way around the inner faces of the fascia board, rafters and the lightbox. The top edge of the support board should fall ½ in. below the top of the fascia and the rafters. Place the lattice in a 6x6 in. pattern.

STEP 7: INSTALLING THE RAILING
The railing encloses only three sides on the gazebo. The fourth side is for the entryway. Cut the railing to fit flush to the face of the corner posts. Fasten two 4x4 intermediate supports, evenly spaced, to each railing with ⅜ in. lag screws.

STEP 8: INSTALLING THE GROUND CONNECTION
The gazebo now is essentially finished. All that remains is to install a step between the finished grade and the deck level. The step, which can be made of stone, concrete or wood, must be well seated for safe use.

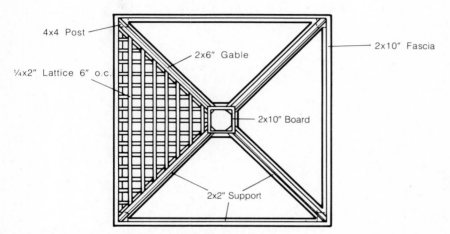

4x4 Post • 2x6" Gable • 2x10" Fascia • ¼x2" Lattice 6" o.c. • 2x10" Board • 2x2" Support

The lattice of this roof lies flush with the upper edges of the gables. The 2x2 roof support is installed along all of the inner edges of the roof openings.

A 45° bevel on each rafter in the gazebo provides a tight fit against the light box in the peak of the roof. The light box will also support the decorative finial.

BUILDING A CABAÑA WITH FENCE

The cabaña with fence extension is a two-room changing space constructed of treated outdoor wood. The structure is rectangular in form, with rooms back to back. Each has a separate entry. Each changing room measures 6x6 ft. so the overall dimension of the cabaña will be 6x12 ft., or 72 sq. ft. of ground coverage. Fence extensions add an additional 3 ft. to each end, making the overall length of the project 18 ft. The overall height of the cabaña is 8 ft. to the top of the plywood panels. The superstructure is a post and beam construction with a flat roof and exterior grade plywood siding as a finish material. The roof is slightly pitched for drainage. The entire unit rests on a concrete slab on grade.

Materials List

8 ¾″ Lead expansion shields with ½ lag bolts
8 4x4 Post anchor assemblies
8 4x4 Posts 8′ long
2 4x6 Beams 18′ long
14 2x6 Rafters 8′ long
4 4x8 ½″ CD Plywood exterior sheathing
60 2x3 Studs 8′ long
8 Sheets 4x8 ⅝ in. plywood
9 2x4 Studs 8′ long (inter partition)
3 4x8 ½″ Plywood
24 2x4x6′ Studs (two benches)
2 Rolls No. 30 felt
2 No. 5 cans cold roofing tar
50 Aluminum gravel stop
4 4x8 Plywood
1 36″ Prehung door frame
18 1x4 Trim door hardware

Step 1: Constructing the Foundation

The cabaña requires a rectangular slab slightly raised above the level of the pool surround with a pitch of at least 1.5 in.

Step 2: Installing the Posts

The design for the cabaña provides a superstructure of 4 posts with beams spanning the posts. These beams extend out further an additional 38 in. on opposite ends. The beams are then capped by the rafters. Lay out the post locations according to the drawings. Once the centerlines of the posts have been located, install lead expansion shields and post anchors (discussed in Step 2 of the gazebo project). Install, align and plumb the posts (see Step 3 of the preceding project). Make sure that the posts are well braced.

Step 3: Installing Beams and Rafters

Install the beams spanning the long dimension and nail them to the post caps. Make sure that galvanized nails are used for all connections. Once both beams have been installed, leveled and nailed, install the 2x6 rafters at 16 in. on center. Attach them to both beams using rafter anchors. (The rafter anchors can be installed before the rafters are in place.) Set a rafter with each end flush with the top of the beam and nail in place.

Step 4: Setting the Roof Sheathing

The roof sheathing is ½ in. CD plywood nailed to the rafters at 16 in. centers. It should overlap the vertical plywood siding by ¼ in.

Cabaña

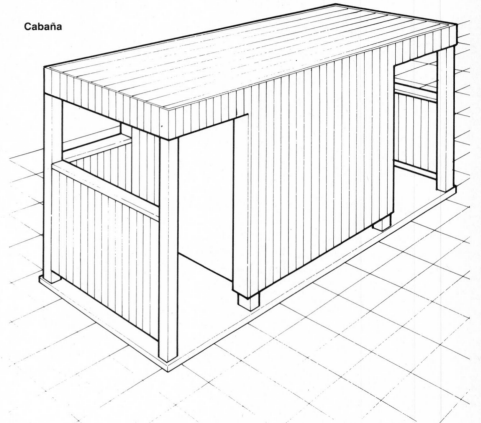

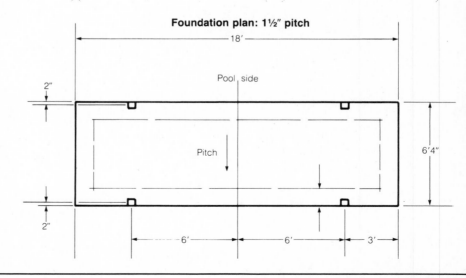

Foundation plan: 1½″ pitch

18′

Pool side

2″

Pitch

6′4″

2″

6′   6′   3′

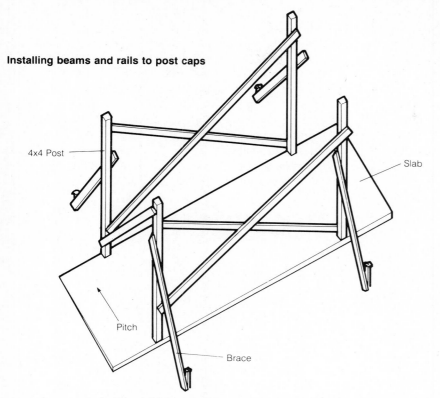

Installing beams and rails to post caps

4x4 Post

Slab

Pitch

Brace

To support the posts before the rafters are in place, use diagonal bracing as shown.

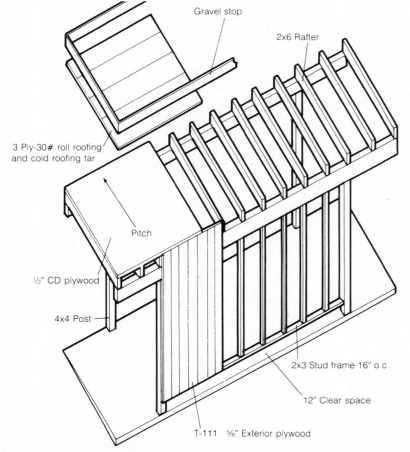

Gravel stop

2x6 Rafter

3 Ply-30# roll roofing
and cold roofing tar

Pitch

½" CD plywood

4x4 Post

2x3 Stud frame 16" o.c.

12" Clear space

T-111   ⅝" Exterior plywood

Pitch the rafters slightly to assure water runoff; fully sheath the roof for longevity.

Step 5: Installing the Infill Panels

The infill panels are supported by 2x3 studs that create a frame. The frame will be placed to fit flush to the outside edge of the posts and will stand 12 in. above the slab.

To build the panels, space all vertical studs at 16 in. centers. Nail ⅝ in. exterior grade rough sawn plywood or T-111 to the frame. Place the entire assembly within the posts and nail it. The plywood should extend up to the top of the rafters. Repeat for each panel.

Step 6: Setting the Roofing

The roof should be fully sheathed. Since this is a flat roof with a slight pitch to the short side, the roof must be sealed using 30# felt.

To lay the felt, start at the lowest edge of the roof. Unroll the felt along the length of the roof, cutting it off so that the ends slightly overlap the end walls. Nail the layer down and repeat the procedure, overlapping at least 6 in. Complete the entire roof.

Now that the first layer is down, mop the entire surface with a cold roofing tar. Then repeat the procedure: tack down the felts again over the cold tar base. Before the third and final layer is installed, a galvanized gravel stop must be installed. This overlaps the side panel and provides a finished edge to the roof. Install the final layer of felt in a manner similar to the first layer. Then mop the entire surface again with the cold tar.

Step 7: Installing the Interior Partition

This partition separates the two changing rooms. It will be the same height off the concrete slab as the exterior ones, 12 in. Construct a 2x4 wood frame with the vertical studs at 16 in. on center. Insert the frame between the two center posts and sheath with either moisture-resistant ⅝ in. gypsum drywall or a treated wood paneling. The wood paneling will last somewhat longer.

Step 8: Framing the Doorways

Using the same method employed for the exterior walls, frame a standard stud wall using 2x3 studs. Allow a 36-

Project continued on next page

in. width for the door. The head of the rough opening for the door will be at the level of the bottom of the beam. Once you cut and install the frame, fasten a precut 4 in. door frame with the lower part of the side jambs cut off so that they are level with the underside of the exterior panel. Then you can hang a 1⅜-in.-thick louvered door. Repeat this procedure for the other changing room. Nail on the exterior siding and finish it to match the other exterior siding already in place. Use 1x4 S4S trim to finish the frame opening and the underside of the panels. To prevent water from forming on the underside of the wall panel, rip an ⅛ in. groove along the entire length of the 1x4. This should be located ¼ in. from the outside edge and will act as a drip.

Step 9: Constructing the Fences

Construct the wood privacy fence with 2x4s for the top and bottom rails and at 16 in. on center for the intermediate studs. Install the frame and frame them to the posts. The farthest post extends vertically to tie into the beam extension from the cabaña. There it is toenailed to the beam. Anchor the base of each post as you did the earlier posts. Use

finish siding to match the cabaña siding. Use the same 1x4 S4S trim for the top and bottom rails. Nail with galvanized box nails.

Step 10: Interior Finishing

After you have installed the door, fences and the roofing, work on the interior benches and lighting. Since the entire wall panel is raised 12 in. above the base of the slab, no additional ventilation is required. If benches are desired, they can be framed into the side wall panels; nailing 2x4 ledgers beams to each side wall and then placing 2x4s on edge with a ¼ in. space between them will do nicely. Pegs for hanging clothes will probably be all that is needed to make the cabaña fully operational. Apply a paint or stain finish.

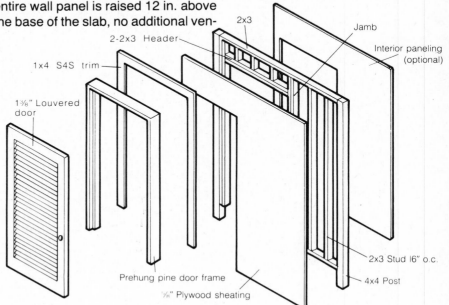

This presents an exploded view of the end walls with the door framing. The head of the rough opening will be at the level of the bottom of the beam. Utilize a prehung door.

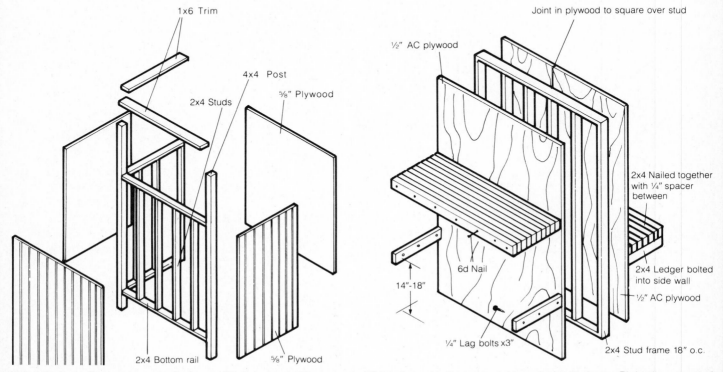

Left: the privacy fences are made of a frame of 2x4 studs set 16 in. on center. This is framed to the posts and toenailed to the beam. Right: the amount of interior finishing is optional. Benches are very convenient. Install ledger boards. Construct the benches of 2x4s set on edge and spaced ¼ in. apart.

BUILDING A LANAI

The lanai will be built of outdoor wood or redwood. The superstructure will be post and beam construction with a wood lattice infill both in the roof and in one wall panel. Six posts support two support beams, which in turn support the rafters. All major connections will utilize the Teco (tm) connector, which is a preformed metal galvanized type of nailable connector. The overall measurement of the lanai is 12x16 ft. in plan and 8 ft. to the top of the support beam. The connections will supply all diagonal stability. The roof will be flat with drop-in lattice panels.

Materials List

- 6 4x4 Post anchors
- 4 2x12 20'
- 6 ¾ Lead expansion shields with ½" lag bolts
- 6 4x4x8' Posts
- 42 ½" Carriage bolts
- 8 4x4x4' Diagonal braces
- 4 4x4x5' Diagonal braces
- 9 2x8x16' Rafters
- 12 2x2x16' Nailers
- 32 2x3x12' Frames and panels Lattice ⅜x1½
- 2 ⅛x3" Steel plate 10' long (optional)

FREE-STANDING MODEL
Step 1: Creating the Foundation
The lanai concrete slab should be quite level, scored on a 4 ft. grid if desired. Have the slab slightly raised above the ground and pitched slightly away from the house.

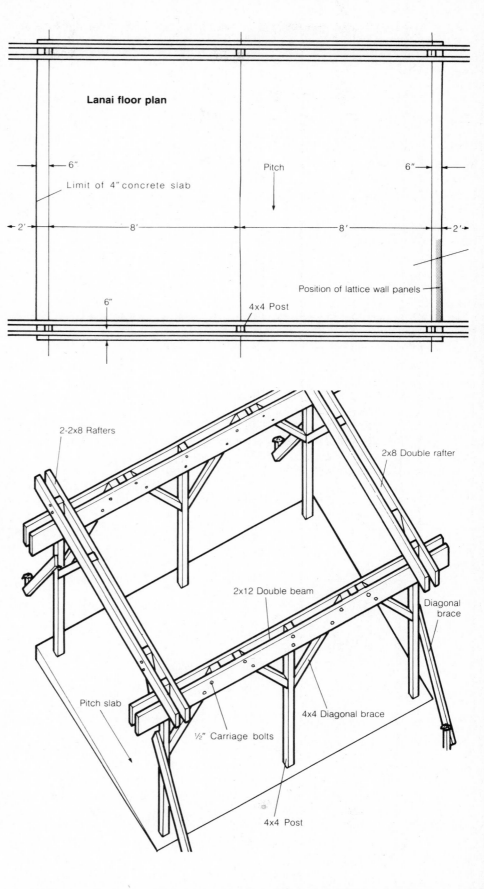

Lanai floor plan

6"

Pitch

6"

Limit of 4" concrete slab

2'   8'   8'   2'

6"

6"

Position of lattice wall panels

4x4 Post

2-2x8 Rafters

2x8 Double rafter

2x12 Double beam

Diagonal brace

Pitch slab

½" Carriage bolts

4x4 Diagonal brace

4x4 Post

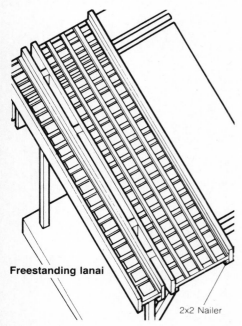

Freestanding lanai

2x2 Nailer

Project continued on next page

Step 2: Installing the Posts

Since this lanai is free-standing, use the same method of anchoring and installing the 4x4 posts to the slab as is described in Steps 2 and 3 of the gazebo project.

Step 3: Installing the Beams and Braces

The two main beams are each composed of two 2x12s, which will be attached to opposing faces of the 4x4 posts. These double beams will be bolted through the post to each other. Diagonal bracing extends down from in between the beams to the post.

Measure 8 in. down from the top of the post. Align the top edge of the beam with this point. Temporarily nail the beams to the posts. Then install two ½-in. carriage bolts per post. Extend 6x6 bracing diagonally to meet the post. The brace will also be bolted to the beam and to the post.

Step 4: Installing the Rafters

The beam assembly is now prepared to receive the rafters. The posts extend a total of 8 in. above the top of the beams. Use two 2x8s to connect the front and back section bolting through to each post. These double 2x8s provide the necessary cross-bracing. The rafters are 2x8s cantilevered over the beams by 24 in. The cantilever allows

the rafter to support more load over its length. Space the rafters on 48 in. centers to allow the lattice panels to be inset between them. Fasten the rafters to the beams by means of rafter anchors.

Step 5: Installing Cross Bracing

The last part of the lanai superstructure is the installation of the cross-bracing. This is accomplished with a 6x6 section that is diagonally connected to a double rafter and that in turn has been bolted to the post. It is then connected in a fashion similar to the lateral bracing by bolting the assembly together. Since this point the superstructure should be completely assembled, remove all temporary bracing.

Step 6: Supporting the Roof Lattice

To build and install the lattice sun screen roof panel and a lattice wall panel, first measure the horizontal distance between the rafters; this distance will be used as the width of the panel section (it should be very close to 48 in). Using 8d galvanized nails, nail a 2x2 finish nailer along the entire length of each side of the rafter. The nailer should be placed 3 in. below the top of the rafter. Try not to bruise or split the wood.

Step 7: Building the Roof Lattice

Cut the lattice as recommended in Step 8 of the Gazebo project. The lattice should measure ⅜x1½ in. wide. Construct a frame of 2x3s. The width should equal the distance between the rafters. The length of the panel should not exceed 48 in. Lay the lattice on a diagonal (45°). The spacing between lattice pieces should equal the width of one piece of lattice. Lay the second layer of lattice perpendicular to the first and finish-nail the edge.

Step 8: Seating the Lattice

After all the panels are complete, lay them in place and toenail into the rafter. Make sure the panels are properly seated on the nailer. Install a 2x2 nailer piece over the rafter to conceal the top of the lattice frame. In the future, should the frame need repair or replacement, the entire panel can be

removed by removing the nails. Then slip the lattice free.

Step 9: Constructing the Wall Lattice

The lattice end wall panel is built in a fashion similar to the roof panel. However, the panels must be constructed on a modular basis. Each module is a multiple of the distance between the two vertical support posts. To determine the size of each module, measure the face-to-face distance between the outside posts and divide by three. This dimension then equals the width of the panel. The height is 6 in. less than the distance between the floor and the underside of the rafter. Construct a 2x3 in. frame to this size. Lay the lattice diagonally, in two layers as described in Step 7. Once the entire panel has been completed, lay another 2x3 over the top of the lattice side and nail to the frame. Refer to the illustration.

Raise each panel into position; square and plumb and attach it to the post and to other panels with ⅜ in. lag screws. To stabilize the lower edge of the three panels, a steel plate ⅛ in. thick by 3 in. wide can be connected to

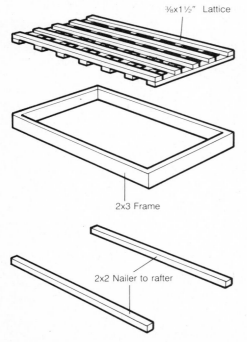

3/8x1½" Lattice

2x3 Frame

2x2 Nailer to rafter

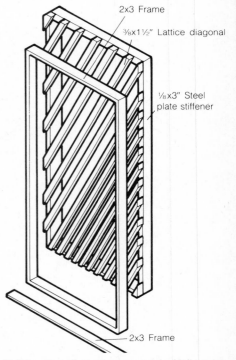

2x3 Frame
3/8x1½" Lattice diagonal
⅛x3" Steel plate stiffener
2x3 Frame

Build each wall panel as a module. Nail the lattice to a 2x3; finish off with 2x3 trim. The attach the module to the framing.

the underside of the panel frame. Screw the plate on at a regular interval along the entire length of the panel.

Step 10: Finishing

Once the end panel is in place, apply a paint or stain finish. Then all that remains to use the structure is to start the vines growing and place some well-built patio furniture in it.

VARIATION: LEAN-TO LANAI

Some homeowners prefer a lean-to lanai to a free-standing one. The inner wall of the leanto is supported by the house. This side connected to the house by a 2x12 ledger board, which bolts to the exterior wall studs with 3/8 in. galvanized lag screws. Space the screws on a maximum of 24 in. centers. If the house is masonry, sink 1/2 in. lead expansion shields on 36 in. centers.

When you build the lanai, be sure to leave enough room between the ledger and the soffit for the beams that support the lattice roof. The roof itself angles away from the house, as shown. Flashing should be inserted, as shown, to prevent moisture penetration. The roof should fall below the eave for snow protection against accumulation and movement due to wind.

With the exception of the ledger, the angle of the roof, and adjustment of the

lattice panel sizes (if desired) the construction of a leanto resembles that of a free-standing one. See the accompanying art for construction details.

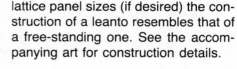

Materials List

3 4x4 Post anchors with 1/2" lag bolts
3 4x4 Posts 8' long
2 2x8x16' Beams
6 1/2" Carriage bolts and washers x 8"
9 2x6 Rafters 12' long
13 1x2x16' Nailers
40 3/8x1 1/2x14' Lattice
1 1x8 Face board 18' long
1 2x12x16' Ledger
   3/8" Lag bolts x 8"
   Valley tin flashing (20 GA)

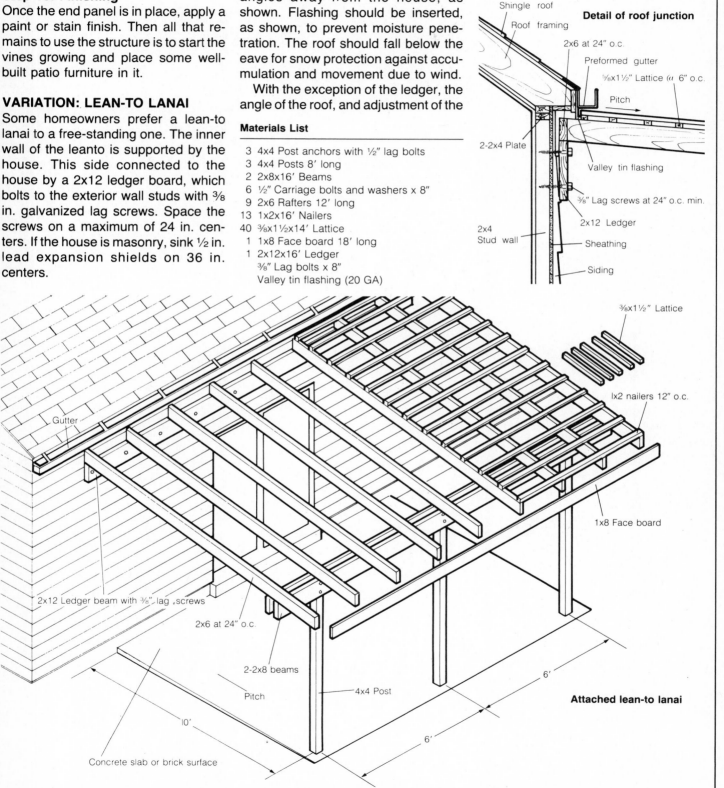

A lean-to lanai is attached to the house by a ledger board at the roof line. Otherwise the construction is the same as for a free-standing structure.

HOW TO BUILD A FENCE OR SCREEN

The first step in planning a fence is to consult local building codes for set-back lines, height requirements and any construction requirements that may exist. Your fence most conform to all restrictions, or you will find yourself having to take down the fence you just put up.

Typical fence posts are 4x4 or 4 in. in diameter. This size is good for most allowable fence heights with typical board or paneling infill. Stringers (the horizontal members to which fencing is attached) are at least 2x4s and perhaps 2x6s or larger, depending on the distance between the posts and the weight of the panel. The infill can range from lath to plywood panels, either flush or with spaces between. The basic example given here is for butted boards, with variations offered at the end of the project.

BUILDING THE FENCE

Step 1: Setting Corner Fence Posts

Posts may be set in earth, gravel-and-earth, concrete or some combination of these materials. The most substantial method is to fill the hole with concrete. Depth is determined by the height of the fence and the climatic pressure that will be exerted upon it. Generally speaking, the deeper the post the better. Also, standard lumber length and height restrictions influence the depth. Usually, a 6-ft. fence will use 8 ft. posts sunk 2 ft. deep.

Creating Post Foundations Always keep post holes straight. Dig a hole about 12 in. in diameter for a 4-in. thick post. Line the bottom of the hole with a base stone and/or gravel to aid drainage and prevent decay.

Setting Corner Posts To align the posts, locate two corners along the run of fence. Set the corner posts in place. Tamp the earth or gravel around each post a little at a time so that the water will later drain away from the post. If pouring concrete around the post, brace the posts to keep them steady while the concrete is setting. Several 4 ft. lengths of 2x4s, nailed to the post and staked at the ground, should hold the posts firmly. Before pouring the concrete, check the posts for plumb by using a spirit level on two adjacent

sides. Let concrete cure several days before you add the stringers and panels to the posts.

Step 2: Setting Intermediate Posts

Aligning the Posts Locate the center of the top of each corner post and drive in a nail so that enough nail is exposed to hold a string. Stretch a line tightly between the posts. Locate the intermediate posts and gate posts, along the string. Mark the locations with tape. Transfer these points to the ground with a plumb bob and drive a stake to mark them. You may dig all the holes at once, or do them as you find the time.

Placing the Posts Stretch two lines along the outside face of the posts, one at the top and one at the bottom, close to the ground. Shim the string out from the posts about ¼ to ½ in. (Use whatever good shim material is at hand.)

Install the intermediate posts, using the strings to keep the posts in the same plane and a level to keep them plumb. To keep the posts the proper distance from the string, insert shims as a spacer.

Step 3: Setting Stringers

Set the top stringer flush with the top of the posts and nail it where you want it — inside, outside or within the frame. If within the frame, use a metal hanger for the stringer. Secure the middle and bottom stringers in the same way. Use a spirit level to keep stringers level.

It is fairly common to see 2x4 stringers laid with the wide side down. However, this should be avoided. Most designs can be achieved by laying the stringer with the 4-in. side placed vertically, which provides twice the strength as when laid on its side. In most cases it is convenient to let standard lumber lengths decide the length

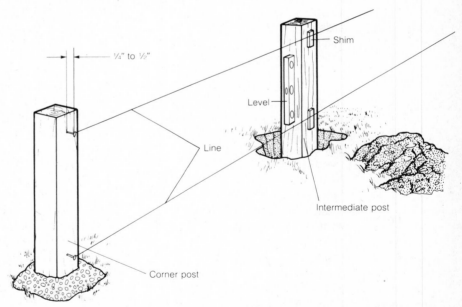

Posts must be carefully aligned, leveled and plumbed. Shim on the intermediate post is the same thickness as the distance between the face of the corner post and the string.

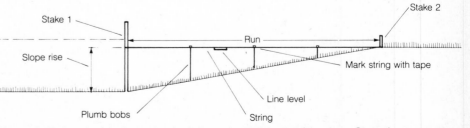

The run is the length of the fence; the rise is the upward distance of the slope. Step a fence on a short steep slope and follow a long angle slope for the best effect.

of fence panels; 8 ft. is most typical. With 8 ft. stringers, it is best to install a set of three — one at the top, middle and bottom of the posts. This method will help keep the fence panels from warping or sagging in a few months. Board fence material should not extend more than a few inches above the top stringer or below the bottom one; if it does, the unsupported boards will warp enough to cause a ragged-looking edge.

Step 4: Nailing the Board Infill

Use rustproof nails, screws, bolts and gate hardware to avoid rust stains on the lumber and to ensure a long-lasting fence.

Do not nail on the boards until the framework is level, plumb, and as you want it. To nail the boards to the stringers, set the first board in place at one end. Use a plumb bob and line to be sure the board is vertical. Butt the next board up against the first one, and so forth. After you attach several, check with the plumb bob to be sure that you are keeping the boards plumb. Adjust as necessary by shifting the boards about an 1/8 in., which will not be noticeable.

Step 5: Building the Gate

Nail stringers across the top and bottom of the gate posts, as you did for the other posts, but leave out the middle stringer. Attach two vertical gate supports; leave about 3/4 in. between the supports and the fence posts. Then fasten the diagonal gate support. This support slopes down from the top toward the hinged side of the gate. It is important that the diagonal support be attached in this way.

Cut 2x4s to fill in between the two vertical supports at the side and the diagonal gate support. Nail the siding boards across the gate posts just as you did between the other fence posts.

Step 6: Installing the Hinges and Cutting the Gate

To install the hinges, saw downward about a foot from the top, between the vertical gate support and the fence post. This permits installation of the top hinge, according to the manufacturer's instructions. Saw upward about a foot from the bottom, between the vertical gate support and the fence post. This cut aligns with the first cut, and allows you to install the bottom hinge.

To free the gate, saw between the vertical gate support and the post — opposite the hinge side. Open the gate; check the fit; sand and smooth raw edges; then make any minor trim cuts needed. Install the latch according to instructions. You may have to trim the gate again after the first rainfall (due to swelling) but this is not hard with a power saw.

VARIATION: SPACED INFILL OR LATH

Although butted boards will afford a great deal of privacy, you can choose from a wide variety of infill materials and patterns, many of which require only a top and bottom stringer. For a staggered look, alternate boards from one side of the stringers to the other. Set the spacing so that air and light can pass through the fence. Or build box frame modules, nail boards on diagonally and attach the panel frames to the stringers. The style of your fence or screen is a matter of personal choice.

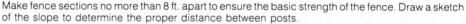

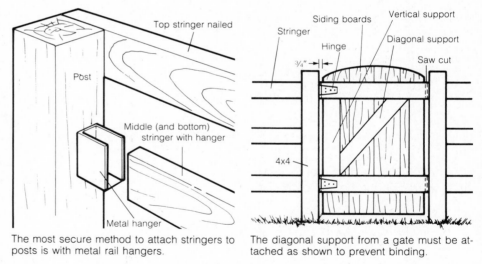

Make fence sections no more than 8 ft. apart to ensure the basic strength of the fence. Draw a sketch of the slope to determine the proper distance between posts.

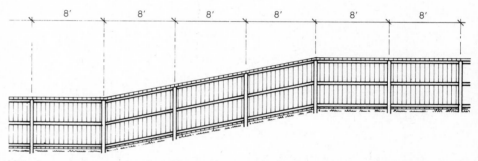

The most secure method to attach stringers to posts is with metal rail hangers.

The diagonal support from a gate must be attached as shown to prevent binding.

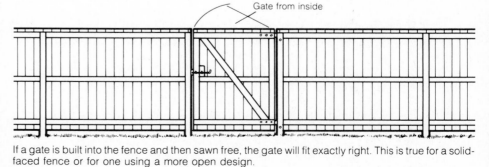

If a gate is built into the fence and then sawn free, the gate will fit exactly right. This is true for a solid-faced fence or for one using a more open design.

APPENDIX: Maintenance and Water Treatment

INGROUND AND VINYL LINER POOLS

Chemical Use in Water Treatment

Common water problems include: algae — tiny plantlike organisms that attach to the walls or float in the water to turn the water green, brown or even yellow; scale — small clusters of waterborne chemicals such as calcium that could cause injury to swimmers; rust — iron oxides suspended in the water to produce a cloudy or rusty coloration.

How to Add Chemicals Always read the manufacturers' labels. Always use the same make of chemicals so that you will know what to expect. Add the chemicals gradually to bring the level to the desired range. Never mix chemicals without professional advice; it could cause serious problems for swimmers.

Chlorine Readily available in many forms, chlorine is commonly used in powder form. The strength of the concentration of chlorine is measured in parts per million, or ppm. The preferred concentration of chlorine in pool water is 0.5 ppm. This value is approximate, since the actual amount of chlorine needed and the frequency of adding it to your pool will vary according to conditions.

When chlorine is added to the pool, it immediately attacks and destroys the bacteria, algae and dissolved organic solids. In doing so, most of the chlorine is expended or is exhausted. The chlorine that remains is called the "chlorine residual." The chlorine residual is important to the continued purity of the water and must be maintained between 1.0 to 1.5 ppm.

pH This is the chemical symbol for the acidity-alkaline balance in your pool water. A very high pH level (alkaline) reduces the chlorine's ability to kill algae and bacteria. A low pH (acid) level results in the chlorine being lost too rapidly, producing a strong chlorine odor. Low pH also causes irritation to a swimmer's eyes, nose and throat, and it corrodes exposed metal parts. Ideal swimming pool water should have a pH level between 7.2 and 7.6. If the alkaline level is low, add soda ash granules. If the test determines that the acid level is low, add sodium bisulfate.

How to Test pH Most chemical or pool manufacturers have a test kit for determining the amount of chlorine residual and the pH balance of the water. To use the test strip method, insert the strip into the water specimen. Simply match the color on the strip against a chart to determine the chemical to be added.

Stabilizer The first chemical that you will add to your pool is a conditioner or stabilizer, which counteracts decomposition of chlorine due to the ultraviolet rays of the sun. The stabilizer level generally is checked twice a year, unless the pool has been emptied or the level has been seriously lowered. A suitable stabilizer level is 50 ppm. Too high a stabilizer level will result in loss of chlorination efficiency.

Super Chlorination Once a week, add three or four times the normal amount of chlorine to the water to clean completely any possible trace of bacteria or algae. This is especially important after a heavy rain or when the pool has had heavy use. The day after you super chlorinate, test for a comfortable chlorine residual range. Do not super chlorinate before using the pool; always perform this operation after the weekend.

Guidelines for Treatment

There are certain recommendations that should be followed for chemical treatment of pool water.

1. Never add water to the chemicals; always add the chemicals to the water. Make sure the volume of water is far greater than that of the chemical.
2. Never add chemicals through the skimmer unless the pump is operating, and do not shut the motor off until you are sure all of the chemicals are fully dissolved in the water.
3. Never add chemicals on top of other chemicals in the skimmer. Always make sure that each has fully dissolved before adding another type.
4. Do not throw chlorine tablets or granules directly into the pool. It could cause severe discoloration of the material that it comes into contact with. Use a dispenser or feeding mechanism.
5. Keep the chemicals in a locked or controlled space; make sure that incompatible materials are not stored together.
6. Always test the water after the chemicals have dissolved.

Troubleshooting Chart

The color of pool water can often tell you if something is wrong. If the water is not crisp sky-blue, you may need to adjust one of your procedures. If in doubt, always consult a professional. The recommendations on the accompanying chart may help you to analyze problems.

Mechanical Equipment Maintenance

Most impurities in water are organic, and it is these impurities that the filter must be able to remove. Inorganic impurities fall to the bottom of the pool and can be easily removed.

Filtration System Maintain the filter system in the order of the stages of filtration. First, clean the skimmer of leaves and small particles. Always check the basket before the day's use. Second, flush the lint trap with water or remove the debris by hand. (Follow manufacturer's recommended procedures). The third and final stage is the actual filter, which removes the smallest impurities from the water. Check the pressure drop to make sure that the filter does not require backwashing or bumping. Backwash the filter on a weekly basis, if the pool is in normal use. Your pressure gauge may indicate the need in a shorter period if the pool is heavily used.

Vacuuming One of the devices that can help the owner clean the pool itself is a

TROUBLESHOOTING: WATER PROBLEMS AND SOLUTIONS

Symptom	Cause	Remedy
White cloudy water	High pH (alkaline)	Add sodium bisulfate
	Hard water	Use de-ironizer
	Algae growth	Super chlorinate
	Combined chlorine	Super chlorinate
Yellow or green water	Dissolved organic materials	Super chlorinate
Dark green or murky water	Algae	Super chlorinate
Yellow, brown or green water		Manganese remover

vacuum or automatic pool cleaner. The most frequently used is the vacuum. The hose connects to the skimmer or the inlet to the filtration system. The water is drawn in through the vacuum; the brush traps the larger dirt particles and deposits those particles in the skimmer trap. Vacuuming should be done at least three times a week, or as often as daily, depending on pool use and size. Select a vacuum head that has the correct suction for the filtration rate in gallons per minute.

Leaf Skimmer or Rake If a pool is located in a heavily treed area, you need a leaf skimmer or rake to sift out debris floating on the top of the water or at the bottom of the pool.

Daily Maintenance

Keep the pool surround free from dirt or other debris. An overloaded filter system will result in greater inefficiency and more backwashing, so the cleaner the area around the pool, the better the system will work. Check the overall condition of the equipment. Make sure the ladders, diving board and slides are firmly attached or anchored and free from objects that could hurt the swimmer.

Skimmer Water Level Make sure that the swimming pool water level is at least half way up the skimmer opening. Most manufacturers have arrows or other water level indicators to help you maintain this water level. Do not start the filter system until this level has been reached.

Skimmer basket and throat Before you start the filter system, lift the basket out of the skimmer and check to see that the opening or throat of the skimmer is not covered or blocked. Place the basket correctly back into the opening.

Pump strainer and lint trap Check the strainer on the pump. If there is debris in the strainer, remove the cover and take out the basket. While the top is off and the strainer is out do not operate the pump. After cleaning the strainer and placing it back into the pump assembly, fill the chamber with water. Replace the cover and make sure that the seal is tight. If you are in doubt, coat the gasket with petroleum jelly.

Filter pressure gauge Start the pump after performing the previous checks. Once the air has been eliminated from the system, the pressure gauge reading should be between 6 and 10 psi (lbs. per sq. in.). This range may vary according to manufacturer. If the indicator vibrates or air bubbles are being discharged into the pool, check the skimmer water level or the pipe connections, because air is getting into the piping. If the pressure reading is in the area of the gauge, indicating backwash or excessive resistance, perform the backwash, bumping or cartridge cleaning procedure outlined in the operating manual.

Seasonal Maintenance

Winterizing Winterizing a pool, even in the coldest climate, is similar for both in-ground and vinyl liner types. Clean the pool and remove all dirt and leaves from the bottom. Make sure the bottom drain is free from any obstructions. Add a gallon of algaecide and allow it to circulate for at least two hours. Then super chlorinate your pool if the water temperature is above 50°F. (below this temperature, algae cannot live). Circulate the pump for at least 5 minutes longer, if possible. Drain the pool by backwashing the filter system until the pool water is 2 to 3 in. below the bottom of the skimmer face plate.

Place winter plugs in the suction and return fittings. Remove all drain plugs from the pump housing, the pressure gauge and the sightglass (if applicable). Use a pump protector compound for the impeller blades to prevent them from freezing.

If you have a solar panel or pool water heater, drain the system and replace all plugs. Remove all pool equipment such as safety rope, ladders, diving boards and slides.

Start-up Procedures As the weather begins to improve, pump or siphon away water that has accumulated on the pool cover. Make sure that little if any of this water gets into the pool. Clear the cover of all debris and remove the cover from the pool. Allow it to dry well.

Bring the pool water level to the proper depth. Remove all winter plugs from fittings and remove any devices placed within the skimmer. Replace all the drain plugs, pressure gauge and strainer on the pump assembly. Make sure that after you have replaced the pump strainer you fill the cavity with water before placing the see-through lid. Backwash the filter immediately. If you have a D.E. filter, charge the system with the powder (refer to the manufacturer's recommendations).

Super chlorinate immediately. Start the pool water heater (if applicable). Test the water for the proper pH balance and chlorine level. Make sure that the chemicals used are still fresh from last season. If in doubt, buy new ones.

HOT TUBS AND SPAS
Daily Care

Tub size, the number of people who use the tub, and the high water temperature all can cause the bacteria in a tub or spa to breed at an alarming rate. Most tub manufacturers recommend a course of water treatment. Follow the instructions to the letter — do not make cuts or substitutions. Run the filter for three hours every day. Use a water test kit daily to determine the hardness of the water, the pH, and the amount of chlorine. Your local tub or spa dealer can tell you the chemical balance recommended for your area.

Water Hardness Water hardness or softness is a major issue to the tub or spa owner. Hard water can cause magnesium and calcium buildup, which in turn can clog the filtration system. If your area has hard water, you may need a water softner. You also may need to drain and fill the tub more often.

Hot Tub Special Needs

A hot tub requires more maintenance than a spa. Clean the filter regularly. Most tub gauges will indicate when it is time to backwash a sand filter, bump the DE filter or change the filter cartridge. Clean out the pump filter trap.

Seasonal Care Hot tubs should never be left to stand over long periods of time without any water in them. The wood will shrink and split. During periods of nonuse, empty the tub to one-half to two-thirds full. Place an insulated cover blanket or a wood insulated tub cover over the tub when it is not in use so the heater does not work excessively.

Oil treatment Several times a year, apply an oil to the exterior finish of the tub. A linseed or danish oil helps preserve the wood. Do not finish the interior, since the wood must remain porous.

Interior scrubbing Four times a year, drain the tub and scrub the interior with brushes and a hose. If the tub has stains from too much chlorine, drain the tub, and let it dry for several days. Use fine grained sandpaper to remove the stains.

Cold climate Most manufacturers

feel that outdoor wood hot tubs can withstand the coldest of climates. The pump, filter and heater assemblies, however, may not. Be sure to check the operating temperature range for the filtration system and heater. If they cannot perform, they may have to be insulated in a protective enclosure.

Minor Repairs The hoops on the tub exterior may need periodic anti-rust paint. Always check for leaks around the base. Some minor leaks can be caulked with a silicone sealant. Others may have to be corrected by resetting the staves on the tub.

Cleaning In a fiberglass or concrete spa, algae and waterline stains need to be wiped away as soon as they appear. A fiberglass spa with an acrylic finish needs frequent cleaning with a soft cloth and nonabrasive cleaners; do not use soap. If a fiberglass spa lacks luster and color, it may require a coat of spa wax. Cracking or blistering of the acrylic surface is a major repair job that should be done by a professional refinisher. A concrete spa can withstand cleaning with muriatic acid.

ABOVE-GROUND POOLS
Daily Maintenance

Check the pH balance of the water with a standard test kit. As a rule of thumb, in northern climates, the pool should be chlorinated from Easter to Halloween. In southern climates, the pool should be chlorinated all year. At the end of the day, add chemicals, check the pool vacuum or sweep, the skimmer, the hair and lint pot, and clean the traps.

Weekly Maintenance

In addition to the procedures outlined above, the filter should be backwashed once a week. Remove a cartridge filter; if you do not have a replacement, soak it overnight.

Seasonal Maintenance

Winterizing In the fall, check the pool for leaks and repair them. Vacuum the pool well. The walls should be clean and free from algae. Drain the pool to 20 to 24 in. below the normal water level. Store pool ladder(s) in a protected space. Super chlorinate as needed until the temperatures fall below 32°F. Install the pool cover.

Store the filter and hoses in a protected place. Clean the filter with a special cleaner provided by the pool dealer. Lubricate the pump motor. Remember to leave the skimmer in the wall of the pool but make sure that it has completely drained. If applicable, drain and winterize the pool heating equipment as per manufacturer's instructions.

Wash and dry solar covers with fresh water, fold up and store where not exposed to the sun. In cold climates, inflate an ice equalizer slightly. Tie it to the middle of the pool and cover the pool with the pool cover. As the ice forms, it pushes against the ice equalizer instead of the walls of the pool. Its pillowlike shape encourages snow and ice to roll away from the center.

Start-up Procedures In the beginning of the season re-install the filter system. Make sure that the pump has not rusted and that the brushes are not worn down or damaged. Uncover the pool and vacuum any dirt from the bottom of the pool. Inspect the filter for any loose connections. Lubricate the motor and backwash valve. Clean all the grids and replace or recharge the system. When all the ice has melted in the pool, give the water a dose of super chlorinater treatment as required. This keeps the chlorine level up and reduces the tendency for algae and bacteria growth. Go around the perimeter and check for tears, wear spots or loose-fitting gaskets. If the exterior pool wall shows any rust spots, it may be the sign of leakage. Make sure that the liner is not damaged, because once the pool is filled again, you may have to start all over again by replacing the liner. Once the leak has been repaired, paint the rusted area with a rust-resistant paint.

Contributors, picture credits

Capital letters following page numbers indicate:
T, top; B, bottom; L, left; R, right; C, center

Armstrong & Schnorr, Landscape architects, 1220 N. Las Palmas Ave., Los Angeles, CA 90038 *(p. 90, 91, 92, 93, 94, 95)*

Mr. & Mrs. Lawrence W. Babb, N52 W34293 Gietzen Dr., Okauchee, WI 53069 *(p. 57)* **Banner Builders,** 10001 W. St. Martins Rd., Franklin, WI 53132 *(p. 46)* **Chuck Baumann, Creative Environments,** 932 Forest Lane, Alamo, CA 94507 *(p. 43, 77 TL, 78 TC, R, BL, 80 L, 96 CR)* **Berkus Group Architects,** 1531 Chapala St., Santa Barbara, CA 93101 *(p. 16, 31 TL, BL, .126 TR)* **Blackthorne Hot Tubs and Landscaping,** Locksine Thompson, 4 Pilot Rd., Carmel Valley, CA 93924 *(p. 76 T, 77 TL, 78 TL, 97 B)* **Jim Blankets,** 240 S. Canon, Beverly Hills, CA 90212 *(p. 28, 44)* **Michael Bliss,** landscape architect, 221 Sunset Dr., Encinitas,

CA 92024 *(6 BL, BR, 18, 24 CR, 84, 85, 89 CL, 113)* **James Brett, Architectural Photography,** 1070 W. Orange Grove, Tucson, AZ 85704 *(p. 5, 6 TL, TR, 8,11,12,13 T, 82 TR, L, 83 RC, 87 T, 88 CR, 96 TR)* **Dennis Buettner, landscape architect,** 9076 N. Bayside Dr., Bayside, WI 53217 *(p. 7 BL, BR, 13 B, 105, 109, 143, 145)* **Lord & Burnham, Costich & McConnell, Inc.,** 225 Marcus Blvd., Hauppauge, NY 11787 *(p. 16, 31 TL, BL)* **Monte Burch,** Rt #1, Humansville, MO 65674 *(p. 41, 114)*

California Redwood Association, One Lombard St., San Francisco, CA 94111 *(p. 132 L, 134, 135)* **Milt Charno & Associates,** 6521 W. Euclid Ave., Milwaukee, WI 53219 *(p. 7 CL, 10 BL, 14 BR, BL, 24 BR, 79 TR, 89 RC, CC, 97 T, 115 T, 120 T, 132 R)* **Copper Development Association,** 405 Lexington Ave., New York, NY 10017 *(p. 31 BR)*

Ted Dayton Photography, 2643 Manana Dr., Dallas, TX 75220 *(p. 6 BL, BR, 84, 85, 89 CL, 113)* **Doughboy Pools,** Cucamonga, CA 91730

EGO Productions, James M. Auer, 1849 N. 72nd St., Wauwatosa, WI 53213 *(p. 57)* **Wayne Eslyn,** N63 W22039 Highway 74, Sussex, WI 53089 *(p. 30, 89 TR)*

Harley M. Frindell, Wauwatosa, WI 53226 *(p. 76 B)* **Richard J. Froze,** designer, 2712 North Maryland, Milwaukee, WI 53211 *(p. 102, 103)*

General Electric, Lamp Division, Appliance Park, Louisville, KY 40225 *(p. 27)* **Green Horizons,** Rt #7, Box 124 MS, Santa Fe, NM 87501 *(p. 96 B)*

Heldor Industries, Inc., One Cory Rd., Morristown, NJ 07960

Kent Keegan, 2219 East Marion, Milwaukee, WI 53211 *(p. 15)* **The Kohler Company,** Kohler, WI 53044 *(p. 57, 81, 82 TR)*

Mr. and Mrs. Anders Lewis, vinyl liner pool

William Manley, interior designer, 6062 North Port Washington Rd., Milwaukee, WI 53218 *(p. 105, 109)*

National Swimming Pool Institute, 2000 K Street NW, Washington, D.C. 20006 *(p. 6 CR, 7 TR, 9 B, 10 BL, TL, TR, 14 T, C, 17, 45, 46, 58, 59, 60, 62, 83 TL, TR, L, 88 B, 89 TL, B, 96 TR, 126 R)*

Pool Boys, Inc., New Berlin, WI 53151

Everette Short, 95 Christopher Street, New York, NY 10014 *(p. 2, 3, 7 TL, 9 T, 86, 87 B, 88 TL, TR)* **Spas Electera by Pool Boys,** 13470 West Greenfield Ave., Milwaukee, WI 53005 *(p. 76 B)* **Sta-Rite Industries, Inc.,** Water Equipment Division, Delavan, WI 53115 *(p. 19, 20)* **Stonelite Tile Company,** 1985 Sampson Ave., Corona, CA 91720 *(p. 77 B)*

Special thanks to: **Marvin Breitlow, Sun Valley Pools,** P.O. Box 442, Menomonee Falls, WI 53051 **Duke Maas, Allied Pools,** 7351 North 76th St., Milwaukee, WI 53223 (Ch. 8 photos) **Ron Thompson, Swimming Pool Services, Inc.,** Waukesha, WI 53186 (Ch. 4 photos)

Metric Conversion Charts

LUMBER

Sizes: Metric cross-sections are so close to their nearest Imperial sizes, as noted below, that for most purposes they may be considered equivalents.

Lengths: Metric lengths are based on a 300mm module which is slightly shorter in length than an Imperial foot. It will therefore be important to check your requirements accurately to the nearest inch and consult the table below to find the metric length required.

Areas: The metric area is a square metre. Use the following conversion factors when converting from Imperial data: 100 sq. feet = 9.290 sq. metres.

METRIC SIZES SHOWN BESIDE NEAREST IMPERIAL EQUIVALENT

mm	Inches	mm	Inches
16 x 75	⅝ x 3	44 x 150	1¾ x 6
16 x 100	⅝ x 4	44 x 175	1¾ x 7
16 x 125	⅝ x 5	44 x 200	1¾ x 8
16 x 150	⅝ x 6	44 x 225	1¾ x 9
19 x 75	¾ x 3	44 x 250	1¾ x 10
19 x 100	¾ x 4	44 x 300	1¾ x 12
19 x 125	¾ x 5	50 x 75	2 x 3
19 x 150	¾ x 6	50 x 100	2 x 4
22 x 75	⅞ x 3	50 x 125	2 x 5
22 x 100	⅞ x 4	50 x 150	2 x 6
22 x 125	⅞ x 5	50 x 175	2 x 7
22 x 150	⅞ x 6	50 x 200	2 x 8
25 x 75	1 x 3	50 x 225	2 x 9
25 x 100	1 x 4	50 x 250	2 x 10
25 x 125	1 x 5	50 x 300	2 x 12
25 x 150	1 x 6	63 x 100	2½ x 4
25 x 175	1 x 7	63 x 125	2½ x 5
25 x 200	1 x 8	63 x 150	2½ x 6
25 x 225	1 x 9	63 x 175	2½ x 7
25 x 250	1 x 10	63 x 200	2½ x 8
25 x 300	1 x 12	63 x 225	2½ x 9
32 x 75	1¼ x 3	75 x 100	3 x 4
32 x 100	1¼ x 4	75 x 125	3 x 5
32 x 125	1¼ x 5	75 x 150	3 x 6
32 x 150	1¼ x 6	75 x 175	3 x 7
32 x 175	1¼ x 7	75 x 200	3 x 8
32 x 200	1¼ x 8	75 x 225	3 x 9
32 x 225	1¼ x 9	75 x 250	3 x 10
32 x 250	1¼ x 10	75 x 300	3 x 12
32 x 300	1¼ x 12	100 x 100	4 x 4
38 x 75	1½ x 3	100 x 150	4 x 6
38 x 100	1½ x 4	100 x 200	4 x 8
38 x 125	1½ x 5	100 x 250	4 x 10
38 x 150	1½ x 6	100 x 300	4 x 12
38 x 175	1½ x 7	150 x 150	6 x 6
38 x 200	1½ x 8	150 x 200	6 x 8
38 x 225	1½ x 9	150 x 300	6 x 12
44 x 75	1¾ x 3	200 x 200	8 x 8
44 x 100	1¾ x 4	250 x 250	10 x 10
44 x 125	1¾ x 5	300 x 300	12 x 12

METRIC LENGTHS

Lengths Metres	Equiv. Ft. & Inches
1.8m	5' 10⅞"
2.1m	6' 10⅝"
2.4m	7' 10½"
2.7m	8' 10¼"
3.0m	9' 10⅛"
3.3m	10' 9⅞"
3.6m	11' 9¾"
3.9m	12' 9½"
4.2m	13' 9⅜"
4.5m	14' 9⅓"
4.8m	15' 9"
5.1m	16' 8¾"
5.4m	17' 8⅝"
5.7m	18' 8⅜"
6.0m	19' 8¼"
6.3m	20' 8"
6.6m	21' 7⅞"
6.9m	22' 7⅝"
7.2m	23' 7½"
7.5m	24' 7¼"
7.8m	25' 7⅛"

All the dimensions are based on 1 inch = 25 mm.

NOMINAL SIZE (This is what you order.)	ACTUAL SIZE (This is what you get.)
Inches	Inches
1 x 1	¾ x ¾
1 x 2	¾ x 1½
1 x 3	¾ x 2½
1 x 4	¾ x 3½
1 x 6	¾ x 5½
1 x 8	¾ x 7¼
1 x 10	¾ x 9¼
1 x 12	¾ x 11¼
2 x 2	1¾ x 1¾
2 x 3	1½ x 2½
2 x 4	1½ x 3½
2 x 6	1½ x 5½
2 x 8	1½ x 7¼
2 x 10	1½ x 9¼
2 x 12	1½ x 11¼

Index

Above-ground pool, building, 120-124
  base cove, 123
  bottom rail, 121-122
  completing the assembly, 124
  deep pool excavation, 121
  design, 120
  seat, 123
  site preparation, 120
  tools and materials, 120
  vertical end caps, 123
  vertical supports, 122-123
  wall panels, 122
Above-ground pools, 9, 10, 11, 115-124
  building, 120-124
  comparison to in-ground, 116
  equipment and functional systems, 117-118
  site considerations, 116-117
  types and designs, 117-118
  work sequence, 115-116
Accent lighting, 10, 25, 62-63
Acoustical privacy, 12-13, 21
Adhesive, 113, 114
Aerator, 125
Algae, 154, 155, 156
American Institute of Architects, 17
Anchor bolts, 69, 70
Attached pool enclosure, 57-66
Automatic pool cleaner, 52,155

Backlighting, 25
Backwashing, 19, 154, 155, 156
Batter boards, 33, 68, 108, 113
Berm, 125, 128
Bottom preparation, vinyl liner, 54-55
  guide board method, 54-55
  hard bottom procedures, 55
  soft bottom procedures, 55
  string line method, 54
Bottom rail, 116, 117, 121
Budget, 17-18, 78, 128, 134
Bumping, 20, 154, 155, 156

Cabana, building, 146-148
  beams and rafters, 145
  doorways, 147-148
  fences, 148
  foundation, 146
  infill panels, 147
  interior finishing, 148
  interior partition, 147
  posts, 146
  roofing, 147
  roof sheathing, 146-147
Cabanas, 9, 11, 22, 27, 28, 130-138, 146-148
  building, 146-148
  climatic design issues, 133-134
  concrete base for, 136-138
  construction options, 135
  cost comparisons, 134
  final touches, 134-135
  site considerations, 134
Cartridge filter, 20-21, 80, 119, 155, 156
Ceramic glazed finish, 41
Ceramic tile, 113-114
Ceramic tile finish, 41-42
Changing space, 132, 146
Chlorine, 14-15, 154, 155, 156
Clay liner, 15, 127, 128, 131
Climate (natural pond), 127
Climatic issues (structures), 133-134
Coating and backfilling walls, 38-39, 44
Concrete base (structures), 136-138
  batter boards, 136
  bracing, 137
  excavating, 138
  fill, 138

forms, 136-137
  pouring, 138
  preparation, 136
  reinforcing, 138
  staking, 136
Concrete block for pool walls, 22
Concrete ornamental pool, 105, 109-112
Concrete spa, 78
Container (in-ground pool), 18
Container (natural pond), 127
Contractor, 17, 58, 61, 63, 66
Contracts, 17
Convection heater, 80
Conventional pump (ornamental pool),
  106-108, 109
Coping, 25, 42-43, 49
  outdoor in-ground, 42-43
  vinyl liner, 53-54
Coping receptor (vinyl liner), 45, 46, 55
Curing concrete, 34, 38, 41, 69, 75, 99, 112,
  113, 144
Cycling, 127

Dam, 125, 130
Darbying, 41, 75
Decking, 10, 11, 51-52, 77, 78, 79, 97, 116, 119,
  132, 134, 144
Department of Natural Resources, 15, 127-128
Design (outdoor in-ground), 22-25
  accessories, 24-25
  concrete, 22
  concrete block, 22
  enclosures, 25
  integration, 23
  site plan, 24
  sizes and shapes, 22-23
  surround, 24
  windbreak, 23
Detached pool enclosure, 57-75
Diagonal bracing (vinyl liner), 45, 49
Diatomaceous earth (d.e.), 20, 80, 119, 155, 156
Diving board, 9, 22, 24, 43, 62, 64, 75, 128, 155
  depths required, 22
  height clearance, 64, 72
  installation, outdoor in-ground, 43
Door installation, 73-74
Drain, 11, 18, 39, 49, 54, 56, 98, 103, 104,
  107, 108, 110, 112, 113, 118
Drainage (soil), 11, 21, 44, 56, 58, 78, 108, 117,
  125, 126-127, 136
Dry niche lighting, 26
Dry packed pool, see Hand-packed concrete
  pool

Electrical needs, 21, 22, 25-27, 63-64, 80, 98
Electrical outlets, 10-11, 21, 64
  outdoor in-ground, 26-27
Electrical pool heater, 27, 28
Electrician, 26, 27, 64, 80, 101, 119, 135
Enclosure (above-ground pool), 119-120
Enclosure (ornamental pool pump), 108
Enclosure foundation, 64-65, 68-69
  batter boards, 68
  excavation, 68
  form construction, 68-69
  form removal, 69
  pouring walls, 69
Enclosure, how to build, 67-75
  adding exterior siding, 74
  concrete floor slab, 75
  construction materials, 67
  covering the roof, 73
  excavation, 68
  finishing the foundation, 71
  finishing the interior, 74-75
  framing the roof, 72-73
  framing walls, 70-71
  perimeter insulation, 70

perimeter pour, 69
  placing doors and windows, 73-74
  removing forms, 69-70
  sheathing roof, 73
  sheathing walls, 71
  sills, 70
  wall forms, 68-69
Enclosure walls, 65
Enclosures, 9, 10, 22, 24, 25, 60-66
  design factors, 64
  greenhouse, 60-61
  greenhouse effect, 60-61, 61-62
  inflatable, 25, 61
  insulating, 61
  rigid frame, 25
  specifications, 64-66
  utilities, 62-64
Environmental Impact Statement, 130
Environmental Protection Codes, 128
Epoxy pool enamels, 41
Estimates, 17
Excavation, 17, 32-33, 39, 45, 46, 47-49, 56, 67,
  99, 109-110, 130, 137
  indoor in-ground enclosure, 64-65, 68
  outdoor in-ground, 32-33
  vinyl liner, 47-49
Excavator, 33, 48-49, 58, 116, 130

Fence, building, 152-153
  board infill, 153
  corner posts, 152
  gate, 153
  hinges, 153
  intermediate posts, 152
  stringers, 152-153
Fencing, 9, 10, 12-13, 22, 23, 25, 78, 80, 97,
  116, 125, 133-134, 135, 152-153
  building, 152-153
  climatic design issues, 133-134
  construction options, 135
  cost comparison, 134
  final touches, 134-135
  site considerations, 134
Fiberglass ornamental pool, 104-105, 109-112
Fiberglass spa, 77-78
Filters, 11, 14, 18, 19-21, 27, 37, 38, 49, 52, 63,
  75, 77, 80, 98, 103, 106, 107, 119, 124, 154,
  155, 156
  cartridge, 20-21
  diamaceous earth, 20
  high-rate sand, 19-20
  rapid-rate sand, 119
  recommendations, 26-27
  throw-away cartridge, 20-21
Finial, 141, 145
Flash heater, 80
Flashing, 73
Flat plate collectors, 27
Float (swimming), 128
Floating blossom light, 26
Floating concrete, 41, 75, 112, 113
Floor, forming (outdoor in-ground), 39-42
Footings, forming (outdoor in-ground), 33-35, 44
  constructing the forms, 34
  finishing, 34
  inserting reinforcing dowels, 34
  placing reinforcing, 34
  pouring concrete, 34
  preparing soil, 34
  setting stakes, 33
  stepped footings, 33-34
  stripping forms, 34-35
Forms, concrete, 34, 35, 36, 37, 67, 99, 112,
  113, 136-137
Foundation (structures), 132, 139, 143, 146
Fountains, 13-14, 105, 107, 112, 113

GFIC (ground fault interruptor circuit), 64, 80,

97, 105
gpm (gallons per minute), 19, 27, 28
Gas-fired pool heater, 28-29
Gate, 10
Gazebo, 13, 27, 80, 105, 109, 129, 130-138, 139-145, 150
  building eight-sided, 139-142
  building four-sided, 143-145
  climatic design issues, 133-134
  concrete base for, 136-138
  construction options, 135
  cost comparisons, 134
  final touches, 134-135
  site considerations, 134
Gazebo, eight-sided, building, 139-142
  beams, 141
  bracing post and beam, 141
  finishing, 142
  foundation, 139
  materials list, 139
  post anchor bolts, 140
  post placement, 140-141
  rafters, 141
  railing and entry, 142
  roof, 141-142
Gazebo, four-sided, building, 143-145
  finial, 145
  foundation, 143-144
  ground connection, 145
  lattice, 145
  posts, 144
  railing, 145
  roof, 144-145
Greenhouse effect, 25, 79
Greenhouse enclosure, 16, 60-61, 61-62
Grout, 113, 114
Gunite pool, 22, 78

Hand-packed concrete pool, 22, 78
Hard bottom (vinyl liner), 46, 55
Heat pump, 61
Heat pump pool heater, 28, 29
Heaters, 11, 12, 14-15, 18, 19, 23, 27-30, 38, 44, 57, 64, 76, 77, 80, 98, 155, 156
  electric, 27, 28
  gas-fired, 28-29
  heat pump, 29
  oil-fired, 29-30
  solar blanket, 30
  solar heating systems, 27-28
Hedges, 10, 24, 25, 78
High-rate sand filter, 19-20
Homeowner's insurance, 10, 18
Hopper, 18, 48-49, 50, 54
Hot tub cover, 97
Hot tub, installation, 99-103
  assembling the tub, 100-101
  excavating the area, 99
  final touches, 102-103
  hoops, 101
  placing fill, 100
  plumbing, 101-102
  pouring and finishing concrete, 100
  reinforcing, 100
  staves, 101
Hot tub kit, 99
Hot tubs, 13, 14-15, 76-103
  characteristics, 76-77
  electrical needs, 80
  installing, 99-103
  safety guidelines, 97
  site considerations, 78-79
  surround, 79
  water system, 80, 97
Hydraulic head, 107
Hydrotherapy jets, 97, 101

Indoor in-ground pool, adding, 57-75

accessories, 62, 64
attached vs. detached, 57
buidling a pool enclosure, 67-75
connection to the house, 65-66
design, attached, 58-59
design, detached, 59-60
electrical needs, 62-63, 63-64
enclosure options, 60-62
excavation, 64-65
heating and cooling, 63-66
maintenance, 66
planning the site, 57-58
pool options, 60, 64
water supply and drainage, 63
Indoor pool-house integration, 58-59
  as addition, 59
  energy savings, 58-59
  new home construction, 58
Indoor pool lighting, 62-63
Indoor pool site, 57-58
  exposure, 57
  slope, 58
  soil conditions, 58
  structural notes, 57-58
Indoor pool, types, 60
Indoor site (hot tub or spa), 78, 79
Inflatable (pneumatic) enclosure, 61-62
In-ground pool, 9, 10, 11, 58, 63, 67, 115, 118, 119
Inlets, 49, 52, 55
Insulating enclosure, 61-62
Insulation, 74
Island, 129, 131

Jacuzzi, 97

Ladders, 9, 24, 25, 43, 51, 62, 115, 155, 156
  installation, 43
Lanai, 80, 130-138, 149-151
  building free-standing, 149-151
  building leanto, 151
  climatic design issues, 133-134
  concrete base for, 136-138
  construction options, 135
  cost comparison, 134
  final touches, 134-135
  site considerations, 134
Lanai, freestanding, building, 149-151
  beams and braces, 150
  cross bracing, 150
  finishing, 151
  foundation, 149
  posts, 150
  rafters, 150
  roof lattice, 150
  wall lattice, 150-151
Lanai, leanto, building, 151
Landscaping, 10, 23, 25
Lattice, 141-142, 145, 149, 150-151
Leaf skimmer, 155
Lighting, 10-11, 21, 25-26, 118
  outdoor in-ground, 25-26
Liner installation, 55-56
Lint trap, 19, 38, 80
Local codes, 10, 11, 21-22, 24, 26, 27, 61, 63, 64, 66, 79, 104, 116, 118, 119, 134
Low voltage lighting, 25-26, 64, 80

Mailbu light, 25
Maintenance, 66, 154-156
  above-ground, 156
  hot tubs, 155-156
  in-ground, 154-155
  spas, 154-155
  vinyl liner, 154-155
Masonry ornamental pool, 105, 113-114
Metal spa, 78
Molded ornamental pool, 113

National Electrical Code, 10, 19, 26, 38, 62, 80, 97, 118
National Swimming Pool Institute, 25
Natural pond, construction, 129-131
  clay seeding, 131
  compacting excavation, 130
  construction permit, 130
  design development, 129-130
  excavation, 130
  filling, 131
  finishing, 130-131
  information gathering, 129
  site survey, 129
Natural ponds, 15, 125-131
  budget, 129
  climate, 127
  construction, 129-131
  container, 127
  Environmental Protection Agency, 128
  natural features, 128
  runoff and drainage, 126-127
  safety, 128
  soil, 127
  structures, 128
  topographical issues, 127-128
  types of ponds, 125
  water sources, 125-126
Natural wetlands, 15, 128

Oil-fired pool heater, 29-30
Ornamental pool, octagonal, building, 113-114
  excavating, 113
  floor, 113
  forms, 113
  tiling procedures, 114
Ornamental pool, square, building, 109-112
  edge forms, 112
  excavation, 109-110
  final touches, 112
  pouring concrete, 112
  reinforcing, 111-112
  site preparation, 109
  supply and drain 110-111
  wood surround, 112
Ornamental pools, 13, 104-114
  building an octagonal, 113-114
  building a square, timber-edged, 109-112
  seasonal care, 108
  site integration, 108
  types, 104-105
  with drainage, 106-107
  without drainage, 107-108
Ornamental pools, types, 104-105
  concrete, 105
  fiberglass, 104-105
  fountains, 105
  masonry, 105
  prefabricated, 104
  vinyl liner, 105
Outdoor in-ground pool, building, 32-43
  batterboards, 33
  coating and backfilling, 38-39
  finishing, 41-43
  floor, 39-41
  plot plan, 32-33
  surround, 43-44
  wall footings, 33-35
  walls, 36-38
Outdoor in-ground pool, planning, 17-30
  choosing accessories, 24-25
  container, 18
  contracting out, 17-18
  design options, 22-24
  drawing a site plan, 24
  electrical needs, 25-27
  enclosures, 25
  heating, 27-30
  planning surround, 24

sites, 21
    water system, 18-21
Outdoor site (hot tub or spa), 78-79
Outfall pipe, 131
Outlets (water), 52, 55, 106
Overflow pipe, 112, 130, 131

pH level, 14-15, 117, 154, 155, 156
Passive solar heating, 67
Patio, 14, 31, 79, 97, 104, 109, 132, 133, 134
Perimeter insulation, 70
Pesticides, 126-127
Plastic piping, 52
Plot plan, preparation, 32-33
    checking vertical level, 32
    drawing the plan, 32
    excavation choices, 32-33
    staking the area, 32
Plumbing, 11, 18, 21, 67, 75
Pollution, water, 126-127
Pool finishes, 41-42
Pool shapes, 22-23
Pool sizes, 22-23
Post anchors, 140, 144, 146
Poured concrete ornamental pool, 13
Poured-in-place pool, 22, 78
Prefabricated coping (vinyl liner), 53
Prefabricated ornamental pool, 104
Property taxes, 18
Pump (ornamental pool), 105
Pumps, 11, 14, 18, 19, 26, 28, 38, 64, 77, 80, 98,
    154, 155, 156

Rafters, 67, 72, 141, 145, 146, 150
Rapid-rate sand filter, 19, 80, 119
Recirculating system, 11, 13-14, 19, 38, 76,
    80-81
Recirculating pump (ornamental pool), 106-108
Regular pump, 19
Reinforcing concrete, 34, 35, 36, 37, 39, 40, 43,
    75, 99, 105, 110, 111, 130, 136, 137, 143
Rim lock coping (vinyl liner), 53
Roof connection, enclosure, 59, 65-66
Roof construction, 72-73, 141-142, 144-145,
    146-147
Roof trusses, 65
Rough openings, 70-71, 74, 148
Rough-timbered ornamental pool, 13
Rubber based enamel finish, 41
Runoff, 125, 126-127
Rural site, 21
Rust, 154

Safety, 9, 10, 15, 25-26, 27, 30, 97, 118, 128
    hot tubs, 15, 97
    natural pond, 128
    lighting, 25-26
    solar blanket, 30
    spas, 15, 31, 97
Sand base (vinyl liner), 45
Sand filter, 19, 80, 119, 155, 156
Scale, 154
Screeding, 34, 38, 40-41, 69, 75, 113
Screens, 78, 132
Seasonal care (ornamental pool), 108
Security, 21, 22, 25, 78, 116, 133
Self-contained pond, 125, 127
Self-priming pump, 19
Setback, 22, 104, 134
Shallow saucer ornamental pool, 106
Showers, 11, 132, 134
Siding, 74
Site considerations (ornamental pool), 108
Site considerations (structures), 134
Site integration, 23
Site plan, 24
Site selection, 11-13, 21-22, 116-117
    above-ground pool, 116-117

acoustical privacy, 12-13
    exposure to sun and wind, 12
    slope and drainage, 11
    soil suitability, 12
    types, 21-22
    water supply, 11-12
Size recommendations, 22-23
Skimmer, 11, 18, 19, 38, 49, 51, 52, 55, 117,
    119, 124, 154, 155, 156
Slides, 24-25, 62, 75, 128, 155
Slope, 10, 11, 21, 31, 108
Soft bottom (vinyl liner), 46, 55
Solar blanket pool heater, 30, 44
Solar panel pool heating, 27-28, 155
Solar water heater, 12
Sona tubes, 143
Spa, installation, 98
Spa cover, 97
Spas, 14-15, 31, 76-98
    characteristics, 76, 77-78
    concrete, 78
    electrical needs, 80, 97
    fiberglass, 77-78
    installing, 98
    metal, 78
    safety guidelines, 97
    site considerations, 78-79
    surround, 79-80
    water system, 80, 97
Stabilizer, 154
Standard coping (vinyl liner), 53-54
Start-up procedures, 155, 156
Storage (equipment), 11
Strainer, 11
Studs, 70, 74
Subcontracting, 17
Submersible pump, 106-108, 113
Suburban site, 21
Sun exposure, 10, 12, 21, 57, 78, 133, 134
Surround, 9, 24, 25, 31, 32, 43-44, 56, 62, 78, 80
    indoor, 62
    installation, 43-44

Tank heater, 80
Throw away cartridge, 20
Toilets, 11, 134
Top seat (above-ground), 117
Topography, 15, 127-128
Trees, 10, 128, 155
Troubleshooting chart, 154
Troweling, 34, 38, 41, 69, 75

Underwater lighting, 26, 50, 62-63, 64, 80
Urban site, 21

Vapor barrier, 74, 79
Ventilation, 60, 60-61, 61-62, 64, 148
Venturi jet, 80
Vertical end caps, 123
Vertical supports, 117, 122
Vinyl liner natural pond, 125, 127
Vinyl liner ornamental pool, 13, 105
Vinyl liner pool, 9, 45-56, 60, 63, 67
Vinyl liner pool, installing, 45-56
    concreting the frame, 52
    coping, 53-54
    excavation, 48-49
    installing accessories, 51-52
    installing plumbing, 52
    installing the liner, 55-56
    pool bottom preparation, 54-55
    pool components, 46
    pool wall erection, 49-50
    preparing for excavation, 47-48
    staking out, 47
    taping joints, 51
    tools and materials required, 46-47

Wall construction, 70-71
Walls, forming (outdoor in-ground), 36-38
    bracing the panels, 37
    finishing the concrete, 38
    installing exterior forms, 36
    installing interior forms, 37
    oiling the forms, 37
    placing reinforcement, 36-37
    pouring walls, 37-38
    stripping the forms, 38
Waste disposal, 11, 22, 63
Water aeration, 13
Water purification needs, 18, 63, 66, 80, 125,
    154-156
Water source (natural pond), 15
Water supply, 11-12, 22, 63, 97, 107, 110, 125
Water table, 12, 55, 126, 128, 129
Water truck, 12
Waterfall, 13, 14, 107
Wall panels, (vinyl liner), 45, 46, 47, 49, 50,
    53, 56
Weir, 125, 126
Wet niche lighting, 26
Whirlpool spa, 80, 97
Window installation, 73-74
Winds, 10, 12, 21, 23-24, 78-79, 128, 133
Winterizing, 119, 155, 156
Wood surround, 112